T0116262

THE BIG THREE

Peter May

SIMON & SCHUSTER

New York London Toronto Sydney Tokyo Singapore

Simon & Schuster
SIMON &   1230 Avenue of the Americas
SCHUSTER   New York, NY 10020

First Simon & Schuster trade paperback edition February 2007

SIMON & SCHUSTER and colophon are registered trademarks of Simon & Schuster, Inc.

Designed by

Manufactured in the United States of America

10   9   8   7   6   5   4   3   2   1

Library of Congress Cataloging-in-Publication Data

For information about special discounts for bulk purchases, please contact Simon & Schuster Special Sales at 1-800-456-6798 or business@simonandschuster.com

ISBN-13: 978-1-4165-5207-9
ISBN-10:   1-4165-5207-3

Photo Credits

Courtesy of the Boston Celtics: 7, 8, 11; courtesy of Centenary College: 3; courtesy of the Golden State Warriors: 4; Stan Grossfeld: 10; courtesy of Indiana State University: 2; Dan Miller: 12; Tom Miller: 1, 9, 13, 14; Frank O'Brien: 6; courtesy of the University of Minnesota: 5

To my own Big Three, Timothy, Patrick, and Kate; to the two who made it possible, my mother and father; and to Eileen, the one and only.

Acknowledgments

In addition to the obvious trio, whose cooperation for this project is gratefully acknowledged, there are many others whose assistance made this book possible. Terry Pluto, the fine writer from the *Akron Beacon-Journal* and a prolific author in his own right, was an early sounding board and advocate. My agent, Faith Hamlin, believed in the project and shaped it through many revisions. Jeff Neuman at Simon & Schuster more than lived up to his reputation as the Larry Bird (circa 1986) of book editors. His associate, Stuart Gottesman, handled the final stages with skill.

Several colleagues at the *Boston Globe* also were helpful. My thanks to Ron Borges, Dan Shaughnessy, Bob Ryan, Jackie Mac-Mullan, Scott Thurston, and Sean Mullin. I am grateful to the Celtics organization and to Jan Volk for his insights.

My thanks to Matt and Dan Bergin, who showed me the ropes in Hibbing, Minnesota, and to John McHale, for setting me up with the two. Paul and Josephine McHale welcomed me into their home and were gracious and helpful. Cliff Roberts, Steve Murray, and Peyton Moore were excellent and informative guides in Shreveport, Louisiana.

And, finally, thanks to four people whose help along the way made it possible for me to even undertake such a project: Ron Grinker, Jon Pessah, and, wherever you are, Steve Weinberg and Brenda W. Rotzoll. None of this would have happened if not for you.

August 18, 1992

The telephone call woke Don Casey in his hotel room in La Costa, California, and he instantly knew that the news wasn't going to be good. You don't get phone calls at 6:00 A.M. unless the message is urgent and unpleasant. Especially when you're on vacation and aren't due back at work for another month.

The caller was Casey's immediate superior, Chris Ford, coach of the Boston Celtics. The news that Ford delivered wasn't wholly unexpected, but it also couldn't wait. In three hours, the Celtics would be making an announcement and Ford was giving Casey advance notice, mostly as a courtesy.

Three thousand miles to the east, Larry Bird picked up his telephone and placed a call to Jill Leone in Florida. For years, she has been the woman who has had the thankless job of getting Larry here or there, making sure the man in Maryland has a signed congratulatory telegram from Bird for his wedding, and so forth. Leone works for Bob Woolf, the Boston-based sports attorney who represents Bird. She keeps track of Bird's whereabouts—no small feat.

"I'm retiring," he told her.

Less than thirty minutes later, Woolf, who also was Bird's neighbor, friend, and one of many father figures in Bird's life, walked out of his redwood ranch house in Brookline, turned onto Newton Street, and walked to Bird's unassuming brick ranch-style home around the corner. Bird had bought the house when he first came to Boston, only because it was close to Woolf.

Bird was by himself. He had sent his wife, Dinah, back to their home in West Baden, Indiana, fearing she would have a hard time dealing with all the emotions of this moment. She, in fact, had wanted her husband to make this announcement a year earlier, after an unrelenting back injury forced him to eat his meals on the floor. But Bird had felt so good after an off-season operation that he returned for another year and even signed a two-year contract extension worth $8 million.

Bird had asked Woolf to bring over some material on another matter, and Woolf had no inkling of what Bird was going to say as he entered the house.

"Oh yeah, by the way, I'm retiring," Bird told him.

Woolf was floored.

The official announcement would be made soon, Bird explained, within a couple of hours. No use waiting. At first, Woolf thought that Bird had just made the decision. He hadn't. It actually had been hammered out a week before, but the Celtics' obsessive penchant for privacy gave the whole thing the air of the Manhattan Project.

Only a privileged few knew. Ford was one. But neither Casey, Ford's top assistant, nor Jon Jennings, the other Celtics assistant coach, was told until hours before the announcement.

The three Celtics owners knew. So did Dave Gavitt, the Celtics' senior executive vice-president; Jan Volk, the team's general manager; and Red Auerbach, the club president, who had drafted Bird fourteen years earlier. The commissioner of the National Basketball Association, David Stern, was told beforehand. So was his assistant, Gary Bettman, now the commissioner of the National Hockey League.

The players had no clue and found out the same way everyone else did. The Celtics were determined to avoid any leaks and they succeeded, for which they were genuinely smug and satisfied. Reggie Lewis, who succeeded Bird as the team's captain, heard the news going to the store. Back in Indiana, Dinah Mattingly Bird was having her hair done when the news came over the radio in the salon. There was silence. And then tears.

The day in Boston was fittingly overcast and rain pelted the streets. Some hoop historian will undoubtedly find some metaphorical significance in that, but the Celtics weren't the only New England institution to take a hit that day. Wang Laboratories, which had prospered in the mid-1980s like the Bird-era Celtics and was one of the state's largest employers, announced it was filing for bankruptcy.

Bird was in no such financial straits. He had earned close to $30 million in salary alone in his thirteen years with the Celtics, including $7.07 million in his final year. Had he merely shown up and played in sixty games in the 1992–93 season, he would have made another $8 million. But he couldn't do it. In fact, he had deliberately backdated his retirement letter because he had been due to receive $3.75 million for the 1992–93 season on August 15. He was raised to work for his money, an admirable quality that never deserted him. In addition, he had done quite well with the vast sums he'd accumulated over the years.

"No one is going to have to throw a benefit for Larry Bird," Auerbach noted.

But there would be plenty of benefits and tributes once the announcement was made public. After sharing the news with his close friends in early-morning phone calls, Bird and Woolf drove to the Boston Garden together. They drove in Bird's blue Lincoln Town Car, which he received from a local dealer for doing some ads. He always preferred paying nothing rather than something. "If it's free, I'll wear it," he once said of an ugly shirt. "If someone wants to buy me a Mercedes, I'll be glad to drive it. But I can't see spending seventy-five thousand dollars on a car."

On the way to the Garden, Bird was nervous. His main hope was that he wouldn't get too emotional, he told Woolf. "I hope I don't break down and I can get through this," he said.

Bird had come to the unavoidable conclusion that he had to retire during a four-and-a-half-hour meeting with Gavitt a week earlier. His back, which had forced him to miss fifty-nine games the previous two years, was not going to get well enough for him to continue playing. Surgery had given him another year, but it was a dysfunctional one at that. Then, when the back acted up again in April, and the team went on a tear without him, people—including some players—began to question Bird's value to the team.

The back was so sore that Bird couldn't even make it through the Olympic qualifying tournament in Portland, the Tournament of the Americas, a weeklong series of games that resembled the Joffrey Ballet more than the NBA in terms of contact and physical play.

It was then that Larry Joe Bird, a three-time MVP and one of the game's greatest players, decided he had quite likely played his last game.

"I just remember lying on my bed in Portland," he says, "and saying, 'God, just get me through the Olympics and I'll give this up and move on to something else.' "

He got through the Olympics. His baby son, Connor, kept him awake at night, but the U.S. team was so dominant his presence hardly mattered. Even his inclusion on the team seemed more of a belated honorarium than a reflection of his present basketball expertise or stature. At one time, it was unthinkable not to include Bird as one of the two forwards on an All-NBA team. But he hadn't made one since 1988, and his participation in the Olympics was akin to John Wayne getting the Oscar for *True Grit*.

Dave Gavitt, who oversaw the selection process of the aptly named Dream Team, noted, "When healthy, there aren't ten better than Larry." But Bird wasn't healthy, hadn't been for years, and now, finally, the sport that had sustained him for the last seventeen years, the sport that had made him a multimillionaire and an idol to thousands, the sport that turned him from a southern Indiana introvert into a global celebrity, would no longer be the focus of his daily life. Quite naturally, he found this troubling.

The night before the announcement, he went back to his house in Brookline and contemplated his brilliant career in between Kleenex and beers. Bird sat alone and remembered. There were plenty of flashbacks. Game 6 against the Houston Rockets in 1986, a game that clinched the Celtics' sixteenth NBA championship, the third and last for Bird. The famed fourth-quarter shoot-out with Dominique Wilkins in the 1988 Eastern Conference semifinals. The masterpiece against the Knicks in Game 7 of the 1984 conference semifinals, a performance so dominating that Hubie Brown, then the coach of the Knicks, still remembers it as Bird's transformation from star to superstar. The fight with Julius Erving. The game-winning basket against the 76ers in the 1981 conference finals. The first ring in 1981. The steal against the Pistons in 1987. The 60-point game against the Hawks in New Orleans. The second championship in 1984. He's lucky he got to sleep at all.

"A lot of tears, that night," he recalls. "And a lot of flashbacks, too. It was a tough one. I woke up throughout the night thinking about it and knowing it's finally going to be over with. I knew at the time I was making the right decision. There just was no way I could go on."

It was the same message he'd delivered to Gavitt a week earlier. The two had returned from Barcelona on August 9 and chatted briefly. Although the dreaded *R* word had been circulating for months, Gavitt said the two avoided it almost as if by mutual telepathy at Barcelona.

"I felt going into the Olympics that he pretty much had decided he couldn't do it," Gavitt said. "He certainly had the desire. And the skills. I realized then that his back just wasn't going to let him play. But I think he actually was having a very difficult time getting himself to actually say it."

The two got together for dinner in Portland and Bird finally did at least allow for the possibility that his NBA career was over.

"All I'm hoping is that there is one more month in this back," he told Gavitt.

Then he said, "If I can't play, what the hell am I going to do?"

The two rendezvoused in Boston two days after the Dream Team's luxury charter touched American soil in Newark. Gavitt asked Bird for his thoughts about the team, the future, the chances in 1992–93. They avoided the obvious like two people on a first date, wondering which one would make the first move. Bird finally did.

"Dave was talking about what they were going to expect of me and I was sitting there thinking about what I've been going through the last couple years and finally I looked at Dave and said, 'We're really wasting our time. I gotta give it up. It's really just a waste of time.' "

Gavitt had been expecting as much, but he wanted Bird to say it, and, more important, he wanted to be sure Bird actually meant it. Are you sure, Gavitt asked? Is this the Rubicon? Bird said it was. "Get everyone together and then let's announce it."

Then came the next question. What did he want to do? Coach? Bird wouldn't even consider it. A nine-to-five job with a jacket and tie? Bird, one of the game's most gifted creators and perhaps the greatest passing forward of all time, a player who, Gavitt noted, played the game better than anyone "from the shoulders to the top of his head and from his wrists to his fingertips," can't even tie a necktie. So that was out of the question.

Finally, Gavitt handed Bird a slip of paper and told Bird to write down the job description. Bird did not write "special assistant to the senior executive vice-president," but that is what he became. Months later, he still didn't know what floor the Celtics' office was on when he visited one day. The job would mostly be advising Gavitt on players seen on tape and representing the Celtics at clinics and functions, something he never did while playing. Some of his teammates felt the position was simply a glorified thank-you. Robert Parish was among them. "I heard he was going to go around speaking," Parish said. "Knowing Larry, we'll see how long that will last."

It didn't take long. Four months later, Bird said publicly that the new job wasn't exactly keeping him busy or interested. "I need a new challenge in my life," he said. "I've got to find something to do." A month later he had back surgery, which would keep him occupied for several months, though that wasn't what he had in mind. And there were rumors throughout the year that the Indiana Pacers, one of the NBA's few struggling teams, were trying to upgrade their image by hiring Bird to coach the team. Bird has repeatedly said that he has no interest in coaching at the professional level and that it would be a disaster. The great ones rarely, if ever, make great coaches because they soon realize the best player on the team is the person they look at in the mirror each day. Bill Russell found that out in Seattle and Sacramento and Jerry West had an exasperating time with the Lakers in the late 1970s. Like Russell, Bird was a legend. Like West, Bird was a perfectionist.

The actual retirement announcement came at midday, and all

three local TV stations went live to the site. So did ESPN and SportsChannel, the cable company that broadcasts Celtics home games. Reporters cut short vacations to cover the event. One *Boston Globe* reporter was on an island in New Hampshire, without a phone, but somehow was found and made it down.

By the time Bird appeared, wearing a red golf shirt with a long white stripe down the left side, everyone knew what was coming. Bird joined Auerbach and Gavitt at a table just to the right of the podium. Seated at the left were the owners, Ford, Woolf, and Volk.

Bird looked worn, tired, and emotion ravaged. Over the years he had grown more comfortable with the media, and he even enjoyed sparring with them on occasion. He was not looking forward to this, however.

"This is a little tough today, but we'll try and get through it as best as we can," he said. "This is not a sad day. It's a very emotional day, but it's not really a sad day. I knew it was going to come. I sort of prepared myself. Once you sign the papers and get up in front of all these people, well, it's a little different."

For the next forty minutes, he answered every question put to him. He talked about his back pain—"I can't shake it. There's no way. Even if I can score sixty points a night, there's no way"—and the Olympics. He reflected on some special moments in his career, including his first title in 1981. Ford was a guard on that team and Bird said, "Chris Ford remembered that because he was playing so long and never won anything."

He even touched on his agonizing week in Portland, when he made a pact with the Higher-up. He got through the Olympics, which was all he wanted, right? "Well, I thought I could lie to Him and maybe play a little more," he said. His sense of humor was still there, and he needed it.

"The reason I stand up here and try to make jokes is to keep myself from crying. I'm not going to cry today. This is a special day for me." That was it. He went over and hugged teammate Dee Brown, who thought he detected some wetness in Bird's eyes. He chatted briefly with another teammate, Rick Fox. They were part of the New Celtics, a team of speed and dynamism for the nineties, as well as friends. Neither one, however, had played with a healthy Bird.

Gavitt then passed around glasses of champagne, a spirit Bird probably drinks about as often as he drinks motor oil. Even before Gavitt could utter a toast, Bird cracked, "How 'bout a beer?" (But no green bottles, thank you. Years ago, Bird had picked up a green bottle of beer at a party, and, thinking it full of beer, promptly downed the contents. The bottle was filled with cigarette butts. To this day, he won't drink a beer in a green bottle.) Then, it was over.

He accompanied the executives to the Celtics' offices, where sandwiches were waiting. Bill Russell called to offer his thoughts. Bird got on the phone and called him "Mr. Russell."

By the end of the day, the two Boston newspapers were scrambling to put together special sections for the next day. The television stations all aired specials on Bird's career. Executives around the league weighed in with accolades, including Indiana Pacers president Donnie Walsh, who compared Bird's retirement to Alexander the Great's decision to not conquer any more countries.

The next morning, Bird was scheduled to fly back to Indiana for his annual golf tournament, which raises money for scholarships for needy high school kids. The phone woke him up at 7:00 A.M., and he couldn't figure out who it might be.

"Where are you? It's time to go to work. I've got things for you to do," Gavitt said.

Bird managed a laugh in his first full day as an ex-player. He was three and a half months shy of his thirty-sixth birthday.

The Big Three. It means different things in different cities. In Detroit, it means General Motors, Ford, and Chrysler. But in Boston, in the 1980s, the Big Three meant only one thing: the greatest frontcourt in the history of basketball. It was Bird, Robert Parish, and Kevin McHale.

Now only two were left, and they were on borrowed time as well. McHale was a year younger than Bird, but, like Bird, he was breaking down because of injuries. He retired after the 1992–93 season, a year of agony and frustration, salvaged by two brilliant playoff performances. Parish, meanwhile, was the oldest player in the league. He was about to turn thirty-nine and was adamant about playing at age forty. After a steady 1992–93 season, he would outlast the other two as he had preceded them into the NBA seventeen years earlier.

And that is part of what made the Big Three so special—they endured as well as dominated. No three players on any team at any time, let alone frontcourt players, had been teammates for such a long stretch.

Theirs was a special bond on the court. Off the court, they were vastly different personalities, although each had been instilled with a work ethic and an inner drive by his working-class parents. All three still returned home in the summer to the towns where they were raised. All three will have their numbers retired and raised to the rafters in Boston Garden, joining the legends of the past. All three are destined to be enshrined in the Basketball Hall of Fame.

When they united in Boston in 1980, Bird was one year out of college, McHale was a promising rookie, and Parish was an uninspiring four-year veteran. Together they won three championships and nine divisional titles, and they made four consecutive appearances in the NBA finals. In their later years they almost redefined the concept of "playing hurt," as McHale limped through the 1987 playoffs with a broken bone in his foot and Bird endured both trauma to his back and surgery on both of his Achilles tendons, which sidelined him for nearly all of the 1988–89 season.

"Today's young athletes who are benefiting from what those three did from a financial standpoint, well, I want to see how all these young guys will respond," Ford said. "Will they give their best? Will they strive to get better? Or will they just be satisfied to have long-term contracts for big money? I want to see what the legacy is going to be. Those three guys put it on the line every single night. They worked to get better and they worked to stay in the league. I want to see if the young guys will have the hunger to get better and to work at it, as those three guys did."

On the court, they complemented each other at both ends. Bird and Parish worked an unstoppable pick-and-roll. Parish, who was rarely an option on offense and never complained about it, would set a pick while Bird figured out the rest. The pick-and-roll can work only if the man with the ball can shoot and pass, and Bird could do both. "No one could run a pick-and-roll like me and Robert," Bird said. "It wasn't even close. Usually, a center sets the pick for you and then just stands there. Doesn't do anything else. Robert would be out there, eighteen feet from the basket, set the pick, and break for the basket. He could get the pass and make the dunk without ever putting the ball on the floor. You never see that. And there was no way to defend that."

Similarly, there was no way to defend McHale, who worked tirelessly on a litany of moves around the basket, a Luis Tiant in the post, always taking advantage of his unique frame, which seemed to be a combination of parts from a tall man's store. He had the reach of someone three inches taller than he was, and at 6-11 he was already one of the bigger forwards in the league. He had the wingspan to stay off a player defensively and the ability to block a shot if challenged from anywhere. Offensively, he developed into an automatic basket by the mid-1980s if he had the ball in the post and wasn't immediately double-teamed.

On defense, Bird would funnel his player into the middle, where Parish and McHale were waiting. Bird was never a solid individual defender, but he could play outstanding "help" defense, which more often than not violated the NBA's rule on zone defenses. But he got away with it.

Teams tried to emulate the Big Three without success; there simply were too many variables at work, and no one had a versatile forward like Bird or a 6-11 forward like McHale who made it all come together by being able to guard the small forward on the other team.

The NBA has never seen anything like them, nor is it likely to ever again. Now, with free agency and multimillion-dollar contracts the norm, it is virtually unthinkable that three superstars in any sport could spend virtually their entire careers on the same team. The two greatest hockey players in the last twenty-five years, Bobby Orr and Wayne Gretzky, ended their careers in different locales from where they started.

The Big Three's confluence in Boston was equal parts miracle, shrewdness, and luck. Of the three, only Bird was drafted using a pick that the Celtics had not acquired in a trade. McHale and Parish came on the same day in the same deal, a trade NBA historians deem the most lopsided in NBA history. But the two deals that put the Celtics in a position to make the McHale/Parish trade and give them wiggle room to take Bird two years earlier were almost as larcenous.

Though sometimes overlooked or forgotten, those two deals represented the pinnacle of Red Auerbach's long and legendary trading career, back when trades could still be made without the suffocating restrictions of the salary cap. Red knew how to take advantage of financially troubled teams and bully them into deals against their better judgment.

All of these factors entered into the assembling of the Big Three. As their careers wound down, the times they appeared together diminished due to injuries and an organizational shift toward quicker, smaller, all-around players. When Bird announced his retirement, McHale had returned to the bench as one of the team's top reserves, a role he relished and played better than anyone else in the early 1980s.

In their heyday, however, they were something. Bird won three consecutive MVP awards from 1984 to 1986 and no one, at any time, played the game better than he did in those three years. McHale was as good a player at both ends as anyone, including Bird, in the first three months of the 1986–87 season. Then, one March night in 1987, Larry Nance stepped on his foot. What started as a small stress fracture grew into something far worse, something that required surgery, the implanting of a screw to keep things together, and began a slow, painful decline for McHale. He was never the same player again.

In the mid-1980s, the Celtics went to the NBA finals four straight years. In 1985–86 they were 67–15 and, as general manager Jan Volk noted, "constituted as complete a team as you could possibly imagine." In two seasons, the team lost a total of two regular-season games in Boston Garden, an unthinkable achievement now, only six years later.

Six years after their great run, Bird stood at a podium at the

Boards & Blades Club in Boston Garden and effectively marked
the beginning of the end of the Big Three. Over the previous two
years, injuries had kept at least one of them out almost continu-
ously, but now one was going to be gone for good. Robert Parish
commented that playing without Bird was going to be like getting
"all dressed for the dance and then finding out you have no one
to go with."

As he reflected on his teammates, Bird noted that Parish was the
best he had ever had. Through the years, Bird had always said that
Dennis Johnson was the best big-game player he had ever seen.
M. L. Carr, he thought, was the most fun. Almost as an afterthought, he mentioned McHale, who he said was the best *inside*
player he had seen. He also mildly chastised McHale for not winning an MVP, something virtually everyone, excluding Bird,
thought was impossible given Bird's larger-than-life presence on the
team and his overall reputation.

McHale and Bird were never close. They had many similarities,
but their personalities were as different as one could find. "Everybody thought Larry and I should be joined at the hip because we
were both tall, we were both from the Midwest, we were both
white, we both played for the Boston Celtics, and we both came
from small towns. But we're two very different people," McHale
said.

Bird was driven, committed, and oriented toward one goal: basketball. McHale was relaxed, fluid, gregarious, and the father of an
always expanding brood. As his boyhood friend Chris Liesmaki
described him, McHale "has never lost sight of what is fun in life.
It's a perfect job for Kevin. He can entertain and have fun. I can't
see him doing anything else. And that's pretty special."

Parish maintained distance from both, though when the team
became fractious in the 1989–90 season, he seemed squarely in
Bird's corner. Like Bird, Parish often wondered how good McHale
really could have been; he thought McHale tended to "coast" during games, although he generally rung up impressive numbers. But
Parish also understood that Bird was something special in the eyes
of management, fans, and virtually everyone else. The double standard, he said, didn't bother him.

McHale and Bird may have gone their separate ways off the court, but they meshed on the floor as few others ever could or would. No one could get the ball to McHale the way Bird could, as McHale found the first time Bird was out for an extended period.

Naturally, over twelve years, there are going to be moments of contention in any relationship, and there were a few among the three. But what made this relationship different is that the conflicts were resolved, forgotten, and deemed inappropriate and counter-productive to the larger goal, getting another NBA championship.

"There's a blip here. There's a blip there. You have arguments with your best friend," said Volk. "It just went away. In this case, the whole is better than the sum of the parts and the parts are pretty good. Rarely do you get three such people able to occupy the same space for a protracted period without friction of great magnitude. And usually that magnitude is sufficient to rend it all asunder. I think we have seen an extraordinary relationship of extraordinary people that in and of itself is extraordinary."

When basketball ended and summer began, these three individuals would part ways and rarely reunite until the next season dawned. Bird would head back to southern Indiana, McHale would return to northern Minnesota, and Parish would visit his college-age daughters in Shreveport, Louisiana, his hometown. But when basketball beckoned, they were almost always united in purpose and dedicated to the task at hand, a mentality that never wavered. Toward that end, their relationship was one, united, and indivisible.

CHAPTER 1

Larry

Despite the retirement of their legendary forward, the Boston Celtics were in much better shape in August 1992 than they were thirteen years earlier, when Larry Bird played in his first NBA game. Bird left a team that still had enough talent and firepower to make the playoffs, although that's hardly impressive when sixteen of twenty-seven teams qualify. Bird joined a team in a state of virtual anarchy, which, after a horrific season that had sullied the proud reputation of the league's most honored franchise, needed a total make-over.

As the Celtics slogged their way through the 1978–79 season, finishing a disgraceful 29–53, both the die-hard get-a-lifers and casual fans kept a close eye on the fortunes of Indiana State University. That was where hope, salvation, and even resurrection resided in the name of Larry Joe Bird. Bird was playing out his senior year under unusual and never-to-be-repeated circumstances: he was a full-time student, but had already been drafted by the Celtics.

Indiana State is located in western Indiana, in Terre Haute. It has never been a major basketball power, except for the three-year period when Bird was there. It had never participated in any Division I postseason tournament before Bird's arrival and it has not done so since he left. A decade prior to Bird's arrival, Indiana State played at the Division II level. A young coach by the name of John Wooden presided over the ISU program in the mid-1940s. He was 44–15 in two years there, 1946–48, and his second team reached the finals of the National Association of Intercollegiate Basketball tournament, losing to Louisville. He was inducted into the ISU Hall of Fame in 1984.

Still, cognoscenti in the state will tell you that any true Indiana high school star who wants to play college basketball at home need only consider three schools: Purdue, Notre Dame, and, of course, Indiana University. At the time Bird was ready for college, Indiana State, although it was a Division I school and about to join the Missouri Valley Conference, was looked upon with almost equal parts scorn and contempt. While recruiting Bird, Indiana coach Bobby Knight told him flatly, "If you're even thinking about ISU, I don't want you to even consider IU." Indiana State was seen almost as a subspecies.

And Indiana State was not Bird's first choice. He initially selected Indiana, but it was a decision partially made out of obligation to the locals of French Lick, his hometown. He had not been heavily recruited in high school, mainly because the competition he had faced while playing for Springs Valley High School was considered a notch below the rest of the state, particularly the more competitive and popular northern Indiana high schools. Springs Valley wasn't as small as Milan (the small school that won the state title in 1954 and was the subject of the movie *Hoosiers*), but the town had a population of only two thousand, and many thought Bird's achievements must have come against subpar competition.

That bias was apparent when Bird was not named to the Associated Press All-State team, a snub that angered him and the Springs Valley coaches. But it was not surprising. "It was such a small school," said Jerry Sichting, who grew up in more populous Martinsdale. "Not many Division I players came out of that part of the state."

Kentucky coach Joe B. Hall saw Bird play in high school; he came away unimpressed and didn't pursue him. Louisville coach Denny Crum visited Bird and challenged him to a game of H-O-R-S-E. If Crum won, Bird would visit the campus. Crum lost, and soon the choices were down to Indiana, Indiana State, and Purdue.

Knight was interested in Bird and went to several Springs Valley games to see number 33. (Bird chose the number because his brother Mark had worn it before him.) After one trip, he returned to campus and rhapsodized about Bird to Quinn Buckner, then a sophomore. Buckner, who considered himself pretty good, too (he also was playing football at IU), wondered what Knight could possibly have seen to make him rave as he did. Knight also sent three players to French Lick to see Bird and to pitch the IU program. He compared Bird to Johnny Bench, the Reds' Hall of Fame catcher, in terms of hand-eye coordination.

There was also a strong Indiana supporter right in French Lick. Bird's high school coach and longtime basketball mentor, Jim Jones, had attended Indiana, and to this day many contend that he was the one who steered Bird to Bloomington. When it was discovered that Bird was being avidly wooed by Indiana, he somehow managed to land a spot on the state high school All-Star team, which played two games against high school stars from Kentucky. Gary Holland and Jones, the two Springs Valley coaches, had done some major behind-the-scenes lobbying for Bird. Making the team was a huge achievement and honor, but Sichting said Bird never would have made it if word hadn't filtered north that Indiana was recruiting him.

The All-Star games against Kentucky were preceded by a game against a touring Soviet team. Bird played fifteen minutes in that game, an easy win for the Indiana high schoolers. The games against Kentucky, however, left him angry and frustrated. In the first game, played in Kentucky, Bird was on the floor for twenty-five out of forty minutes. A large contingent from French Lick had made the short trip and were rewarded with a 23-point, 7-rebound performance from their local hero. But in the second game, in Indianapolis, Bird played only fifteen minutes in the first half and then was either forgotten or ignored in the second half. When the coach, Kirby Overman of New Albany, finally remembered Bird, he called for him to reenter the game in the closing minutes. Bird, who inherited his mother's stubbornness, felt humiliated and refused.

Ten years later, while on a road trip in Dallas, Overman showed up at the Celtics' hotel looking for tickets. He ran into Sichting in the lobby and the two had a pleasant "Glory Days" chat. When he asked Sichting for his tickets, Overman was told they were already spoken for. "But," Sichting suggested, "why don't you go up to Larry's room? Here's his room number. Maybe he'll give you his."

Sichting, of course, knew of the historic All-Star snub of Bird and must have felt a perverse sense of satisfaction as he watched Overman get into the glass elevators in the Hyatt Regency for the trip to Bird's room. Bird was there and he finally got revenge. He does not forget.

"I did basically the same thing I'd do to anybody who'd treated me like that. I told him I didn't have time and I didn't have tickets and that I wasn't interested in talking to him. Nice seeing you and have a good life," Bird said. "At the time [in high school], I was from a small town. He really didn't look at me like a big-time player because I didn't have all the publicity. But I was playing as well as anybody on that team. I had a great camp. I was playing just as well as Mr. Basketball. I played well in the first game. In the second game, he just forgot about me. I thought he overlooked me because he never thought it would come back to haunt him. Well, I guess he was wrong."

Before the high school All-Star series with Kentucky, Bird had publicly committed to Indiana, even though his friends and family members thought his choice was mostly out of duty and obligation. His mother said that Bird did not want to go and she would have preferred he go to Indiana State. His father (the Birds had been divorced in 1971) was a big IU fan, as were most people in the state. Although Bird did not know it at the time, he was a late recruit. He did not commit until April.

"I was a small-town kid with an opportunity to play for a big-time school. That's what it's all about," Bird said.

Knight recalled an incident when he was visiting the Bird home and the phone rang. On the other end was Fred Schaus, the Purdue athletic director. Knight could sense that Schaus was making a heavy pitch for Purdue.

"Schaus browbeat him on the phone," Knight said. "The kid really stood up to him. He was polite, but did not back down. His whole demeanor impressed me. That's what I'll always remember about Larry: that phone call from Fred Schaus. Boy, he was tough the way he handled it."

Bird wasn't fit for Purdue. Or, as it turned out, for Indiana. He lasted only twenty-four days in Bloomington before he suddenly hitchhiked back home. He never participated in a single practice, not to mention a game. He informally worked out with the team and remembers getting the cold shoulder from Kent Benson. Bloomington, though not far from home, might as well have been Mexico City with its sprawling campus, throngs of students, and large buildings.

Bird arrived with $75 in his pocket, a scant supply of clothes, a pair of tennis shoes, and an inferiority complex. He just felt out of place socially. His roommate, Jim Wisman, had clothes, shoes, and sophistication. Even though he, too, was from a small town (Quincy, Illinois), to Bird he looked like the sultan of Brunei.

"He was all the things that Larry wasn't at the time," Knight said. "It was a very difficult transition for him from French Lick to IU and I didn't help him at all. But I don't think anyone could have stopped him."

Bird was comfortable on the basketball court. But nowhere else.

"The whole experience of being there was intimidating," he said. "The size of the campus, the size of the classes. To me, it was pretty amazing."

Knight, who now regrets not handling the situation differently, simply didn't have time for his freshman and didn't see any need to coddle the newcomer. He had not done so for Benson, Buckner, Scott May, or Bobby Wilkerson. Why was this kid any different? And besides, it wasn't as if Bird was going to start or make a significant contribution right away. The 1974–75 team lost only once all year, to Kentucky in the NCAA tournament. The next year the team went undefeated and won the NCAA title. It was deep, talented, and arguably the best college team since UCLA dominated with Lew Alcindor and Bill Walton.

"That was a helluva team," Knight said. "Larry was kind of on the fringe that year, even if he had stayed. He just wasn't going to play as a freshman."

When Bird hears that today, he gives you one of his "What are you crazy?" looks.

"I think I would have played," he said. "Maybe not all that

much my first year. But Scotty May had a wrist injury. I don't know. I think I might have done a little better than anyone anticipated. You can say what you want, but I had a good feeling about my game. I was coming around at that time."

When Bird returned to French Lick, many people felt betrayed. He moved back in with his grandmother, whom he'd lived with for much of his adolescence, to avoid his mother's withering stares. "No question, I think people felt I let them down," he said. "But if I had to do it over again, I would do the same thing." He hasn't talked to Knight about the episode since. "Why bother? Everything worked out for the best," he said.

Two years later, after Indiana had won the NCAA title, Knight was heading to a coaches' clinic in New Orleans. When he hailed a cab at the airport, he was joined by Hubie Brown, who had just finished his second year as head coach of the Kentucky Colonels in the ABA. They had won the league championship in 1975. He was making the jump to the NBA that fall, to take over the Atlanta Hawks.

Knight got into the front seat and Brown took the back as the cabdriver took them to their hotel. The conversation, as one might expect, centered on basketball.

"Bobby," Brown said, "you've had some great players at Indiana. But who in your opinion was the best?"

"Larry Bird," Knight said without hesitation. "He was with us for only a month, but Larry Bird is the best."

"He never played for you?" Brown asked incredulously.

"No. But he was the best player to come to Indiana," Knight said.

This was before Bird had ever played a college game. He had transferred to Indiana State after taking a year off, but sat out the 1975–76 season as a transfer.

"I didn't want to sound stupid," Brown says now, "so I didn't say anything more. But I had never heard of the kid. It's just an incredible testament to Larry's career."

After leaving Indiana, Bird attended the nearby Northwood Institute for two weeks before deciding he'd like to have some money in his pocket and some time on his hands. That was when he got a job with the French Lick Public Works Department and drove a garbage truck once a week. He never stopped playing basketball, however. There was a local AAU team and Bird even practiced during the workday in the Public Works Department garage, hanging a basket to the wall. He enjoyed his brief stint as a city worker. "I had a blast," he said. He made about $150 a week and bought his first car, a 1964 Chevy.

Before he decided on Indiana State, Bird's AAU team played a game against the Indiana high school All-Star team, the same team he had been on the year before with Overman. The Indiana team was on its way to Louisville and had stopped in Mitchell, Indiana, to get a tune-up.

"Larry just killed us," said Sichting, a member of the team in 1975. "Then I played against him again later in the summer in an outdoor tournament in Lebanon. They eliminated us. He was with some Indiana State guys. We were playing on concrete and Larry dives for a loose ball. He gets it, sits up, and, while still sitting, makes the shot."

There was also a lot going on in Bird's personal life at that time. His father committed suicide in 1975, an event Bird speaks frankly about today. "He made his decision on how he wanted to live and how he wanted to die. I still can't believe it. All I can hope for is that we'll meet up again."

There also was an affair of the heart that would prove ruinous. He was engaged to Janet Condra, a cheerleader at Springs Valley High, and they got married in November 1975. It was an ill-advised marriage from the start, and eleven months later they were divorced. A month later, Janet discovered she was pregnant and, in August 1977, while Bird was overseas playing in the World University Games, she gave birth to a little girl, Corrie. At first, Bird contended the child was not his, but Janet Condra went to court and won a paternity/child support judgment. She has since remarried and lives with her daughter outside Terre Haute.

Indiana State hired a new basketball coach for the 1975–76 season, Bob King, who had come from the University of New Mexico. His biggest achievement of the year came before the season started, when he convinced Larry Bird to come to ISU. It was not an easy sell, mainly because there were doubts that Bird wanted to go to college. He was having fun at home, hanging out with his buddies, making enough money to keep him happy and out of the public eye. Even when Bird became a celebrity, he still preferred hanging out in French Lick with his buddies.

King dispatched assistant Bill Hodges to resume the chase. When Hodges made his first visit to the Bird house, Georgia Bird, Larry's mother, shooed him away. Hodges came back again, this time with Tony Clark, a childhood friend of Bird's and a former high school teammate who had gone to Indiana State and made the team as a freshman walk-on.

"[Hodges] said to me," Clark recalled, " 'Let's see if we can't get Larry to come.' Finally, [Bird] agreed."

Bird soon discovered, however, that he was in financial trouble. The money from his NCAA scholarship was barely enough to keep him going. For the first year, he was living with Janet. After they divorced, Bird convinced his brother Mark to move in with him in Terre Haute and to get a job to help support him. Mark wasn't working in French Lick and had just left college. He found a job with Columbia Records in Terre Haute and that provided enough money for both of them to exist. Mark Bird stayed at Columbia until the plant was moved to Georgia in 1982. He then took over the management of Larry's hotel in Terre Haute.

Bird's college career at Indiana State lasted three eventful seasons. After sitting out the 1975–76 season (ISU went 13–12), Bird suffered a collapsed lung in the summer of 1976. He was incapacitated for two months, but he was ready for the season opener. Indiana State went 25–2 and wound up being ranked sixteenth in the country. Its only losses were to Illinois State and Purdue, each by 6 points and each on the road. Bird averaged 32.8 points a game, and thus became only the twelfth player in NCAA history to average 30 or more points as a sophomore. He also averaged 13.3 rebounds and shot 54 percent from the field and 84 percent from the line. Except for his rebounding figures, these were the best numbers of his college career.

The paths of the Big Three never crossed in college. Robert Parish was finishing up at Centenary the year Bird sat out as a transfer. Interestingly, Indiana State and Centenary played every year from 1972 to 1975, took the 1975–76 year off, and then played twice in 1976–77, Bird's first season at ISU, but by then Parish was in the NBA. And after the two games in 1976–77, Centenary and Indiana State stopped meeting. But the Centenary coach at the time, Riley Wallace, vividly recalled the two games in Bird's sophomore year.

"The first time at our place, it was a close game, but we lost [74–71]. And Bird didn't hurt us all that bad [Bird had 28 points]," Wallace said. "And I said to myself, 'I'll just box him when we play them again at Indiana State. Then he won't hurt us.' So what happens? He fouled three guys out. He had a huge game [37 points, 19 rebounds, 5 steals] and they just killed us [88–70]. I decided then and there that the best thing to do with him was lay low and not stir him up."

Indiana State had never been to a major postseason tournament, but the NIT called. (At 25–2, how could they not?) Having just joined the Missouri Valley Conference, Indiana State had to wait a year to be eligible for the conference title and an automatic NCAA berth. The Sycamores eagerly accepted the NIT bid. "Pack your bags for Houston," said King. They did and lost, 83–82, when Bird's last-second off-balance shot missed. (Bird felt he was fouled on the shot, but there was no call.)

In the summer of 1977, Denny Crum led a United States team to Sofia, Bulgaria, for the World University Games. The team went 8–0 and Bird was named the Most Valuable Player. He hated the trip—his first of any duration outside Indiana—and was more than happy to return. His life until then had been still relatively tame, but that was about to change.

For the cover of its college basketball preview issue on the 1977–78 season, *Sports Illustrated* used a photo of Bird with two ISU cheerleaders. The women had their index fingers on their lips, urging everyone to keep quiet. That was because Bird was deemed to be college basketball's secret weapon. Once the magazine was out, though, Bird was anything but a secret weapon. He was visible, known, and from that point on his life became an open book, much to his regret.

"It was like a gold rush after that. That picture changed my life," he said. "From then on, everyone was coming to get their story."

And in the beginning, Bird and Indiana State made *Sports Illustrated* look like a prophet. The team came out of the blocks in the fall of 1977 and won its first thirteen games. Bird's name was quickly becoming a household word, at least in basketball homes, and he again put up impressive numbers, averaging 30 points and 11.5 rebounds a game. The Sycamores rose to fourth in the national rankings, then hit the wall and lost five straight. They finished the season at 22–8, losing to Creighton in the Missouri Valley Conference tournament.

Again, the NIT beckoned. After a first-round win over Illinois State, the Sycamores lost to Rutgers and Bird got into a fight with a fan leaving the floor after the game. As was the case the year before against Houston, Bird missed a last-second shot. As was the case the year before, he felt he was fouled, but there was no call.

Between his junior and senior years, Bird again ran afoul of Joe B. Hall, the Kentucky coach who hadn't even deemed Bird worthy of recruiting in high school. This time, the situation was the World Invitational Games, a round-robin tournament involving college All-Stars, Russians, Yugoslavs, and Cubans. The games were played at three college sites in the United States and the U.S. team was heavily laden with Kentucky players (Kentucky had just won the NCAA title). Hall started four Kentucky players, keeping players like Bird, Sidney Moncrief of Arkansas, and a sophomore-to-be from Michigan State named Magic Johnson on the bench most of the time. The United States won anyway.

"The practices were the best part because Larry and Magic were the dominating players," recalled Rick Robey, a member of the team. "They were on the second team, but they used to clean up in practice."

There also was something else looming between Bird's junior and senior years: the NBA draft. All season long, teams had dispatched scouts to check on Bird. The Celtics first heard the name Larry Bird when longtime scout and assistant coach John Killilea, then in his final season with Boston, had seen Bird play in St. Louis the year before. He came back to town raving about "the best passing forward I've seen since Rick Barry."

"I thought he was the best forward I ever saw," Killilea said. "It was enough to make me say that he would be better than Rick Barry. We were out on the road when I saw him. Tommy [Celtics coach Tom Heinsohn] and I would go out if we had a chance, and we saw him at a game in Kiel Auditorium. At the time we were so thin, when you got a chance to see someone, anyone, you saw him. I was thoroughly impressed with the guy. I thought he was the greatest natural player I had ever seen.''

Auerbach dispatched K. C. Jones, then a scout, to watch Bird and the same reviews came in. Auerbach himself saw Bird only once in college. ''I was very impressed, but I had no illusions how great he would turn out to be,'' he said.

Bird was available for the NBA draft in 1978 because of the league's junior eligible rule. At that time, a player became eligible for the draft four years after his college career began, regardless of his college eligibility status. Once a student enrolled in a school, as Bird did at Indiana in the fall of 1974, he became a member of the class that would be seniors in four years. By attending Indiana for twenty-four days, Bird had become a member of the class of 1978 in the eyes of the NBA. So even though he had a year of eligibility left at Indiana State, he would probably be playing that season while an NBA team held his draft rights.

Prior to 1976, a team lost its rights to a junior eligible if the player returned to college and played in a game. Thus, a team had to have a pretty good idea the player would sign if it drafted him. Elgin Baylor was a junior eligible pick by the Minneapolis Lakers in 1958, the first pick overall. He left Seattle University and turned pro. Bird was the first major player to become available under the new guidelines, which went into effect with a new collective bargaining agreement in 1976.

Had the old rules been in effect, Bird would never have been drafted in 1978 because he had every intention of returning for his final season at Indiana State. The pick would have been a waste.

The new rule gave the team that drafted Bird a year (until the next draft) to sign him. If it couldn't, he would go into the 1979 draft pool. The league thought a player would not be ''solicited'' by other teams if he stayed in school and only one team held his rights. But the rule gave a player incredible leverage. If he didn't like the money, the traffic, the teammates, the uniforms, or the restaurants, he could say, "Sorry boys," and there was nothing the team could do about it.

"It was a twofold risk," Celtics general manager Jan Volk said of the Bird situation. "The first is that you ran the risk of waiting a whole year if the player returned to college. The second risk was not getting him at all."

At first, Auerbach was still under the impression that the old rule was still in effect. He never bothered with the finer points of labor agreements; that's why Volk was around. After some internal discussions, a call was placed to the NBA office and league counsel David Stern informed the Celtics that, yes, Bird was a junior eligible under the guidelines, meaning that Boston would not lose his rights the moment he returned to Indiana State and played for the Sycamores.

There was no doubt as to Bird's value or talent. There were some concerns about his speed, jumping ability, and, incredibly, his toughness. But had he been leaving Indiana State after the 1977–78 season, he might well have been the number one pick in the draft. He never would have slid to number six, which is where the Celtics took him.

The sixth pick was Boston's own and the Celtics had it for a reason: they were awful. They had won only thirty-two games, one less than Bird's Indiana State team would win the following year. The team had gone through eighteen players, had fired a coach for the first time in the Auerbach era, and, by all accounts, was getting worse, not better. John Havlicek was retiring; Dave Cowens had taken a "leave of absence" the season before; Sidney Wicks and Curtis Rowe, acquired to bolster the sagging team, instead became a symbol of the team's futility and sloth. And the owner, Irv Levin, was desperate to leave town and get back to southern California.

But the Celtics also had an extra pick in the 1978 draft, the eighth overall, which had come from the Lakers, who in turn had gotten it from New Orleans. The company line nowadays is that Bird would have been Boston's choice at number six even if there had been no number eight. But the fact is that the Celtics had a cushion that only one other team (Portland, which had the first and seventh picks) had.

"Red couldn't have done it with just one pick," Bill Fitch said. He was the coach who would inherit Bird and the 29-53 team from 1978–79. "They needed help right away. They were so damn bad. A lot of people at the time thought Red was nuts. Now, of course, they say anyone would have done the same thing. That's just not true."

The story of how the Celtics acquired the eighth pick adds to the Auerbach lore, for it was one of his great moves. The Celtics at the time were awful, the butt of jokes, the object of pity, and yet Auerbach was secure. He was the personification of the teams that, through the 1960s and 1970s, won eleven NBA championships, despite going through ten ownerships in twenty years. He was the one constant link to all the banners. The unconditional reverence extended to down time as well. He always escaped culpability, blaming the referees, the league, or any convenient target and generally getting away with it. There was always an expectation in lean years that Auerbach would reverse things with one bold move. He usually did something right; the Celtics were an ongoing success on the court. But because the Celtics weren't drawing well at the box office, his moves seldom drew much attention or public scrutiny.

Celtics history is littered with examples of Auerbach moves that at the time seemed risky. Not all of them worked. Many did. But he was never afraid to try.

Auerbach traded a popular, productive player (Ed Macauley) and the rights to a legitimate college star (Cliff Hagan) because he saw something special in Bill Russell. He didn't care that Russell wouldn't be available until midseason because of an Olympic commitment. He didn't care that Jo Jo White had a supposedly ironclad military commitment; hadn't anyone heard of the reserves? Danny Ainge wanted to play baseball? He couldn't hit the curve, could he? And the storied Celtics might be able to change his thinking. He took a flyer on Charlie Scott, even though Scott was in the ABA— what did he have to lose, especially in the seventh round? The pick eventually would get them Paul Silas. The one time he was indisputably lucky was when, after first bypassing him in the draft, Auerbach drew Bob Cousy's name out of a hat during a dispersal draft and got the Cooz to Boston.

"You know, it's the old saying, 'Nothing ventured, nothing gained.' We had one thing going for us over the years that the others didn't," Auerbach said, "and that was reputation. Most players then, and now, would love to play in Boston. We have enough ego to think that it's the organization, but it's not all that. It's the city, too. But it's the Celtics, too."

Looking at the disaster in the making in 1977, Auerbach traded Charlie Scott to the Lakers. In return, he received Kermit Washington, who at that time was on indefinite suspension for rearranging Rudy Tomjanovich's face. That in and of itself would have made the trade worthwhile. But he also got Don Chaney, who was nearing the end of his career but managed to play for three more seasons. And, at the time, it was announced that the Celtics had received "future considerations" from the Lakers.

No one divulged what those considerations might be. The Celtics' owner, Irv Levin, said only that "it's something that we think is really going to help our team." Eventually, of course, word leaked out that the "future consideration" was the number one draft pick in 1978 that the Lakers had received from New Orleans. The Lakers had received that pick fifteen months earlier in a transaction that, given the players it eventually touched—Bird and Magic Johnson— may have been the biggest deal in NBA history.

The Jazz had won thirty-eight games in their second season in the league, 1975–76, and were determined to keep improving. The team made an ill-fated move for Sidney Wicks, promising Portland $50,000 a year for ten years. Wicks never reported, stayed in Portland, and eventually was traded to Boston. The Jazz also targeted a veteran free agent, Gail Goodrich, whose contract with the Lakers had expired. Goodrich was still well known and could still play. The Jazz signed him to a contract.

In those days, a team that signed a free agent had to arrange compensation with the free agent's team. And, in those days, the Lakers had money, clout, and history. The Jazz had nothing. Dave Fredman worked in the front office with the Jazz at the time and recalls that the one fear among the New Orleans shakers and movers was that the compensation would include cash. Why? "Because the Jazz didn't have any," Fredman said. "They felt that any deal that didn't involve money was, therefore, a good deal." They knew that the Lakers had had to part with more than $200,000 after signing free agent Keith Wilkes from Golden State. The Jazz were determined to avoid paying a cent. Toward that end, they succeeded. Instead, they paid with their future.

When the dust settled, the agreement called for the Lakers to receive first-round picks from the Jazz in 1977 and 1979 and also swap first-round picks with the Jazz in 1978. And since New Orleans would probably finish with a worse record than the Lakers in 1977–78, the advantage would tilt toward Los Angeles in 1978 as well. Each team also threw in a second-round pick to finish the deal. The Jazz never revealed the extent of the transaction, saying at the time only that compensation with the Lakers had been agreed upon and that it involved a number one draft pick in 1979. The truth got out seven months later.

Magic Johnson eventually went to the Lakers with the number one pick in 1979, the second of the two Goodrich compensation first-rounders. The flip-flopped pick in 1978 was the one the Lakers sent to Boston as the future consideration from the Scott–Washington/Chaney deal. That pick turned out to be the eighth overall—New Orleans had gone 39–43 in 1977–78—giving Boston what it needed to take a risk on Bird.

Now, with two first-round picks, the Celtics felt confident. They then made things even better by signing Kevin Kunnert, a free-agent center from Houston, as insurance in the event that Bird wasn't available when Boston picked. He became a Celtics footnote because he never played a game for the team. Now the Celtics simply had to wait and hope that Bird would still be around when they picked sixth. They had already decided that they could not afford to wait until number eight because Portland, which had considered drafting Bird first overall, would definitely take him at number seven.

"The original thought process," Volk recalled, "was to get the better available player at six and go for Larry at eight. But we began to get a real strong feeling that Portland would take Bird with the seventh pick, and that no one else could afford him or afford to take a chance on him. There were a lot of question marks about Larry, even back then, and his plan to go back to school was risky. Most teams needed a player right away. But with Portland, the more we heard, the more we thought they would use that seventh pick on Bird. So we decided to take him at six.''

Portland had talked to Bird. But the Trail Blazers needed a center, having lost Bill Walton. They had also traded Johnny Davis to Indiana to get the number one pick and they felt they needed to get someone to show for it. Mychal Thompson, the Minnesota center who played with Kevin McHale for two years, was their pick. It made sense. The next day, the consensus was that Portland, which had the NBA's best record the year before, had gotten even stronger. And it still had the number seven pick, which was going to be used on Bird, even though general manager Stu Inman had some misgivings about him.

''I didn't think his body would hold up,'' Inman said. ''He had the beer-drinking, softball-player image and you wondered how well he took care of himself. How well can he jump? Is he for real? Did I think he was good enough to be taken number one? The answer is yes. I even had a short conversation with Larry that spring. I suggested we get together for coffee. He said he was playing softball. I said I'd get back to him, but I never could. His phone was disconnected. The athletic department said they'd take messages, but you know how that went. I never did get back to him.

''I never had any doubt about Magic. Or Bill Russell. I think we realized this kid might be good. Did any of us at the time think he'd be that good? Well, if anyone says yes, they're lying.''

The Kansas City Kings were next. They had a money crunch, and if Bird was to be lured out of college—and he had been adamant in saying that would not be the case—then the team would have to break the bank. The Kings were in no position to do so. They also needed help right away.

Kansas City had just hired a new coach, Cotton Fitzsimmons. He had been in Atlanta when the Hawks drafted both David Thompson and Marvin Webster in the first round and hadn't been able to sign either. "We never recovered from that," he said. He was determined not to go through the same thing with Bird. "If we take Larry and Larry not only waits a year, which is a problem in itself, but then goes back into the draft, then the Kings have a very serious problem. And money was always a problem in Kansas City. That's why the team isn't there anymore."

Kansas City took Phil Ford, even though Fitzsimmons said the Kings had been warned not to do so by both Ford's agent, David Falk, and his college coach, Dean Smith. "They told us he'd never play there," Fitzsimmons said. "Finally, I just told them that we were going to take him and he'd play with us. And he did."

And he played well. He is the answer to the trivia question "Who was the NBA Rookie of the Year in the year Larry Bird was drafted by the Celtics?"

The Indiana Pacers had the next pick and planned to draft and wait for their favorite son. But the Atlanta Hawks intervened at the eleventh hour and signed Pacers free-agent forward Dan Roundfield to a contract back-loaded into the twenty-first century. Their new coach, Hubie Brown, had fallen in love with Roundfield in the ABA and the Hawks put the double squeeze on Roundfield, with GM Mike Gearon out making the pitch while team counsel Stan Kasten stayed back in Atlanta, crunching numbers.

"We had Danny in our sights all year long," Kasten said. "He was young, athletic, and as soon as we could talk to him, we did. We got it done in twenty-four hours, flew him down to Atlanta for the draft. It was going to be the greatest day in the history of the franchise. We drafted two NCAA stars in Butch Lee and Jack Givens and we also got Danny. It didn't take too long for us to realize the best thing we did that day was sign Danny."

And the Pacers, cash strapped like the Kings, did not have the resources to compete. They were $200,000 short of appeasing Roundfield, a pitiful sum in today's NBA but a mother lode back then. Now, with Roundfield gone and Bird not available for a year, Indiana coach Bob "Slick" Leonard had to deviate from his plan. He selected Ricky Robey, a 6-10 bruiser from Kentucky, the NCAA national champion. It was a widely applauded, logical choice, but not the one Leonard wanted to make.

"Here's how bad it was for us," he said. "Even then, with compensation, we could either get a [1978 first-round] draft pick or cash [for Roundfield]. We took the cash. One hundred thousand dollars. It was a struggle. That's how hard up we were. [The Pacers did get Atlanta's number one pick the following year, however.] Teams prey on you when you are weak, in that position. And we were weak. I don't know if it'd been better had we taken [Bird]. We soon got a change in ownership, but the way he finished up [at college], we'd have had troubling finding the money."

Kasten, now the Atlanta Hawks' president, to this day remains envious of Boston's success, having tried admirably but unsuccessfully to duplicate it in Atlanta. He had a love-hate relationship with Boston during the 1980s, hating the outcome of most Boston-Atlanta games but loving the many fans who would buy Celtics jackets, shirts, and hats at the concourse shops at the Omni. When Bird was on the cover of *Time* in 1985, Kasten's reaction was typically quick and sharp: "I went out and bought *Newsweek.*"

And how does he feel knowing that the Roundfield raid helped get Bird to Boston?

"He would have tormented us wherever he ended up," Kasten said. "But if those two guys [Roundfield and Bird] had ever been together, I'm not sure that wouldn't have been even scarier. Danny could run like the wind. They would have played well together."

The Knicks had the fourth pick, courtesy of a Treaty of Versailles–like indemnity settlement with the Nets, who had joined the NBA and intruded on the Knicks' territorial hegemony. Money was not the issue here; the Knicks were owned by Gulf & Western. But the company's board of directors, one of whom, Donald F. Gaston, would later purchase the Celtics, had to answer to stockholders. As part of the settlement the Knicks received $400,000 from the Nets, but the corporate bigwigs also wanted a player who was available right away. And Bird, while coveted by both GM Eddie Donovan and coach Willis Reed, was deemed a no-go by Gulf & Western.

"I wanted to take Bird," Donovan said. "I thought there would be a good chance we could get him signed before the next draft. What kid wouldn't want to play in New York?"

Bird might have been one. He had visited New York in college for a photo shoot and was appalled at having to pay $6 for a Coke and a hamburger. He told an Indiana State official traveling with him that he could never play in New York. When he dined in New York one night with Robey during his rookie year, Bird got the bill and saw it was for $50. He was aghast. He was further stunned when Robey suggested an extra $15 for a tip. "Sixty-five dollars for one dinner?" Bird said incredulously. "You could eat for a week on that in French Lick." (Years later, with some $20 to $25 million in the bank, Bird was in Monte Carlo, preparing for the 1992 Olympics, and was equally appalled to discover it cost $7 to buy a beer. It wasn't money. It was principle. He didn't spring for the beer.)

The Knicks took Montana guard Micheal Ray Richardson. Reed thought the Celtics wanted Richardson as well, and to this day thinks that Richardson, not Bird, was Boston's preferred pick. "That's bull," scoffs Auerbach. "I never even saw Micheal Ray Richardson play."

The only team now remaining before Boston selected was Golden State. The Warriors did have two first-round picks, but their second was the twenty-second choice, the last one in the round. Thus, it could hardly be construed as insurance, as the Celtics' number eight pick clearly was. And Golden State needed immediate help, not future help. It selected a scoring machine from Jackson State named Purvis Short, who ended up having a reasonably productive NBA career for the Warriors and, later, the Houston Rockets.

"The Celtics had the best of all worlds," said Al Attles, the Warriors' coach at the time. "They weren't dependent on getting a player right then. They could allow him to play that year in college. We needed a guy right now. It wasn't that we didn't think Bird was a great player. We all knew he was. But everyone was afraid of losing the pick. You couldn't negotiate with the guy when he was in school. I'm sure a lot of us are looking back now. But we had Rick [Barry] already."

The grin began to form on Auerbach's face as soon as the words "Purvis Short of Jackson State" came out of the mouth of NBA commissioner Larry O'Brien. Without equivocation, he picked up the telephone at the Celtics's draft headquarters in Boston and connected with Volk, who was in New York. The message: Larry Bird of Indiana State.

"I'm not sure of how aware I was of how significant this was going to be," Volk said, "but I do remember a surge of excitement. So I wrote down 'Larry Bird' and sent it in. Red is pretty good at calculating risks and we felt the upside was worth it. And I don't think any of us, even Red, understood how big that upside was."

Auerbach to this day denies taking any credit for being anything other than a gambler that day. "We weren't stupid," he said. "If there had been any chance that he would have come out, we never would have gotten a chance to draft him. If there had been any chance of him playing, we never would have gotten near him. Not even close. But the way I looked at it was this: how many times do you get a chance to sit at the table and get the player who has the number one ability in the country?"

The Celtics knew little about Bird, other than what they had seen on film and in person. In those days, the draft was considerably less scientific. The Celtics brass never had Bird in for an interview, never met with him in Indiana. They would go another eight years before they started interviewing draft picks; McHale was never brought in. Now it's routine and taken to almost ridiculous lengths. The Celtics had the twenty-fourth pick in 1990 and brought in fifteen players for interviews.

Once the pick was announced, people around the league shook their heads and wondered. Bill Fitch, in Cleveland, thought to himself, "That goddamn Red. He's done it again." Little did Fitch know that he would be Bird's first pro coach in Boston a year later. Jimmy Rodgers, who was with Fitch in Cleveland and later would coach Bird in Boston, was surprised because junior eligibles were generally regarded as late first-round picks or second-rounders, especially if they were not going to be immediately available. "Yet you knew he was a good draft pick if the Celtics were willing to wait."

Then there was the other side, the theory that the Celtics had nothing to lose, given that they also had the eighth pick. That theory gained more supporters each year as Bird's ability and Boston's success made Bird seem like a natural choice.

"I don't think it was a brilliant move by Boston," said Indiana's Bob Leonard. "And let's be honest, they got more than they bargained for. No one had the slightest idea he'd turn out to be as great as he turned out to be."

On Draft Day 1978, Bird was playing golf, appropriately, in Santa Claus, Indiana, when he was approached on the course and told the Celtics had taken him. He had absolutely no idea what that meant. Did it mean he'd have to leave college? Did it mean he'd get paid? There was no one more unaware and, frankly, unconcerned about impending celebrity than Larry Bird on that June day. He didn't even know that there was an NBA draft that day, let alone that he'd be selected. And the thought of going to Boston, which might as well have been Vladivostok, had no allure whatsoever. He got a better read on the situation when he returned home that night, turned on the local sports in French Lick, and found out just what had happened. He then got a further rundown from the folks at Indiana State.

He had no intention of leaving school. He wanted to finish and become the first member of his family to get a degree. (He did, getting a bachelor of science degree in physical education.) And, more to the point, he was enjoying college. Bird could have considered leaving when coach Bob King was forced to step down after suffering a heart attack and then a brain aneurysm. Bird wanted Bill Hodges, an assistant, to take over, but another assistant, Stan Evans, had come to Indiana State expecting to be King's replacement. Evans, who had hired Hodges, was originally supposed to take the coaching reins the year before, but with Bird's arrival and the team's success, King decided to postpone his move to athletic director.

King, thinking he might yet recover enough to return to coaching, selected Hodges to take over. Evans promptly left and former Pacers star Mel Daniels was hired as an assistant. The promotion of Hodges gave Bird something he might not have had under Evans: almost complete control over the team. But then, who better?

Once the Celtics realized Bird was staying, they were careful not to exert any pressure on their future prize. Auerbach briefly flirted with getting Bird signed for the playoffs, if there were any. As it turned out, the Celtics finished in last place. Bird now somewhat regrets not hitching on with Boston for the final month or so, if for no other reason than the fact that no one else had done it or likely will ever do it. He would have been the first—and last.

Other than knowing something about Bill Russell, Bird was astonishingly ignorant about the team that had drafted him. He had no idea it had won thirteen NBA titles, including eight in a row. Basketball may be king in Indiana, but the NBA is somewhere way down in the kingdom. High school hoops, men's and women's, and college basketball all are more important than the NBA in Indiana. Bird had no idea who Auerbach was, or most of the other Celtics greats. He was in his own comfortable world in southern Indiana, and neither the NBA in general nor the Celtics in particular held any attraction.

It was Jim Jones who guided Larry Bird through the various stages of basketball, as well as life. And he has a ready-made definition of a true Indiana Hoosier: "He's the one dribbling the basketball around the Indy 500 speedway with a mushroom sack over his shoulder."

Bird didn't have much use for the Indy 500 (once, in 1986, he suggested that fellow Hoosier Jerry Sichting was more concerned about the upcoming Memorial Day race than about the soon-to-begin NBA finals against Houston). But he loved basketball and he loved to hunt mushrooms. The latter is a preoccupation in Indiana. People plan their vacations to coincide with the spring arrival of the fungi, which are also called morels. Every house, or so it seems, has its own recipe and batter for deep-frying them. You never divulge the recipe. And, Jones noted, "you never tell anyone where your mushroom patch is, either."

Sports in general and basketball in particular was Bird's outlet from a dark, economically deprived childhood. He was the fourth of six children (five boys) and he was forever following around big brothers Mike and Mark, who played football, baseball, and basketball and hung out at the local pool hall.

"Larry was a little cottontop," said Jones, who organized the town's youth basketball program (Biddy Ball) and coached Bird through his junior year in high school. "All three of the boys were. They were always playing sports. Always involved in something. The mom was always working and the boys were always over at their grandma's house. They kind of took their turn living there, one following the next, making the house less crowded."

None of the Big Three came from wealth or privilege. Bird not only had neither, he also had the largest and most troubled family. His father, Joe, battled unsuccessfully for years against the ravages of alcohol until, inevitably, he was divorced by Georgia Bird. Joe later committed suicide in the most lurid fashion, calling Georgia on the telephone and letting her hear the sound of a shotgun blast as it ended his life.

In a television interview on the Celtics-owned station shortly after her son retired, Georgia Bird said of the suicide, "It's a lot how it was done that makes it so terrible. If it had been a car wreck or something, it would not have been as bad. But to think that maybe we all could have done something, especially me. I always thought if I could have done one little thing, maybe that could have changed the whole thing."

The Birds lived in French Lick, a name that became synonymous with Bird throughout his career. The town abuts West Baden, which is where Bird built his new house after turning pro and where he spent much of his adolescence living with his grandmother. They are two totally separate incorporated towns. The main industries in the area are the Kimball piano factory and Kimball Electronics, both subsidiaries of Kimball International, which, between them, employ about a thousand people. The region also has agriculture and wood-working and a resort hotel that was famous long before Larry Joe Bird ever arrived.

Bird grew up not in the flatter country of northern Indiana, but in an area of hills and valleys. And poverty. Orange County was among the state's poorest at the time. Joe Bird was a redhead with a receding hairline who chain-smoked but was well liked. Said Jones, "When Joe was right, he'd give you the shirt off his back. But when he wasn't . . ." Joe Bird held a variety of jobs: he worked at a gypsum plant and at his brother-in-law's chicken farm, and he also did odd jobs. But he never was able to keep a job for a sufficient amount of time because of the unrelenting strains of alcohol and creditors, his two lifelong nemeses. Georgia Bird also went to work at the chicken farm, as well as at a shoe factory and a nursing home, to support the six children. As is the case when everyone in a community is pretty much in the same economic lot, Bird felt neither deprived nor bereft growing up, though he now recognizes he was both.

"I thought it was the greatest. I really did," he said. "Everyone played ball. Every sport. Whatever was in season. I had a lot of freedom as a kid. My parents worked, so I could come and go as I pleased, just as long as I was home in time to go to bed. That's what I think life is all about. My mom was working, but all she had to do was go by the fields if she wanted to find us. French Lick is in a poor area, but everyone had basically the same things. No one had anything real lavish. I used to quarter my mom and dad to death. 'Can I have a quarter? Can I have a quarter?' Some days I got one, some days I didn't."

The area is known for its mineral springs, which prompted the construction of two lavish hotels, the French Lick Springs Resort and the West Baden Springs Hotel. Both were built in the late 1840s and catered to the barons and baronesses of the time. A separate railroad spur was even built to accommodate the bigwigs who would make the trip by train, and they included the likes of Al Capone, Franklin D. Roosevelt, Jack Dempsey, Tom Mix, Howard Hughes, and Jacob Ruppert, then owner of the New York Yankees. The primary attraction of the hotels was casino gambling, but Indiana clamped down and sent in the state police in 1949. Baseball teams also practiced in the area in the early part of the twentieth century, as did several boxers, including John L. Sullivan

The springs and mineral waters also produced a very powerful natural laxative called Pluto Water. It was so named by the builder of the French Lick Springs Resort Hotel because it came from underground. (In classical mythology, Pluto was the god of the dead and the lower world.) The water was supposed to cure as many as fifty-five ailments, and the saying "If nature won't, Pluto will" was common and widespread in the area.

But the lure of the valley was gone by the time Bird grew up in the 1960s and 1970s. The Pluto Water bottling plant had begun to produce Blue Lustre Carpet Cleaner and packaging materials. The West Baden Springs Hotel was closed after being sold for $1 to the Society of Jesus, which in turn sold it to the since-closed Northwood Institute in 1966. The town is now restoring the hotel and plans to reopen it, however.

Joe Bird did a stint in the service and returned to West Baden after the war. There, he got a job at a factory and met Georgia Kerns, who was in the same car pool. When war broke out in Korea, Joe reenlisted and Georgia ended up working at a paper company in town that also employed Joe's mother, Helen. Joe and Georgia were married in September 1951 on one of his leaves. The two both came from large families—Joe had eleven siblings, Georgia had seven. They quickly had four children within five years; Larry Joe was born on the fifteenth anniversary of the bombing of Pearl Harbor, December 7, 1956.

Bird inherited his toughness from his father, who, like Paul McHale and Robert Parish, Sr., rarely missed a day of work. He also inherited a stubborn streak from his mother, although he says he doesn't stay mad at someone or something for as long as she does. When he left the University of Indiana after staying there for just over three weeks, Georgia Bird was so upset she wouldn't speak to her son for a month. He also became a neatness nerd, a trait that carries over to this day. When he was young, his mother called him "Mr. Clean." And, she said, "he still is that way today."

Bird learned the fundamentals of basketball through the Biddy Ball league and from Jim Jones, a graduate of Indiana University. Jones had a passion for baseball, not basketball, but he knew the Indiana basketball tradition, and he also knew the sport. He got the boys playing by the third grade, teaching them to box out, shoot free throws, and, more than anything, practice, practice, and practice. He would see his players in the summertime, when he technically wasn't allowed to coach them, and simply say "Hi" as he passed by. He told them he'd be back soon, but never exactly when. This was how Jones got his future players to practice and work at their game continually. There was nothing worse than a coach's distrust, so Bird, Mike Cox, Tony Clark, and the others would always be playing hoops—none of them wanted to be the one who wasn't there when the coach came back. And Jones also knew the boys liked to be watched. The more they worked, the better their chance of being watched. "We instilled the work ethic in them," he said. "It's good in the game of life, too."

According to Bird, "When I was in seventh grade, Jim Jones came to me and said, 'Everything you do is with your right hand. You are not going to be able to play the game unless you use both hands equally. So from that day on, if you've ever seen any pictures of me bringing the ball up, I'm always using my left hand. Now my left hand feels more comfortable with a basketball than my right hand. [Bird writes and eats left-handed.] You ever seen Bob Cousy? He always used his right hand. He never used his left hand. He could have been in a farm accident and lost his left arm and still been able to play basketball.

"But I was always practicing something. And Jim Jones would stop by to watch and he'd say, 'Larry, you're always playing basketball. And that's great. You shoot twenty thousand free throws and that's great. But there's always one kid down the road or in the next state over who is shooting twenty-one thousand. You're never going to be the best because there's always someone out there trying to be a little better than you.' That made you want to work that much harder. Unfortunately for me, I ran into that guy. His name is Magic Johnson."

Larry always followed Mark and Mike to games in the local park. "You had to figure one of us would make it," Mike said. "And Mark and I beat Larry up enough that eventually it sunk in." One advantage of staying with his grandmother was that her house was near a streetlight and they could play at night. And, when Bird was in junior high school, he would sometimes get the privilege of playing in games involving the blacks who worked at the hotel. They would gather at the park in the afternoon. It was Bird's only exposure to blacks growing up; there were none on his high school team.

"Those guys were great," he recalled. "Sometimes they would let us in their games, and it was a great experience for us. We had to learn to pass and rebound and do the little things because they liked to do all the scoring. It was great."

Bird still shakes his head in amazement over one of the black players, Mike Odon. A lot of towns and cities have Mike Odons, players of legendary local proportions who simply vanished. Odon attended Northwood Institute. At 6-5, he could play above the rim, and Bird and his friends thought he was just about the greatest thing they'd ever seen on a basketball floor.

"We thought for sure he'd be a pro one day," said Clark.

"He was just an unbelievable player," Bird said. "Unbelievable. He would get forty a night, easy. One night, we all went over to watch when Kentucky State came in. They had Travis Grant and Elmore Smith and the two of them scored about a hundred that night. But Odon played basketball nonstop. He was a lot like Scotty May [an All-American at Indiana]. He was something. Then he got mono. I never heard of him since. But he was unbelievable."

The Birds never left the area for vacations or trips. Larry worked at the local grocery store or his uncle's gas station simply to have some money in his pocket. Occasionally, Jones would organize trips to see ABA games in Louisville. Bird went to one and didn't even know it was a pro game until he returned and someone told him. His travels were basically limited to the Sunday trips he and Clark would make to Bedford, a twenty-five- to thirty-mile round-trip, just to get some Kentucky Fried Chicken. Then they'd immediately turn around and head back to French Lick, get the keys to the gym, and play basketball.

"Money wasn't that big an issue because most of us didn't have any," Bird said. "The only way you did is if you had a job. And even then, I couldn't make enough money to go out and buy a pair of sneakers or a pair of pants. But I always had a few bucks in my pocket. I never knew what existed beyond ten miles. I thought it was great."

The insularity of the area and the passion for basketball combined to produce this most introspective and introverted person. His shyness was legendary, to the point where he avoided crowds at the local high school games when his brothers were playing. And even when he was starring at Springs Valley High and putting up big numbers, he was virtually ignored by the supposedly more savvy northern basketball folk who regarded the southern Indiana players almost with contempt. They were underdeveloped, and as a result were underpublicized.

"He always was very quiet, with a heavy concentration on basketball and trying to become the best," Clark said. "I can remember him shooting outside in the rain, all by himself. And I remember when he broke his ankle and he was determined to play on the varsity. He would be out on the court, standing with a crutch, and practicing his shot. Basketball was real important to him."

It was between his freshman and sophomore years in high school that basketball went from a season diversion to an obsession for Bird. Making the varsity as a sophomore was of paramount importance. He did. And then, in his second game, he went up for an offensive rebound, came down, and broke his left ankle. He stayed in the game. Jones told him it wasn't serious until it swelled up, and then he knew differently. Bird was put in a cast, which, because of the excessive wear and tear from, among other things, playing basketball, fell off before it was supposed to be removed.

He struggled to make it back on the team in time for the final games and the state tournament. In Indiana, every team participates in the tournament, which is divided into sectionals, regionals, semistates, and then the championship in Indianapolis. Jones saw Bird working to get back. Bird was a skinny 6-1 at the time and weighed about 135 pounds. At the end of the season, Bird still wasn't ready and Jones made a deal with him: if Bird could do a suicide (a running drill detested by basketball players worldwide) in thirty seconds, he'd put him on the Springs Valley playoff roster.

"He didn't know I already had submitted his name," Jones said. "But he finally did it."

And then Bird made two free throws to win Springs Valley's first-round game. The team lost in the second round.

In his junior year, Bird grew to 6-6, and the Springs Valley Black Hawks went 19–2. Bird averaged 16 points and 9 rebounds a game. "He could have led the team in scoring and rebounding, but he didn't," Clark said. "He made sure everyone got involved. All five starters averaged in double figures." At one point, Bird came off the bench in a blowout to help Steve Land set the school scoring record.

"He made three passes. The guy got three baskets and the record. And Larry came back to the bench," Jones said.

The team, however, was upset in the tournament and Bird vowed to come back bigger, stronger, and better. To signal his new commitment, he even tried to skip the team banquet and practice instead. Eventually, he was persuaded to attend, but he got there late. Every day in high school, Bird would report to the gym at 6:00 A.M. At 6:15, he and the rest of the basketball team would do nothing but shoot free throws for seventy-five minutes. Jones provided milk and doughnuts for early-morning sustenance.

"It was three guys in a circle going around and around," Bird said. "Every single morning. No matter what season it was. The gym was open at six. We'd start shooting at six fifteen and go right up until seven thirty."

Bird started to attract college scouts in his senior year. He was now 6-7. Before the season started, he was confronted with a shocker: while he was bowling one afternoon with Cox, Jones stopped by to announce he was leaving his position as head coach to become the athletic director. His assistant, Gary Holland, would take over. Bird was stunned. But he went out and averaged 30.6 points and 20.7 rebounds a game and the team went 18–3. It got to the sectional finals and lost to Bedford when Beezer Carnes, one of Bird's best buddies, missed two key free throws. Carnes had always been a reluctant and arbitrary participant in the morning free-throw drills and Bird had warned him that one day he'd pay for it. The Bedford game, a 63–58 loss, was the kicker.

Throughout his high school and college careers, Bird's seasons invariably came to an end with a stinging, disappointing, and unacceptable defeat. He would never win a championship at any level until his second pro season in Boston, a championship he still relishes as much as any because it was his first. The Bedford loss ended his high school career. There were the two 1-point NIT losses to Houston and Rutgers following his first two years at Indiana State. And then there was THE LOSS. It was the most-watched college basketball final in NCAA history, and it closed not only Bird's college career, but one of the most remarkable seasons in NCAA history.

They still call it the Dream Season in Terre Haute, and who can blame them? Has a school with virtually no history of basketball success ever done what Indiana State did in 1978–79? And done it solely because of one player, a Hope Diamond surrounded by some Woolworth stones? This wasn't merely a Cinderella team, as, say North Carolina–Charlotte was the year before or, maybe, Dayton was a decade earlier when it became the first sacrificial lamb to Lew Alcindor's UCLA team. This was a team that went 29–0 in the regular season and then made it to the NCAA finals, only to lose to a Michigan State team that included not only Magic Johnson, but future pros Greg Kelser and Jay Vincent.

By the time his senior year began, Bird was a legitimate phenomenon. The Celtics had drafted him and were patiently waiting for him to finish his career and get his degree. And Indiana State was becoming *the* basketball school in the state, dwarfing heretofore kingpin Indiana as well as Purdue and Notre Dame.

On one trip to play the Pacers in Indianapolis, Doug Collins, then a guard for the Philadelphia 76ers, figured he would see what the excitement was all about. He had played his college ball at Illinois State, a regular rival for ISU, and the stories had made their way back east.

"My college buddies kept saying, 'You gotta see this guy Larry Bird. He's so much like Rick Barry,' " Collins recalled. "So one night in Indiana, we have an off night and Chuck Daly [then a 76ers assistant] and I decide we'll drive to Terre Haute and watch him play. It was an awful night. Snow. Ice storms. We went over a hill on the interstate and a semi starts to spin. We skidded a quarter mile, went off the road, and wrecked the car. We decided then we'd better forget about it and we rented a car and checked into a Holiday Inn in Greencastle. We watched the game on TV and that was the first time I saw him. And all I could think of was, 'Oh, my word.' "

Indiana State was not expected to win its conference or make a national splash, despite Bird's presence. The team had a new coach, Hodges, who had taken over for King. Two transfers, Alex Gilbert and Bob Heaton, were new and expected to play big roles. Gilbert was going to be the center, even though he was only 6-7. None of that mattered. Bird put on his pack-mule clothing and simply carried and willed Indiana State to victory after victory.

By now, everyone knew about Bird and knew that his competitiveness was something to behold. At one point that season, he told the president of the university to leave the locker room when the unfortunate man stopped by for a halftime pep talk. Bird's drive was best known in basketball, but he was also a fierce competitor in everything else. He would fume when he lost a Ping-Pong game to Jones's daughter, as he did once, or, worse, when he lost a bet. Generally, when Bird says the word "Betcha" at the start of a sentence, the wisest thing to do is say, "No, thanks." Clark and Bird once got into a discussion over the worth of Bird's rookie NBA trading card.

"I was into those things so I had a pretty good idea. Larry had no idea," Clark said. "I asked him what he thought it was worth and he said, 'Probably a thousand at the minimum.' I said, 'No way, it's no more than five hundred, five fifty tops. He said, 'What have you got in your pocket?' I had thirty dollars. He said, 'I'll betcha that.' That was fine with me. We called his brother Jeff in Indianapolis and had him check on the card. And it was five hundred. I don't know if he ever paid the thirty. He was so mad."

On the court, however, there was no one to contest Bird's dominating will. And he was quickly becoming a celebrity. He had no control over the press, which started to infiltrate his life as he never could have envisioned. And he had no control over the alleged cognoscenti, who remained skeptical about Indiana State because of its schedule. The team had raised a few eyebrows when it opened its season with an 83–79 victory over a touring Soviet team, becoming one of four college teams to beat the Russians. But, despite a win at Purdue, the overriding feeling was that Indiana State simply was no match for the teams of the Big Ten or Atlantic Coast Conference—or even for a reputable independent such as Notre Dame, which started the year ranked number one.

One of the most satisfying wins that year was an overtime victory at New Mexico State. ISU was 18–0 and trailed, 83–81, with three seconds to play. Bird had already fouled out, but Heaton threw in a fifty-foot Hail Mary heave at the buzzer to send the game into overtime. Indiana State prevailed, 91–89, and did so with its best player on the bench in extra innings.

Bird had tried, without success, to convince people that Indiana State was more than just a one-man team. He even stopped talking to reporters because he didn't want to dominate the conversation at the expense of his teammates. The New Mexico State game proved him right, or so he thought. The team won the Missouri Valley Tournament at Terre Haute and then was named the top seed in the Midwest Regional. It disposed of Virginia Tech (89–69) in a sub-regional and then went to Cincinnati and beat Oklahoma (93–72) and a good Arkansas team (73–71), which featured Sidney Moncrief. Heaton won that game, too, with a last-second shot.

In the Final Four at Salt Lake City, Indiana State eked out a 76–74 win over De Paul while Michigan State destroyed an over-matched Penn team. Then the dream died. Bird, who had fractured his thumb in three places in the Missouri Valley Conference clincher over New Mexico State, had seen the Michigan State Spartans early in the season and thought they were the best team in the country. And the Spartans won, 75–64.

Six months later, it all hardly seemed to matter. He was now in the NBA with the Boston Celtics, possessor of a record rookie contract and destined to turn around a franchise and, with some help from Magic on the other coast, a league. One night in his rookie season, he and Rick Robey were in New York and Bird was in a contemplative mood, lying on his bed in the hotel.

"All I want out of this game is to play five years and have a million dollars in the bank. That's my goal, Rick," he told Robey.

"I think he did a lot better than that," Robey said.

He did. But for a while there were events happening both within and beyond his control that could have prevented him from signing with the Celtics. There was the expected and customary but at times shocking and distasteful sight of Red Auerbach and Bob Woolf, Bird's agent, insulting each other during acrimonious and very public negotiations. And there was a bizarre transaction in the summer of 1978 that could have changed everything.

A month after Bird was drafted, in what still remains an unprecedented move, the Celtics and Buffalo Braves swapped franchises.

The Boston owner at the time, Irv Levin, yearned for a franchise in southern California and eventually saw the best way to do it. He would exchange teams with Braves owner John Y. Brown (who had been an ABA owner in Kentucky) and move the Braves to San Diego, which had not had an NBA team since the Rockets moved to Houston in 1972.

The swap was played out among the owners, Levin, Brown, and Harry Mangurian, who was Brown's silent partner. (Brown was the epitome of a meddlesome owner and thus any partner was, by definition, a silent one.)

At the end of June 1978, Volk and Auerbach made a trip to Washington, D.C., for a highly unusual exercise. There, they met with two different agents in one place and signed deals with Kevin Kunnert (the Rockets had received cash and a second-round pick in 1981 as compensation for the signing) and Kermit Washington. At the time, the two Celtics executives had no idea what was in store once the signings were done. They do now.

"We left that night after we'd spent all day doing the contracts," Volk said. "Red called Irv Levin to tell them contracts were signed, and what we didn't know was that that was the go-ahead call. That triggered everything. The next morning I woke up and found out the franchise had been sold. We had done their dirty work for them. I felt like the Japanese ambassador in Washington, D.C., going to the White House on December 7, 1941."

It was an anxious time for the Celtics. Not only did they have new owners, but the franchise swap involved more than just the teams. There were also players who changed teams, and one of them could have been Bird. As Brown and Levin discussed players, Bird's name came up. Only Levin's uncertainty about being able to sign Bird prevented him from taking Bird with him to San Diego.

"I absolutely could have had Larry Bird if I wanted. No question about it," Levin said. "John Y. and I were choosing sides and giving and taking and Bird was a big factor. But if I had taken him to San Diego, I would have only had two or three months to sign him, and I was fearful at the time that I might be unable to do that. Then I'd have nothing.

"Plus, I also knew that Red was very high on the kid, and I felt that if I took Bird to San Diego, Red would in some way make sure that he never signed with me. So I made up my mind that it simply was too risky. We were starting a new franchise. Of course, had I known then what I know now, I would have taken that risk. But no one knew. We knew he was a good college player, but that was all. And John Y. offered no resistance. None whatsoever."

Levin instead took with him the player the Celtics selected two picks after Bird, Freeman Williams of Portland State. Williams had been a prolific college scorer—he had games of 81, 71, and 66 points, and scored 50 or more points six times—and the Celtics saw him as their future shooting guard. Levin also took the two players Volk and Auerbach had just signed, Kunnert and Washington, and Sidney Wicks, by then a pathetic creature in Boston. The Celtics ended up with Billy Knight (whom Brown had agitated for), Nate Archibald, and Marvin Barnes.

Once again, the Celtics were lucky. The men who scouted Bird, sweated out the draft, and later would haggle over money and then triumphantly announce his signing could have been left with nothing before Bird's career ever really began.

"Levin and Brown did what they wanted to do," Volk said. "The fact that we ended up with Larry Bird as part of the deal was simply fortuitous for us."

The Celtics deliberately hadn't approached Bird all through the 1978–79 season. As Bird's fame and success grew—his talent was now beyond reproach—he became more than just a daring draft pick. He became a "must-sign." The Celtics were even worse during the 1978–79 season than the year before, winning just twenty-nine games, changing coaches (again), and going through eighteen players (again). However, there was one significant positive development. In April 1979, Mangurian took complete control of the team, buying out Brown, who decided he'd rather run for governor of Kentucky. He did and he won.

The ownership change was critical as the hourglass emptied on the Celtics in the spring of 1979. Auerbach was fuming over details of the contract negotiations and maintained his position that Bird, as good as he might be, was still just a forward. Woolf, knowing that the Celtics needed Bird more than Bird needed the Celtics, pressed for a record rookie haul, in the $800,000-per-year area.

Bird and Woolf seemed an unlikely alliance. How they came together was in and of itself unusual, given Bird's exalted status and the Celtics' desperate need to sign him. To further distance himself from the pros, Bird established a committee of four Terre Haute businessmen whom he knew and trusted and who would take care of him. Their mission was to get an agent for Bird who wouldn't fleece the unsuspecting rookie or undersell him. The choice came down to Woolf and Reuven Katz. Woolf, who was Boston based, was one of the trailblazers in the athlete representation business; at times, he had represented many of the biggest names in Boston sports, including Carl Yastrzemski, Jim Plunkett, and John Havlicek. Katz, a Cincinnati-based attorney best known for handling Pete Rose, had no NBA players.

Woolf had his first meeting with the Gang of Four at a Terre Haute country club in April, and it lasted for a mere eight hours. He was asked about fees (hourly or percentage) and everything else imaginable. He then got summoned back for a second, four-hour session at the same country club, which is when he first met Bird. After Woolf was selected, Bird told him that he had been picked "because the other guy was so much smarter than me."

If drafting Bird was a gamble, signing him turned out to be an ordeal of name-calling, accusations, and counteraccusations. It became known locally as the Hundred Days' War. Both sides were under tremendous pressure to get the deal done. Woolf had initially come in with what Volk said were "inappropriate" demands, one of which, according to Auerbach, was that the Celtics pay for Bird's college tuition (he was on a scholarship). Auerbach said Woolf wanted an extra $10,000 if Bird made the All-Rookie team. Auerbach retorted, "You want to pay the guy eight hundred thousand dollars, he should make the All-Rookie team." Auerbach had yet to see a forward turn a team around and, at least publicly, doubted that Bird would be the first.

In the past, Auerbach had always cited the Celtics' tradition, family atmosphere, and history of success in swaying potential signees. None of that meant a thing to Bird. Tradition at any level meant little to him. He had refused to attend the ceremony in Los Angeles at which he was to receive the John Wooden Award as the nation's top college hoopster because he had student teaching obligations in Indiana. Snub the Wizard of Westwood, an Indiana man to boot? Hey, the kids needed teaching and he needed the credits for his degree. And he had never had money as a kid, so the obscene figures being tossed around meant nothing to him. He showed his austere side in a three-day visit to Boston in April. Woolf still has the hotel bill from that stay and it shows room and tax and nothing else. No phone calls, room service, or restaurant expenses. Not even a six-pack of beer.

As the 1979 draft approached, things intensified. Word leaked out of Indiana that Bird had mangled his right index finger playing softball. He had. To this day, it is still mangled. He adjusted. Woolf was stopped at a traffic light in Worcester and a Celtics fan recognized him. The fan gave Woolf a single-digit greeting that could be interpreted only one way.

"There was a tremendous amount of concern," Volk said. "Larry had a tremendous amount of leverage. But we didn't feel like we had to pay him for performing under that contract. That's what he was there for. There was an awful lot of animosity that developed."

Woolf and Auerbach were old antagonists and Auerbach only recently had begun to soften his opinion that agents were the lowest possible life-form. At one point in the negotiations, Bird and his then girlfriend Dinah Mattingly (now his wife) sat in briefly on a negotiating session and were appalled at the language, tone, and general hostility. Bird thought to himself, "I don't need this," and was genuinely shocked to see people fighting over his services. All he had known prior to this was the college recruiting scene, which, of course, is vastly different. In that case, the prospective head coach is fawning, obsequious, and even deceptive if that's what it takes. "I couldn't believe what was going on," Bird said. "Everyone was screaming and hollering."

Then Mangurian, sensing a new voice was needed, stepped in and cooler heads prevailed. One week before the 1979 draft, and 364 days after Boston had made its historic selection, Bird and the

Celtics agreed to a five-year deal worth $3.25 million. It was the largest contract ever given to a rookie in any sport.

It was an especially traumatic day for Volk, who had to get the paperwork done and finalized. His father happened to be undergoing bypass surgery that same day, and he could have been forgiven for something other than Celtics loyalty. But his father came through the operation and Bird signed on the dotted line. "It turned out to be a good day," he said.

Having watched the Bird affair from afar, the NBA decided that there had to be a better way to draft and sign underclassmen. In May 1979, shortly before Bird signed but in the middle of the contentious negotiations, the league's board of governors changed the junior eligibility rule. Beginning with the 1980–81 season, a player would have to renounce his college eligibility before the draft if he wished to be selected. Otherwise, he could not be drafted until his eligibility expired. Kyle Macy was the last player of any repute to be drafted under the formula Boston had used to take Bird. He was drafted in 1979 by Phoenix and started NBA play the following season.

From 1976 to 1980, there were three different rules on the drafting of college players who still had eligibility remaining. Had either the first or the last been in effect in 1978, Larry Bird would never have been drafted by the Celtics. It was more evidence that forces beyond wisdom and derring-do had conspired to land Bird in Boston. The gamble had paid off and would continue to do so, more than anyone had any right to think on that June day.

CHAPTER 2

1980, Parish, and The Trade

On the night of October 12, 1979, the Boston Garden was filled with people, anticipation, and cautious optimism. All three had been missing the previous two seasons, when the Celtics, due to a series of poor draft choices in the 1970s (Steve Downing, Norm Cook, Glenn McDonald), retirements by veterans (Don Nelson, John Havlicek), and bad trades (Paul Silas), skidded to the bottom. In 1977–78 and 1978–79, the team had managed sixty-one victories, fired two coaches, made some ridiculous trades, and ended up being an utter disgrace.

But things were different that night, primarily because of the presence of Bird. But the Celtics fans were still understandably hesitant to embrace this "new" team. After all, they had been told that the previous two teams were the "new" Celtics. The club even adopted a new advertising slogan: "No More Games." In other words, it was time to work.

Bird, of course, embodied the supposed renewed commitment. But the Celtics had other new faces as well, none more critical than the man at the end of the bench. Bill Fitch had left Cleveland the year before, and he was a specialist at something out of nothing jobs, having built the expansion Cavaliers from the ground up. But he was tired of the Cleveland situation and wanted out. He did, however, want to stay in the NBA and was seriously considering the Lakers job (Jerry West was moving upstairs) when Red Auerbach called and persuaded him to become the first "outsider" to coach a Celtics team.

In addition, the team had signed a free agent from Detroit, M. L. Carr, who had led the league in steals and would become an ideal sixth man in the storied Celtics tradition. Nate Archibald was healthy and slim after a disastrous season the year before. Dave Cowens, who had wound up coaching the team over the final half of the 1978–79 season, was back, too, and without the dual burden of being a player-coach.

The newspapers were also reluctant to anoint this team as a contender. A .500 season seemed acceptable, given the tumult from the year before and the fact that Philadelphia was loaded and experienced and the Bullets, two years removed from an NBA championship, were still strong. But this team would be very different from the previous two teams, and Bird above all personified that change.

Soon after the Celtics signed Bird, the *Boston Globe*'s Bob Ryan wrote, "Now all the Celtics need is 11 mirrors." And when Bird showed up at rookie camp, despite having had surgery to fix his finger, he was dominant. But that was a group of pretenders and wannabes. What would happen when he showed up to play against the real guys?

Bird had already figured out that he could play with the established pros because a few had shown up at rookie camp, anxious to get a shot at the newcomer. And when training camp opened in September, any doubts in anyone's mind about the rookie's talent were erased quickly.

"Very quickly," said Chris Ford, then a guard on the team. "You could tell right away. The passing. He would do things at practice that would make your eyes pop open. It was amazing. And to be there when it all began, and after what we had been through the year before, that was amazing, too."

A couple of weeks into the exhibition season, the Celtics played the 76ers. The reigning Eastern Conference deity was Julius Erving, and he was asked about Bird. "I guess the best thing you can say about him is that he can play," Doc said. "You can feel the intensity he has, the moves. He can create his own offense. He was talking all the time out there. I have a very favorable opinion of him as a basketball player."

It would be the first of endless tributes to Bird, and it came after the Celtics' first exhibition game. Boston went 7–1 in the exhibition season, and Bird not only showcased his variety of offensive skills, he also averaged 4 steals a game, including 5 in each of the final two games.

Thus, there was reason to believe that things would change. The season opener that year drew a sellout, as had the opener the year before. This time, however, it wouldn't be the season's last, as it had been in 1978–79.

The Houston Rockets were the opponent on opening night. As Bird was introduced, he was met with a standing ovation, and a flock of birds was released from the balcony. Bird was already established as a phenom, but he had also come with a set of personal ground rules enjoyed by virtually no other athlete in Boston. He would not allow reporters to call him at home. Or visit him at home. Once he left the Boston Garden, or the team's practice site at Hellenic College near his Brookline home, he was off limits.

Bird occasionally would relent, but only to a favored, select few. And he never thought it capricious or arbitrary to allow someone to penetrate his self-constructed wall when others were denied such access. He made himself available after games and, usually, after practice. That was enough, wasn't it? He even made it known that he would not receive visitors to his home in Indiana in the off-season, if they were so bold as to try to capture something of his nonbasketball life.

Those were the rules. If you didn't like them, tough. No one complained. And with basketball season about to begin, there would be plenty of Bird to appease the most thirsty of reporters.

In his first pro game, Bird didn't lead the Celtics in scoring or rebounding. He played only twenty-eight minutes because he was in foul trouble all night (Dick Bavetta had his eye on the rook). He picked up his fifth foul with 6:28 to play and was on the bench when Ford and Carr keyed a late Celtics rally and a 114–105 victory. Bird finished with 14 points, 10 rebounds, and 5 assists. Afterward, Rick Barry, then with Houston and finishing up his career, noted, "They've finally got to the point where they have more people who are, quote, Celtics, unquote." The inference was clear.

Little was made locally of Bird's debut. *The Boston Globe* ran a game story that noted Bird's contributions, but focused instead on the fourth quarter. There was no columnist or second writer assigned to chronicle Bird's first night. As was the case throughout his rookie year, Bird's milestones came at times when the sporting eyes and minds were focused elsewhere. Opening night coincided with the World Series. A February tear coincided with the Winter Olympics (and the gold-medal hockey team). The playoffs ran up against baseball's opening day and the dominant Red Sox.

The Celtics' season had opened successfully, but their second game provided a clue as to how good they were. It was a road game in Cleveland, and it was significant because the Celtics had been such an awful road team, and because Fitch would be returning to the town he had just left.

Bird set the tone from the outset, making 11 of his first 15 shots, and the Celtics won easily, 139–117. Bird played forty minutes and led the Celtics in scoring with 28 points. He also added 7 rebounds and 5 assists. And, when the Cavaliers attempted to get back into the game in the second half, he shredded a Cleveland press with his passing.

Soon, it was clear that this would not be a .500 team. In his fourteenth game, Bird registered his first triple double. The term *triple double* was coined by a Los Angeles publicity man to highlight Magic Johnson's versatility. It referred to double figures in points, rebounds, and assists. Bird had sixty-seven triple doubles in his career, including playoff games. On this night, he had 23 points, 19 rebounds, and 10 assists. But the concept meant nothing to Bird. He once sat out the fourth quarter of a game in Utah when he was one steal away from a quadruple double. And he saw no significance in the fact that he had a triple double at the half in a game against the Bullets at the end of the 1986–87 season.

By the end of 1979, the Celtics had established themselves as a legitimate contender for the division championship. They were virtually unbeatable at home (16–1) and were playing better than anticipated on the road. They were leapfrogging with the 76ers for the lead of the Atlantic Division, although things looked bleak in January when Dave Cowens went down with a foot injury. He would miss fourteen games. The Celtics did not suffer, because Bird took over the team and wouldn't allow it.

The Celtics won seven of eight after Cowens was hurt and then prepared for their annual February road trip out west. Each February, Boston Garden welcomes the ice show and the Celtics and Bruins hit the road. It is a brutal time to travel, given the weather and the fact that every plane is jammed because the trip usually coincides with winter vacations. Bird loved these trips, which took the Celtics to the cities of the Western Conference. He was acutely aware that the Celtics made only one visit per season to these outposts, and he felt an obligation to perform. Some of his greatest games came on these trips, including his first visit to Phoenix on February 8, 1980.

The Celtics lost the game, 135–134, blowing a 9-point lead in the final 1:57. Fitch was furious after the game. But the talk in the Suns' locker room was Bird, who had scored 45 points, the fifth-highest total in Celtics history. He had made 19 of 32 field goals, including 3 three-pointers. He had 13 rebounds. Afterward, Paul Westphal said, "That Larry Bird, I think he's going to be a player someday."

The Celtics had lost two straight only once all season and they didn't want it to happen again in Portland. Bird would not allow it. He had 28 points and 15 rebounds and Boston won easily. He then followed that one up with a 21-point, 13-rebound performance in a 109–108 loss to Seattle. Boston closed the trip with wins at Utah (Bird had 33 points) and Denver (he had 13 points and 11 rebounds) and headed home, never to be caught by the Sixers. Bird was named Player of the Month in February, having averaged 28.4 points and shot 52 percent on the road trip.

Boston finished its season with a 61–21 record. The Celtics' thirty-two-game turnaround was the greatest in NBA history, and would remain so until David Robinson arrived in San Antonio and presided over a thirty-five-game turnaround. Bird was third in MVP balloting and was a runaway winner for Rookie of the Year. (Magic Johnson did not make first- or second-team All-Pro; Bird made the first team.) Bird led the Celtics in points, minutes played, rebounds, steals, and, typically, turnovers.

In addition, fans flocked to Boston Garden to see the Celtics as never before. Even in their glory days, the Celtics had only once averaged as many as 10,000 fans a game (1966–67, the one year in ten they did not win an NBA title). Attendance had peaked in 1975–76, averaging 13,446. Then, with the team's decline, it dropped: the year before Bird arrived, the slothful Celtics averaged only 10,193 a game, and that was stretching it.

Now things were different. The team set an attendance record. Both of the Celtics' "home" games in Hartford were sold out. The Garden was filled to 91 percent capacity. Midway through Bird's second season, every Boston Garden game would become an automatic sellout, a streak that extended throughout his career and even into the first year of his retirement.

But even with their remarkable season, there still was some doubt as to how strong the team was as the playoffs arrived. The Celtics had not beaten either the Lakers or Seattle. They had split their season series with Philadelphia, 3-3. But they also were 35–6 at home and had the homecourt advantage throughout the playoffs.

The Rockets provided opposition for the Celtics in the first round. It was Houston's last year in the Eastern Conference before the team moved to the Western Conference.

Boston had had no trouble with Houston in the regular season, going 6–0. That trend continued in the playoffs. Despite a ten-day layoff (the Celtics had a first-round bye while Houston needed the three-game maximum to eliminate San Antonio in a miniseries), the Celtics swept the Rockets in four. Bird gave Boston the jump start it needed when he made his first five shots in the opener. In Game 4, he keyed a run with two hoops and two assists that put the game away. The Celtics' average margin of victory was 18 points. The Sixers, who had won a five-gamer from Atlanta, were next.

Again, the Celtics had every reason to feel confident. They had beaten the Sixers in all three games the teams had played in Boston. All three had been blowouts with an average victory margin of 20.3 points. Yet before the series began, Julius Erving prophetically noted, "Boston played for the regular season. We play for the playoffs." He was right.

In Game 1, the Sixers won 96–93 in Boston, putting the Celtics in a quick hole. Bird then helped Boston salvage a split, scoring 31 in Game 2. In one incredible twelve-minute sequence, he scored 21 points as Boston expanded a 12–8 lead to 47–35. But the Celtics could not break through in Philadelphia, and then the Sixers closed the Celtics out in Boston, 105–94, as Bird struggled (5 of 19) through what would be his final game as an NBA rookie.

With 3:28 to play, Bill Fitch sent in M. L. Carr to replace Bird, who had scored only 12 points and committed 6 turnovers. Slowly, Bird started to walk from the foul line under the Philadelphia basket to the Boston bench. The crowd, sensing what was happening, erupted into a standing ovation—a thank-you. Afterward, Bird spent an hour talking about the game and the season, and then said, "I'm looking forward to training camp."

The Celtics' organization was looking ahead, too. Despite Boston's amazing turnaround, they knew their team had problems. Philadelphia wasn't going to go away, and it was clear that the Sixers were too big and too strong for the Celtics. They needed to add muscle if they were going to compete. Besides Rick Robey, a 6-10 reserve, the Celtics had no one to match up against a bruiser like Darryl Dawkins, a seven-footer, and Caldwell Jones, who was 6-11 but played a lot taller.

"There was an urgency there," Fitch said. "Even though we won sixty-one games, we lost to Philly. And they had beaten us because we couldn't handle Dawkins or C.J. [Jones]. They were too damn much for us. We were going with Larry, [Cedric] Maxwell, and Dave [Cowens]. We just weren't big enough. Dave had as good a year as he could have had. But he couldn't rebound with them. And Larry was still basically a power forward. It was evident that if we were going to get better, we had to get bigger. And we desperately needed a center because Dave wasn't going to last that much longer."

Boston had no worse than the second pick in the upcoming draft, but the team felt that there wasn't a franchise center available. A trade seemed like their best route, and Fitch knew who he wanted. During the 1979–80 season, the coach had casually remarked to a writer that he would "love to get my hands on that Robert Parish." The writer nearly choked, which wasn't surprising given Parish's reputation for uninspiring play. But Fitch explained that he wanted to be Henry Higgins to Parish's Eliza Doolittle; he was utterly convinced there was something worth extracting from the lethargic seven-footer from Golden State.

"I always try to look three or four years ahead," Fitch said. "You want to put a team on the floor that's better than the one you have. But that was going to be tough. We had won sixty-one games. But I'd liked Robert in college and I always thought there was a little more there than what you saw. We wanted him in Cleveland when he came out of college, but we just couldn't get him.

"He also didn't know how good he could be," Fitch went on.

"But I followed him, watched tapes of him, and he was always there. If you look at what he did in Golden State, he'd have some great games and a lot of valleys. My thinking was that if he can do it once, he can do it more than once. And that if he can do it ten times in a row, he'll be the best. Because on his best nights, there was no one better."

In his years in Boston, Parish developed a reputation as a consummate team player who never complained about minutes or shots and who willingly sacrificed his game to become a defensive stalwart. He was little of the above with the Warriors. He was a different player in Boston.

"There aren't a lot of guys," Danny Ainge said, "who really don't care at all about stats. We all know Kevin and Larry loved to score and break records, but Robert didn't care at all about individual accolades. All he cared about was going about his job. He never complained about not getting the ball, about being taken out, yet he always was there when we needed him. We'd ignore him for four games and then we'd need him and he'd get twenty-five points for us."

Or, as Bird put it, "Robert sometimes got left out as far as shots and minutes were concerned, but he didn't care. He just wanted to win."

That was what he thought would happen when he played for Golden State. But the team began to go steadily downhill the moment he got there, and it still has not advanced past the second round of a playoff series since 1976.

Parish hadn't expected to end up with the Warriors for at least two reasons. First, they held the eighth pick in the 1976 draft, and seven-foot centers with Parish's promise and impressive college careers historically don't last that long. (Benoit Benjamin was the third pick in the 1985 draft, Rik Smits the second pick in the 1988 draft.)

But Parish suffered from lack of exposure—remember, this was the mid-1970s and there was no ESPN, there was little scouting, and Centenary, where he attended college, was banned from tournaments and television. Word of mouth and advice from trusted hands often meant as much as anything; in 1972, Auerbach drafted Paul Westphal out of Southern California with the Celtics' first pick, the tenth overall, despite never having seen Westphal play.

Parish also may have been hindered by the perception that Centenary's schedule was less than onerous and by the fact that the NBA and the ABA were about to merge, meaning such prizes as Moses Malone, Maurice Lucas, Artis Gilmore, and Marvin Barnes would soon be available to NBA teams. They all had pro experience while Parish had none.

Atlanta had the first pick in 1976 and also had its eyes on Parish. The Hawks dispatched GM Bud Seretean to begin talks with Parish's agent, a Shreveport attorney named Peyton Moore. The two met several times, but Atlanta wanted a deal loaded with incentives and short on guaranteed salary. Moore hadn't had any experience representing NBA draft picks, but he sensed a deal should be the other way around for a number one pick. He then retained someone who was wise to the ways of the NBA and his suspicions were confirmed.

Negotiations never got all that serious, or close to an agreement, and then Moore was absolutely floored when Atlanta traded the pick, along with Dwight Jones, to Houston for Joe C. Meriweather, Gus Bailey, and the Rockets' number one pick. The Hawks now had the ninth pick and, as it turned out, came close to getting Parish anyhow. Instead, they selected Armond Hill from Princeton.

The Rockets, now with the first pick, were preparing to sign Moses Malone after the merger so they went for the versatile guard John Lucas out of Maryland. The Bulls had Artis Gilmore coming in, so they took Scott May, who had a brilliant career at Indiana but never did much after that. Kansas City, drafting third, took UCLA center-forward Richard Washington, and Detroit, which had Bob Lanier and didn't need a center, went for Alabama power forward Leon Douglas.

Those picks all made sense at the time. So did Portland's choice of Wally Walker, because the Trail Blazers had Bill Walton. And even Buffalo, with Bob McAdoo playing center, saw no need for Parish and took Adrian Dantley with the sixth pick. The seventh pick belonged to Milwaukee, which selected Indiana's versatile guard Quinn Buckner. The Bucks had traded Kareem Abdul-Jabbar the year before and acquired Elmore Smith, a 7-2 center, in return. Smith was eighth in the league in rebounding that year with 11.4 a game. They also had Swen Nater, who had played behind Walton at UCLA, and he would finish seventh in the league in rebounding the following year at 12.0. Neither player, however, was with the Bucks for the 1977–78 season, which would have been Parish's second year.

Parish was monitoring the proceedings from the Centenary coaching office and, after Atlanta chose Lucas, he had no clue as to his future whereabouts.

"After Atlanta, I really had no idea where I was going to end up. But I was happy to be chosen by Golden State," he said. "I really was. I thought I was going to a winner. They had won the championship two years before that. They had the best record in the league that year. I was happy to be going there. I thought they would keep winning."

Instead, the Warriors were on a slippery slope that saw them slide out of the playoff picture entirely in just two years. Parish was taken under the protective wing of Clifford Ray while at the same time getting a shocking introduction to the NBA in general and to Rick Barry in particular. The onetime de facto franchise forward was on his way out (after the 1977–78 season, Barry signed with Houston and the compensation was cash and John Lucas; what goes around comes around), and Parish was astonished at what he saw.

"I was like shell-shocked," Parish said of his experiences with Barry. "His personality. The way he would speak. He was *extremely* arrogant. He was the most arrogant person I ever met in my life. I think there are some arrogant people in Massachusetts, but they are children compared to him. Some of the things he got away with . . . I can't believe management even tolerated it.''

Parish, of course, played with Bird, who was also known to be arrogant, for twelve years, but when he compares him to Barry, Bird comes off looking like George Sanders.

"Oh, Larry was a lamb,'' he said. "Let me give you an example [of Barry's behavior]. He got pissed off at Al Attles. He [Barry] didn't want Gus Williams to start. He wanted Charles Dudley and Charles Johnson in the backcourt. And Al started Gus and Charles Johnson. And he [Barry] didn't take a shot the whole game. Refused to take a shot. And you know what the paper said the next day? That he wasn't feeling well. A virus or something.

"As great as he was. And there was this other time, it was like three games after he had been called into the office and told that he had to sit down to rest an injury or whatever, and again he went the whole game and didn't take a shot. Then, in the last two minutes, he throws up a shot like one of those [underhanded] free throw shots he used to take. And management didn't say nothing.''

Parish has seen Bird throw a temper tantrum on the court. He has seen Bird get mad, insult people, throw chairs. What he has never seen Bird do is what he thought Barry was doing in those games.

"Rick Barry just *gave up*. And he was one of the best forwards to ever play the game. But he gave up.''

The Warriors were 46–36 in 1976–77, 43–39 in 1977–78, 38–44 in 1978–79, and 24–58 in 1979–80. The decline came even though the team had two first-round picks in 1976, 1977, and 1978. But of the six players, only Parish could be construed as a legitimate star. Rickey Green and Purvis Short had their moments, but Wesley Cox, Sonny Parker, and Raymond Townsend were short-termers at best. And in 1979 the Warriors had no first-round pick.

As the team slowly deteriorated, Parish somehow statistically elevated his game. By 1979, he was averaging 17.2 points and 12 rebounds a game. He duplicated those numbers the following year, his last at Golden State. The Warriors had scorers—Phil Smith, Parker, and Short—but they were a woeful defensive team and utterly bereft of chemistry. Parish usually maintained his celebrated cool, but on one occasion his frustration boiled over. On his way to the bench for a time-out, Parish was so sick of battling three and four opponents for every rebound that he took a plastic jar of talcum powder, slammed it on the press table, and shouted, "Will someone out there fucking rebound?" He then sat down, looked straight ahead, and became Parish again. It was an uncharacteristic blip on his control screen. There would be others—his 1983 contract hold-out, his 1987 pummeling of Bill Laimbeer, his 1993 arrest for marijuana possession—but they were rare.

"Early on," Clifford Ray recalled, "Robert had to learn just like everyone else. You would tell him about certain players and what they did, but until you actually saw it, it was hard. Once, we were telling Robert about Earl Monroe and how Earl can basically undress you if you're out there on the floor. Well, that's what happened. Robert comes into the game and sure enough, the ball pops out and Earl has it. Robert is standing at halfcourt and immediately goes into his defensive stance. Then, he looks back, sees how far away from the basket he is, and he freaks out. And Earl just looked at him and said, 'Sorry, baby, it's just you and me,' and spun Robert every which way. We all broke up on the bench."

That was the Warriors. Just one big fun bunch. In a game against the Bulls in Chicago Stadium, the team discovered that Ray wasn't available to start the second half. In fact, he wasn't even around. Coach Al Attles dispatched trainer Dick D'Oliva to find Ray, and he did—in the locker room. Ray had found sanctuary in the bathroom during halftime, but was still there when the team went back on the floor. And in Chicago Stadium, the locker rooms are locked, bolted, and almost hermetically sealed during the game. He was banging on the door, to no avail, when D'Oliva found him.

Attles, the Warriors' longtime coach, had to leave the bench in the 1979–80 season when he tore an Achilles tendon—he was practicing with the team because he didn't have enough players. And when acting coach Johnny Bach took over, he wasn't successful either. During halftime of one rout in Philadelphia, Bach looked at his sorry team and saw no hope in the second half. "Gentlemen," he announced, "the gates of mercy are closed."

By then, Parish was tiring of the mess and had heard the trade rumors. He had no desire to leave, but he also didn't want to stick around if things remained the same.

"For me, it was getting to be very aggravating in Golden State because, first of all, they weren't serious about winning. And they didn't have the finances to make, not necessarily a championship team, but a winning team. It was [owner Franklin] Mieuli. Owning the Warriors was like a play thing. Just to say, 'Hey, I got a sports team.' He wasn't serious about winning. He wasn't competitive. If they win thirty, thirty-five, maybe forty games, hey, that's a helluva year in his eyes."

Parish rarely vocalized those sentiments, which was consistent with his demeanor and behavior. He was not a boat-rocker. He has always preferred the background to the spotlight, and if his stoicism bothered someone, so be it. If nothing else, the man Cedric Maxwell nicknamed Chief (after Chief Bromden, the silent giant from *One Flew Over the Cuckoo's Nest*) was consistent and inscrutable. And unconcerned about what others might think, be it Bird for not joining a fight with Erving, or his first coach at Union Junior High in Shreveport for not wanting to play the game that eventually would lead him to stardom and riches.

Cotton Fitzsimmons remembers the first time he saw Robert Parish. It was while Fitzsimmons, a longtime NBA coach with an engaging manner and a long résumé (Atlanta, Buffalo, Kansas City, San Antonio, Phoenix), was coaching at Kansas Sate and running a summer basketball camp. Parish, who was about to enter his junior year in high school, was one of the campers.

"Everyone at this camp was small. Everyone, that is, but Robert," Fitzsimmons said. "He's on the break and someone throws him a lead pass. He has to turn back to see the ball and there is this little kid in front of him. I'm about to close my eyes because I know what's gonna happen: Robert is going to collide with this poor kid. But he caught the ball, turned, saw the kid, went behind his back, floated in, and dunked it. I said to myself, 'I think this kid has a chance to make it.' "

By then, Parish was certain to make it. He was about to lead Woodlawn High School in Shreveport, Louisiana, to consecutive appearances in the state finals and be named Player of the Year in the state in 1972. He also would be one of the most sought-after players in the country.

But Parish was a reluctant convert to basketball. There was no hoop in his driveway at home because there was no driveway. Hattie's Perry Park was nearby and that's where the games were played—but by others. There was no organized youth league to groom him, as Bird and McHale had been groomed, at least not for blacks in Shreveport. He had no inner passion or even sense of obligation to play, as he might have had had he been born in Muncie, Indiana, or Owensboro, Kentucky.

Shreveport is tucked into the northwest corner of Louisiana and is closer to Dallas (which is 180 miles west) than New Orleans (which is 285 miles southeast). In 1970, when Parish was in high school, Shreveport had a population of slightly more than 182,000. Twenty years later, the population was nearly 200,000, with a racial breakdown of 54 percent white and 45 percent black. It is the third-largest city in the state after New Orleans and Baton Rouge, the state capital. It served as Louisiana's capital when the state joined the Confederacy during the Civil War.

The city was named for Henry Miller Shreve, who, in 1833, was commissioned to clear a monumental blockage on the Red River, which now runs along Shreveport's eastern border. The blockage was called the Great Raft, and for a good reason: it was a 160-mile logjam that covered the area where Shreveport is now located. It took forty years of hard work to clear the entire 160-mile mess. But five years into the project, Shreve had removed enough of the logjam to get some movement on the river.

In its early years, Shreveport was a center for cotton and lumber. Later, petroleum discoveries prompted oil exploration and related industries to locate there. Today, only about 13 percent of the labor force is employed in manufacturing jobs. Barksdale Air Force Base, located just across the Red River from downtown Shreveport, is the area's major employer. The largest private employers are General Motors, AT&T, and Morton Thiokol.

The Parishes moved to a tiny, one-floor, wood frame house on Clanton Street (pronounced "Clinton" by the locals) when Robert was two years old. It is located in what is known as the Hollywood section of town, but any resemblance to the real Hollywood is strictly coincidental. Across the front of the Parishes' property was a huge drainage ditch. The only way you could get to the front door was over a large wooden board. The ditch and the board are still there. The house had six rooms and Parish described it as "tight. Very tight."

Robert Parish, Sr., held many jobs over the course of his thirty-plus years at Beaird Industries, where he helped build and test storage tanks and railroad tank cars. He also was a sandblaster and general handyman. Like Joe Bird and Paul McHale, he rarely missed a day of work. The one exception was when he needed two months to recuperate after getting pinned between two flatcars. One of his foremen along the way was the father of Pittsburgh Steelers quarterback Terry Bradshaw, who also grew up in Shreveport.

Parish's mother, Ada, started to work when Parish was in junior high school, first as a maid and then as a cook for the school system at Union High. Part of the reason she went to work was to raise money to help her rapidly growing son buy special clothes. She'd take the money over to a friend, who would make the long clothes for her growing son.

Ada Parish was from a family of seven—six girls—and met Robert Parish, Sr., when the two were introduced at a Shreveport store by her brother-in-law, Johnnie Ball. She was not a local, having been raised in Corey, Louisiana. Robert Parish, Sr., who is 6-4, was raised across the Red River in Bossier City before settling in Shreveport. The two were married in 1951 and settled into a house on Portlein Street. They lived there for four years, welcoming Robert junior, Tommy, and Doris into the family. A fourth child, Liz, came along later.

Football is king in Shreveport and always has been. The high school games on Friday nights draw some fifteen thousand fans at the state fairgrounds. The gym at Woodlawn High School, where Parish played his final two years, seats about two thousand. Ken Ivy, who coached Parish in basketball at Woodlawn, also coached football there. Eventually, he left to go to a nearby school where he made more money just coaching football. Bradshaw went to Woodlawn High, although he played only one season. He was followed by Joe Ferguson, who played three record-shattering years there. In those days, if Woodlawn had a running play, it was usually a draw.

This is not to imply that Louisiana in general or Shreveport in particular is bereft of basketball history or tradition. It is not. Notable Louisianans who have played professional basketball include Karl Malone, Elvin Hayes, John (Hot Rod) Williams, Bob Pettit, and Joe Dumars (who, like Parish, was born in Shreveport). Bill Russell was born there, in Monroe, but played his high school ball in Oakland. NBA Designated Icon of the Nineties Shaquille O'Neal played collegiate ball at LSU, although he was an army brat and went to high school in San Antonio.

When Ferguson was quarterbacking Woodlawn High, it was an all-white school. Parish went to an all-black school, Union, which had both the junior and senior high classes in the same building.

Parish ran some track, usually the 880. He played football and baseball. But basketball?

"I never liked it," he said. "I never had any interest in basketball whatsoever. I never even played it. And it showed, too, the first time I went out on the court. If it wasn't for my junior high school coach, I would not be where I am. He literally forced me to go out for the team."

That man is Coleman Kidd, now a minister in Benton, outside Shreveport. He was the basketball coach at Union Junior High School in the late 1960s and he kept wondering who this tall youngster was whom he saw walking by the school every day.

"I figured he must be going to work," Kidd said. "He was exceptionally tall. I started asking around and I was told he was going to the Hollywood elementary school. He was in the sixth grade. I couldn't believe it. Sixth grade and I had to look up to him. The only thing I could get out of him was 'Yes, sir' or 'No, sir.' I asked him if he was coming to Union. 'Yes, sir.' Are you going to play basketball? 'No, sir.' Why not? 'Don't know how, sir.' Ever played? 'No, sir.' I told him. 'I'm Coach Kidd and I am going to look you up next year.' "

The next year, Parish arrived at Union and Kidd was there, ready for his new center. But his new center, now 6-4, still wasn't interested. Parish had told Kidd he would come to practice, but when the club gathered there was no sign of him. Kidd reminded Parish of his agreement and mildly admonished the youngster that he had better not continue to be a no-show. Parish continued to be a no-show.

Kidd then led Parish into the locker room and produced a small, half-inch-thick oak paddle, which the shop teacher had made for him. He made Parish bend over so he could get "better leverage." Then, Kidd said, "I warmed his pants real good. He rubbed his backside when I was finished."

And the next time the junior high basketball team gathered, Parish was there. Kidd was so pleased he even let Parish wear cutoff blue jeans instead of basketball shorts. There weren't any around that fit, anyway.

"He gave me a couple of good, strong whacks and said, 'I expect to see you here tomorrow,' " Parish said. "And then I decided to come out. Back then, you could do that stuff."

"We had our way with the students back then," Kidd said. "The parents expected you to do it and never complained or asked questions."

Now he had Parish. But he soon began to wonder if this was a case of "Be careful what you wish for because you might get it." Parish wasn't kidding about his utter lack of basketball skills or knowledge. He may as well have spent his first twelve years in Antarctica.

"I really didn't have a clue about the game," Parish said. "They threw me the ball and I started to run with it. And that's only when I was able to catch it. A lot of times it would hit me in the face or go right through my hands. I mean, I was bad."

Kidd said Parish's skills were as bad as Parish described them. Maybe worse. He was forced to use Parish only in late-game, blowout situations. In his first year of organized basketball, Robert Parish, perennial NBA All-Star and future Hall of Famer, was strictly a garbage-time player.

"I was so disappointed," Kidd said. "I'm saying to myself, 'Here is a boy that could go places but he just doesn't have the skills. Or the potential.' He couldn't catch it. He couldn't dribble it. He was clumsy. He had hard hands and no coordination and I almost gave up on him. I did everything I could. Jump-roping drills. Everything. I'd make him take a basketball home. Then he started to show a little promise at the end of the seventh grade, and after playing all summer in the city he came back and was a totally different player. He was phenomenal."

So good, in fact, that Parish played for Kidd only one more year before he was promoted to the Union varsity in the ninth grade. As a freshman at Union, he led the school to the state semifinals. He did the same thing as a sophomore. But he did it while playing only with black teammates and only against all-black competition. The following year, a court order changed everything. In an attempt to integrate the schools, Union High was closed and turned into a career vocational center. Its student body was dispersed, mostly to Woodlawn.

Few were happy with forced integration. For the previous two years, Shreveport had had a "freedom of choice" option that allowed blacks to attend the white schools. But few did. Before that, blacks went to one of three schools (Union, Bethune, or Booker T. Washington) and whites attended one of four schools (Woodlawn, Fair Park, Captain Shreve, and Byrd). The school system consisted of two entire, separate, and insulated worlds whose paths rarely crossed. Cliff Roberts, the point guard at Woodlawn in the first year of integration, had never heard of Parish until they played together at Woodlawn.

Freedom of choice had, however, allowed a trailblazer named Melvin Russell to become one of the first blacks to play for a previously all-white school in Shreveport or anywhere in northern Louisiana. Russell had to wait a year at Woodlawn before he could play, but when he did, his team won the state title in 1968–69. He played with Parish in college and later coached Woodlawn to a state title.

"It could not have opened up without Melvin Russell," Ivy recalled. "By the time Robert got there, we had been through all the stuff—people refusing to feed us, things like that. Melvin made it possible. And it was kids like Robert that came along after that that made it go."

Parish didn't want to leave Union. It was a short walk from home. He was comfortable there, but it was closing and Woodlawn was more than a mile away.

"None of us wanted to be there," Parish said. "It was a huge transition. I would have preferred to stay where I was. I didn't like being broken up and separated. I resented that."

So did Roberts. He lived in the Woodlawn district, but had attended Fair Park under freedom of choice and because his older brother, Bo, a high school hoop star, went there. But he had to attend Woodlawn in his senior year while his friends remained at Fair Park. He even tried to circumvent the order by leasing an apartment in the Fair Park district, where he planned to stay with his mother. But dual residences were not allowed and he was ordered back to Woodlawn.

"It was a very, very traumatic year for everyone, blacks and whites," said Roberts. "The blacks didn't like it. The whites didn't like it. We had never been exposed to blacks and they had never been exposed to whites. There was some violence, but not too much. On the team, it was OK. But beyond that, there was no camaraderie whatsoever. Basketball was the only time we were together. And it was hard for me because none of my friends from Fair Park was there. I became a Woodlawn Knight. But I was still a Fair Park Indian at heart and always will be."

This wasn't simply the students being reshuffled. It was, as nearly as could be managed, a fifty-fifty split among students, faculty, and administration. Teachers at Woodlawn had to move to previously all-black schools. Coaches had to go, too. (The vaunted Woodlawn football staff took a big hit.) The changes were sweeping and widespread, but the courts felt they had to be instituted because freedom of choice hadn't produced the anticipated integration of black and white students.

To make things even worse, a new high school, Southwood, which was supposed to handle the overflow of students at Woodlawn, was not ready to open in September. So, for the first semester, the two thousand Woodlawn students went to school from 7:00 A.M. to noon and the soon-to-be Southwood students went to Woodlawn in the afternoon. The Woodlawn basketball team had to find practice sites every day until Southwood was ready. Often, the team would practice at Centenary. After practice, Roberts and Parish, who lived near each other, would climb into Roberts's 1953 Ford and head home. Roberts would drop off the gangly teenager whom everyone called "Slim" and the two would do their nightly routine.

"What you doin' tonight?" Roberts would ask.

"Gonna find a warm woman, two packs of [pork] skins, and a cold Schlitz," Parish would laugh. He then headed home.

The Woodlawn team itself was awesome. All five starters from the Union team were on it, including Parish and a 6-1 wunderkind named William Wilson, who, Roberts said, was by far the best player on the team. Roberts was a starter from Fair Park. And Woodlawn had four returning starters from its team the previous year. Roberts was one of four whites on the team. The next year, two years after integration, the basketball team would have no whites.

While Wilson was dazzling—he eventually went to Southern University, but dropped out—Parish, who was closing in on seven feet, was the certifiable star. The Woodlawn Knights were almost unbeatable: they went 36–2 in his junior year, the best year in Shreveport prep history. Most of their home games were played not at the high school but at the Hirsch Coliseum, miles away, because authorities were worried about crowd control after the integration edict. Parish also played many of his games the following year on the road.

The 1970–71 team was, by all accounts, a superior team to the one the following year, although it failed to win the state title. Parish, who practiced his rainbow jumper by shooting over a broomstick held by coach Ivy, broke the school scoring record for a single season (881 points) despite playing in the second half in only eight games. "The scores were so lopsided," Ivy said. "He played his half and that would be it. He didn't care. He didn't care if he scored thirty points or if he scored five points. As long as we won. But I never liked to score a hundred points on anyone because it can come back to haunt you."

Woodlawn's biggest win came in the state semifinals, where it beat Booker T. Washington of New Orleans, which featured future (ABA and NBA) pro Bruce Seals. Woodlawn trailed by 11 and Parish fouled out, but the team rallied to win, 79–73. Woodlawn then came up flat against an inferior team from New Orleans,

Brother Martin, and lost the final, 65–62. (Rick Robey, a future teammate of Parish's, was a freshman that year at Brother Martin, but he was ineligible because he had transferred from another school in town. His team would win the state title and he would become the state Player of the Year in 1973–74, his senior year, two years after Parish won the award.) Parish got into foul trouble in that game, too. "The referees had absolutely no clue how to call a game with a seven-footer in there," Ivy said. "He only played a few minutes in that game. He'd block a shot, they'd call a foul."

Woodlawn got redemption the following year. Before the season started, Parish and Ivy huddled and it was agreed that Parish would play at least three quarters in each game because it was critical to his development. All Parish did was average 30.7 points and 19.9 rebounds a game as Woodlawn went 35–2 and won the state title. In one game in Lake Charles, Parish scored 52 points to set a school record. He established the mark only because the team manager mentioned it to Ivy when Parish was given a rest with 48 points and the team comfortably ahead.

"I told Robert to go out there, get the record, and then get off the floor," Ivy said. "I didn't want to keep him out there. The other coach was a good friend of mine. Well, sure enough, we put Robert back in after a time-out and what does he do? He throws the ball back out after getting it inside. So I call another time-out and tell him, 'Robert, get the four points, will you?' He scored a couple quick ones and that was that."

Woodlawn was almost like a road show that season. At one point, the team was 17–0 and had played only four home games. For good reason, no one wanted to play the team at its own gym, or even at Hirsch. That was a close to an automatic loss as you could get. So on Woodlawn's many road trips Parish would fold himself up and climb into Ivy's Volkswagen as the two drove to games. "He went with me," Ivy said, "because I wanted to make sure he got there."

One of Woodlawn's two losses that season came against Hughes Springs, Texas, 56–54. Ivy said it was the worst-refereed game he'd seen in thirty years of coaching. Another visitor that night, Indiana coach Bobby Knight, later told Ivy the same thing.

"It was unbelievable. At that time I'd play anybody, anywhere.

We'd drive all over east Texas," Ivy said. "Well, in the first two minutes of the game, Robert picked up three fouls and he still hadn't touched anyone. And the referee making the calls is someone I'd never seen before. Robert probably played about seven minutes that night. Every time he moved, there was a foul. All five of our starters fouled out and we're still only down two points at the end. Then, one of our guys gets called for traveling while he's still dribbling the ball. They get the ball back and run out the clock."

The postgame scene was almost embarrassing. Even the fans sensed that Woodlawn had been shafted, and they consoled the players afterward. The Hughes Springs players apologized and shook hands. Knight came up to Ivy and said, "I've recruited in twenty-eight states and I thought I had seen everything. But I don't think I ever saw anything like I saw tonight."

Parish looked up at Ivy after the game and said simply, "Do we have to count this one, coach?" The coach found out later that the unknown referee was not a referee at all, but a friend of the Hughes Springs coach who had been visiting over the holidays and had been pressed into service due to a still unknown "emergency." Hughes Springs was scheduled to play Woodlawn later that season, but —surprise—canceled the game.

"I saw Bobby Knight the next year," Ivy said. "He was across the room. And as soon as he saw me, the first thing he said was 'Ken, have you been to Hughes Springs, Texas, lately?' "

Woodlawn rolled through the first three games of the state tournament, including another victory over Booker T. Washington/New Orleans in the semifinals. This time, however, Woodlawn eked out a 50–49 victory in the finals over Rummel. Again, Parish's contributions were limited by foul trouble. "The officials were trying to make the game even," Parish said. "That's why I was always in foul trouble. Same thing in college. They try to restrict the big man. But the win was very satisfying, especially after the year before."

As he finished his record-setting career, Parish had coaches around the country drooling, hoping to land him for college. Jerry Tarkanian, then the coach at Long Beach State, had seen Parish play at Woodlawn when his team arrived in town to play Centenary. He told assistant coach Riley Wallace of Centenary, "If that kid ever gets out of town, they should fire you all." Wallace was concerned about Houston, which had successfully recruited Lou Dunbar from Minden, outside Shreveport. He remembered being excited when he was invited to Dunbar's home for the letter of intent signing, thinking Centenary had bagged a good one. He quickly discovered that was not the case when he entered the house and saw Houston coach Guy Lewis there along with a horde of cameras.

But Wallace told Ada Parish that Houston had a reputation for not graduating its players, and Ada Parish wanted her son to graduate. He would be the first in the family to do so. Countless other schools drifted in and out of the picture, and Wallace visited the Parish home one day to ask where Centenary stood and who was behind the decision-making process.

"Honey, I'm going to tell you something right now," Ada Parish said sternly. "Robert Parish is a man and is making his own decision."

Parish also had become a father. He would become a father again in his first year in college. The children, LaToya and Tomika, were the product of a three-year engagement to Annie Jones, which eventually dissolved.

"I wanted to wait until I got out of college to get married," Parish said. "But she didn't want to wait. So she gave me an ultimatum: get married now. But I said, 'Why get married now when I can't take care of my responsibilities? So let's just wait and do it right.' She didn't want to wait and that is understandable.

"Three years is a long time," Parish went on. "I didn't feel like it was fair to the kids, or to her. I didn't have two nickels to rub together. I got fifteen dollars a month from scholarship [the NCAA didn't allow student athletes to have jobs]. I can't even feed myself on fifteen dollars, let alone two kids. Looking at it from her point of view, now that I'm older and more mature, I can see where she was coming from. But back then, I thought she was being selfish."

The two daughters were raised by their mother, graduated from high school and went to Northeast Louisiana in Monroe. Parish attended their high school graduations and sees them when he visits Shreveport in the summer. He is equal parts surprised and gratified that the children turned out so well, "because I was never there.

"That's one thing I always say when people ask me what I'm going to do when I retire: I definitely want to spend more time with my children, even though you can't make up for all the time that was lost. I feel fortunate because most kids, when they turn their back on their parents, they don't turn back around. But my kids came around as they got older. They changed their minds once they saw the whole picture."

While Parish was dealing with fatherhood for the first time as a teenager—or trying to deal with it—he also was being courted by virtually every major college in the country. He eventually whittled his choices down to five schools: Centenary, Indiana, Florida State, Jacksonville, and Illinois State.

Knight was one of many persistent pursuers of Parish and got Parish and Ivy to make a visit to Bloomington. The weather was horrible and nothing Knight could do could make up for Mother Nature.

During the interview, Knight sat Parish down and asked him what he wanted. "How much money do you want a month?" Knight asked. "What kind of car? What kind of clothes?" Parish, typically, said nothing, though he was wondering where this all was leading. He and Ivy had had an agreement that any time a coach promised something that looked shady, he would tell the coach without mentioning names.

"The reason I'm asking you if you want all of this is because you'll get none of it if you come to Indiana," said Knight. "You come here, you come here because you want to play for a national championship. If you want that other stuff, I can give you some phone numbers because I know guys who can and will give you that stuff."

Knight also told Parish something more important and more critical to Parish's short-term future. It was something Parish would hear elsewhere: we can't take you on scholarship because your grades and test scores are too low.

The NCAA was watching Parish closely. The organization knew he was being heavily recruited and wanted to make sure everything was on the up-and-up. It dispatched a young employee named David Berst to oversee the matter. He met with Parish at Woodlawn and, sitting in the bleachers after a faculty game, advised him on what was proper and what was not. "I interviewed him because he was a seven-footer and in those days we all tried to figure out if there might be a problem," Berst said.

Ivy said he also chatted with Berst, and related one telling exchange: "David came into my office, and he wanted to know where Robert was planning on going. I told him five schools that were interested, and he said that of the five, the only one where Parish could go and still probably be eligible to play was Centenary. He said it would be no problem. The guy told me, eye to eye, that it was the one place he could go."

Berst, however, emphatically denies ever having such a conversation.

"That's impossible," he said, "and completely contrary to our procedures. I don't think I ever, under any circumstances, advised anyone if there was trouble at any school. When I recognized that Centenary was involved, and that if they were going to enroll Parish, that they needed to [obey the rules] to ensure compliance. It doesn't make any difference [to me] where a guy goes."

Centenary and Parish were, are, and always will be an utterly unfathomable mix. There is no other instance of such a valuable high school commodity—he was, at worst, the number two recruit in the country—selecting a school so utterly devoid of basketball tradition or excellence. It would have been like Lew Alcindor choosing Hunter College. There simply is nothing that even comes close. (Bob Lanier and St. Bonaventure might be the closest.)

"It was totally his decision," his mother said. "All I told him was that he could go all across the country, but what he might need the most would still be in his own backyard." Parish was an incorrigible homebody. Had he lived in Monroe, he probably would have gone to Northeast Louisiana.

In Parish's days, Centenary was the smallest Division I school in the country—its student body consisted of only seven hundred students. Today, it has eleven hundred students. It is the oldest private liberal-arts college west of the Mississippi and has a beautiful campus of brick Georgian buildings and flowering magnolia trees. It also has a three-thousand-seat gym, the Gold Dome, which opened the year Parish arrived.

Centenary started playing basketball in 1921 and has, with the exception of the World War II years, had a team ever since. Through its first sixty-seven seasons, it has won twenty or more games only six times. Three of those times came during Parish's stay. The school attained Division I status in 1960, and thirty-three years later it still hasn't made an NIT or NCAA tournament appearance. Even more bizarre, Centenary won the Trans America Athletic Conference championship in 1980, the year before the conference's champ began receiving an automatic NCAA tournament bid. (At 15–14, the team's record wasn't good enough to warrant an at-large bid.) Once the conference champ became eligible to receive an automatic bid, Centenary lost five straight TAAC championship games. In 1989–90, Centenary went 22–8 but again went nowhere.

Parish is the only Centenary basketball alum to have made any kind of splash in the NBA. Former Atlanta Braves pitcher Cecil Upshaw, golfer Hal Sutton (his father is a big Centenary booster), and gymnast Kathy Johnson also attended Centenary.

Curiously, however, despite its reputation as an academic institution, Centenary's procedures for admitting freshman scholarship athletes were among the most lenient and favorable in the country. And that played a big part in the Parish courtship.

In those days, an incoming freshman had to predict to a 1.6 grade point average (out of 4.0) to be eligible for an athletic scholarship. The school arrived at this number by taking the player's grades, high school rank, and test scores, throwing them into an education Veg-o-Matic, and getting a numerical result.

To this day, there are two very different views on Parish's projected eligibility. He says it was not a problem, and Wallace, who recruited Parish, concurs. The NCAA, however, did not see it that way, nor did the federal courts. The disagreement occurred when Centenary converted Parish's American College Test score to a Scholastic Aptitude Test number after being advised repeatedly, in writing and by phone, that such conversions were not allowed and would result in Parish's being declared ineligible.

The killer wasn't Parish's grades; he had a 2.1 average at Woodlawn. It was his score on the ACT. The test, which is administered in all fifty states, is not an aptitude test. It's more a snapshot of a student's development at that point. The ACT covers four subject areas: English, math, science, and social studies. Each student who takes the test gets a composite score from the four disciplines, ranging from 1 to 36. The statistical mean is 18. In 1992, the national average was 20.6.

Parish took the ACT twice. His highest score was an 8, which put him in the first percentile for men. In other words, 99 percent of the male students who took the test did better. The low score was a red flag to several schools, which decided there was no way Parish could be eligible or predict to a 1.6. Indiana was one of those. Florida State told Parish he would need a 21 on the ACT to project to a 1.6 and suggested he take it again. But Parish was tired of taking tests, and Wallace agreed, calling him "gun-shy."

Another option Parish did not consider was attending a state school—LSU or Northeast Louisiana were two possibilities—which he could have done merely by graduating from high school. And he could have become eligible for a scholarship at a state school once he had an academic track record. But Parish said he could not afford to pay for college, even a state school.

Centenary, which saw a chance to land a premier player and knew that Parish wanted to remain close to home, went hard after the homegrown talent. As it had with many athletes before—including twelve the previous year, when conversions also were not allowed—Centenary converted Parish's ACT score to an SAT score. The problem was that Parish was being watched, and so Centenary was playing with the big boys. No one had cared or noticed before, and Centenary had never revealed anything, either.

The NCAA had ruled in 1969 that, effective May 1970, two years before Parish enrolled at Centenary, conversion tables no longer would be allowed. All NCAA member institutions, including Centenary, were informed in writing. In June 1972, with the courtship of Parish well under way, the NCAA again wrote to remind Centenary that conversion tables were a no-no. That missive came after Wallace told Berst that Centenary was converting the ACT score to an SAT number, as it had done before without recrimination or punishment.

Berst again warned the school in August, a week before Centenary announced that it had landed Parish. Berst said he even suggested that Parish take the SAT so there would be no problem. Parish, however, was never told about the eligibility questions or advised by Centenary to either retake the ACT or try the SAT. He didn't hear anything until he and four other basketball players admitted via the conversion table method were well into their freshman year, after the basketball team began practice but before it had played any games.

"The school president came to us and told us that the NCAA was being picky," Parish said. "I did not know anything about them [the conversion tables] being outlawed. They also said the NCAA said nothing about it."

That simply is not the case. Centenary was warned. It simply chose to ignore the NCAA, and it did not take advantage of any appellate proceedings within the NCAA guidelines. On January 9, 1973, the NCAA lowered the boom, putting Centenary on indefinite probation. If the players were quickly ruled ineligible, the probation would last two years, but if the players continued to play, the sanctions would stay in effect until two years after they left. Included in the sanctions were bans on postseason play and television appearances.

Centenary maintained its loyalty to the players and kept them on scholarship. The school's records and the records of all its players were stricken from the NCAA's books. (Parish's last official entry in NCAA stats is from a release dated January 27, 1973, when he was averaging 23.3 points and 17.4 rebounds. The next week, there is no mention of him. And the NCAA record books do not note that Parish is the leading rebounder in Division I since 1973, either.) Parish also achieved impressive scoring numbers without aid of the dunk, which was outlawed at the time. Before his final game, a local columnist pleaded for him to dunk, just once. Parish didn't. He remained curiously averse to dunking in his pro career, too.

Centenary was powerless. It was an independent and clearly out of its league in this instance. It also was dead wrong on the conversion table issue. The NCAA determined that Parish needed a 450 SAT score (you get 400 for spelling your name correctly) to qualify, but he never took the test. Even if the conversion tables had been in effect, and using Centenary's most favorable rate, the 8 on the ACT would have translated to somewhere between 403 and 443 on the SAT. And that still would have made Parish ineligible in the eyes of the NCAA.

The battle soon shifted to the courts. After the probation decision came down, the Gents Club (Centenary's teams are called the Gentlemen) asked two local lawyers (both members of the booster club) if there was some way they could get a court to overturn the 1.6 rule or stop the NCAA temporarily from enforcing it because Centenary stood a chance at a postseason bid. The lawyers, with the booster club paying expenses, took the case.

They first questioned whether the NCAA had any jurisdiction in the case; the judge rejected that contention but granted a temporary restraining order on the 1.6/eligibility question. The team, however, was not good enough (19–8) to receive a berth in a postseason tournament, and eventually the restraining order expired.

But the court case went on. The lawyers were buoyed by two other cases in which the 1.6 rule was either questioned or ruled inadequate, one involving Isaac Curtis, the other involving athletes at Sacramento State College. In Curtis's situation, he enrolled at Cal–Berkeley without having to take either the ACT or SAT. (That is known as the 4 Percent Rule in California, under which students are admitted on the basis of need, maturity, and ability to catch a ball in traffic or go to the boards.) With no test score, a student cannot predict to a 1.6, regardless of his GPA in high school, so Curtis, technically, did not predict to a 1.6. Curtis was allowed to transfer to San Diego State with impunity. He also had established a good GPA at Cal. In the other case, eleven students at Sacramento State sued after the school did what Centenary did not do and declared them ineligible. They won at the district court level, but the appeals court ruled in favor of the NCAA.

In Centenary's court case, there was testimony for two days in April (Ivy still can't understand why he wasn't called to testify about his version of his chat with Berst, but it did not pertain to the 1.6 question); and then, in July, U.S. District Court judge Benjamin Dawkins ruled against the players' request that their eligibility be reinstated. He saw nothing wrong with the 1.6 rule, going so far as to say, "Members of the black race [Parish was the sole black among the five litigants] have been perhaps the greatest beneficiaries of numerically disproportionate participation in intercollegiate athletics; and they have done so under the aegis of the 1.600 rule."

The players appealed. With one season gone and the sanctions still in place, they stressed in arguments that they would suffer harm if the NCAA kept its ban on television and tournaments. In January 1975, or midway through Parish's junior season at Centenary, the Fifth U.S. Circuit Court of Appeals upheld the lower court on every issue.

The irony in all of this is that the celebrated 1.6 rule quickly became moot. At its annual convention on January 13, 1973, four days after the NCAA hit Centenary with its sanctions, the organization amended the 1.6 rule. Beginning in the 1974–75 academic year, an incoming freshman had to have a cumulative 2.0 grade point average over his high school career to be eligible to play varsity sports as a freshman. But the NCAA kept Centenary on probation because the old 1.6 rule applied in Parish's case.

"They threw it out because it wasn't working," said Peyton Moore, one of the Shreveport attorneys who represented the players. "The judge never thought it was discriminatory, but the whole basis of our suit was that it did discriminate against people like Robert. He was not prepared to take the ACT. His grades were OK, and once he got to Centenary he did fine. We knew the thing was a long shot. But the whole suit was about Parish. Had he not been involved, no one would ever have known or cared. The NCAA brought out all its vindictiveness on him. And he didn't do anything wrong."

In what to Centenary sure looked like a contradiction, the NCAA promised the five players immediate eligibility if they transferred. (By then, however, the players all had sufficient college credentials to be eligible.) They did not. Parish would not even consider it. He still had his daughters nearby. He also didn't think he or the school had erred in any way. And he was comfortable at Centenary.

So for four years Parish was the best invisible man in the country. "They made him a nonperson," said Moore. Centenary became the Leon Trotsky of NCAA basketball, also ceasing to exist in that stretch. In his final three years at Centenary, the team went 21–4, 25–4, and 22–5, with a 35–2 record at home. The team had a school record eighteen-game home winning streak. Under most conditions, all of those teams would have been invited somewhere. "We were good enough to get to the Final Four," Wallace contended.

But not without Parish. Why did Centenary refuse to revoke Parish's scholarship and declare him ineligible? The athletic director at the time, Orvis Sigler, was gone shortly after the incident. The answer may be that the school honestly felt it either was being victimized or had acted in good faith.

Or it could be that it knew it would never have a chance to get another player like Parish and it might as well risk the wrath of the NCAA. Or maybe it thought it could slide by on good faith. As one person involved said, "If I'm the coach of that team, I'd want to get Parish, too. Do you think Centenary is going anywhere without Robert Parish? Or be on TV without Robert Parish?"

Without Parish, the team had no chance of postseason play or tournaments. With him it at least had a good team and inevitably would attract interest. Wallace made sure all the weekly voters in the Associated Press poll (sportswriters) knew about Centenary and Parish; he mailed out the team and individual statistics to them on a weekly basis. *Sports Illustrated* did a piece on Parish in 1976. *The New York Times* called the school "unknown and unwanted." None of that would have been forthcoming had Parish been declared ineligible. As one college scout observed during Parish's senior year, "Without Parish, they would not be on probation, but no one would have ever heard of them, either."

And although they could not have known it then, the school would long be remembered for its association with Parish. Before each Celtics game through the years, he received the following introduction: "Starting at center, from Centenary, Robert Parish." What the school still can't understand is why Parish's eligibility was not restored once the NCAA abandoned the 1.6 rule and why the five players were told they could transfer anywhere and be eligible immediately.

"The coaches told me that they would understand if I transferred," Parish said. "But I chose to stay because I had made a commitment to Centenary, and I think that was my first sign of showing loyalty. I had gone there because it was small, it was close to home, and the program was on the way up. And once I made the decision, that was it. I think it's something my father instilled in me at a very early age. He always had told me during recruiting that once I've made the decision to stick with it. And it definitely was the right decision for me. It was the best four years of my life. And if I had gone to a bigger school, there's no way I would have gotten my diploma. Not in four years, anyway.''

That was the final irony of all. Parish had a 2.33 grade point average when the case went to trial at the end of his freshman year. And he eventually graduated on time and got his degree, despite the fact that four years earlier the NCAA had ruled him ineligible for a scholarship because of an inadequate academic record.

"Robert graduated on time. He failed one course, English 101. He missed three classes his freshman year," Wallace said. "My wife tutored him in English. He'd call her and say he had a paper due in two weeks. Now, they call and say that it was due last week. He wanted an education. He wanted a degree. He got both."

Leaving Centenary for another college with postseason hopes and television dates (for that was all he was missing by staying) wasn't Parish's only choice. Another, far more lucrative one (we can assume, anyway, without knowledge to the contrary) was the American Basketball Association. The league had not hesitated to snap up promising underclassmen in the 1970s (Julius Erving being a most notable example) while they still had college eligibility. Many players jumped; the money was too good to pass up. One day while Parish was still at Centenary, Wallace got a call to go to Parish's dorm room and found two men with professional ties chatting with Parish. He knew they weren't there to talk about Watergate and asked them to leave.

At the end of his freshman year, Parish was drafted by the ABA's Utah Stars, and every year while he was in college the Stars' director of player personnel and assistant coach, Larry Creger, would visit Shreveport. On his first trip, he brought legendary center Zelmo Beaty, who was making the jump to Utah from the NBA, for impact purposes. Creger would watch the Gentlemen and lay out his position for Parish to consider. The money was good, six figures, maybe more than he would get when he did turn pro (the merger knocked down salaries). Creger had first noticed Parish in the state high school tournament while he was scouting center Edmund Lawrence of McNeese State. Lawrence had Parish-like numbers in college, but his NBA career was limited to three games with the Pistons in 1980–81.

"I immediately thought, 'This guy [Parish] is NBA material. Or ABA,' " Creger said. "When he went to Centenary, I called his coach and told him that we were going to try and get Robert into the pros. During most of that time, the ABA was allowing most anything. We could have signed high school players, and we did sign Moses [Malone, who joined the ABA straight out of high school]. But I was always very careful not to be unethical if I could help it."

Money was no object in the Stars' pursuit of Parish. Creger would spend a month in town, making frequent visits to the Parish house. Some nights he would show up and the call would go out for dinner. "There was always a house full of people. Someone would say, 'Why don't you go out and get sixteen cheeseburgers?' That's what we'd do." But every year, the answer was the same: no. But that doesn't mean Parish wasn't tempted.

Parish felt he stagnated in his last two years at Centenary. He felt coach Larry Little was not a "big man's coach" and felt that the sanctions began to hit home. Still, the team was good, and Parish's numbers would have been eye-opening at any level (he averaged 18.9 points and 15.4 rebounds in his junior year).

"After my junior year," he said, "I was tempted [to join the ABA]. I wasn't getting any better, I didn't think. I felt like I grew my freshman and sophomore years, but the last two years I felt I stayed at the same level. I think that's why it took me a couple years to catch up in the pros. But my parents would have broken my back if I had left. Getting that degree was more important to them than the money. And we definitely could have used the money."

"I presented the family with the whole situation every year for three years," said Creger. " 'Here's the money. Here's the guarantee.' But I don't know how much it would have cost us to get Robert because his mother insisted he finish." The feeling at the

Parish house was that they hadn't been rich all their lives and that another year or two wouldn't make a big difference.

"I told Robert, 'You're going to get the money anyway. It'll be there for you. The education is more important,' " Ada Parish said. "I took my children to church. I taught them right from wrong. I taught them that school comes first. If you learn all that, you won't have too much to worry about."

While Parish and Centenary remained persona non grata in the eyes of the NCAA, the folks who put together the 1975 Pan American team, the 1975 Intercontinental Cup team, and the 1976 U.S. Olympic team wanted Parish. The school, however, had to pay Parish's way to Salt Lake City in 1975 for the Pan Am trials after he was initially snubbed. Once there, he impressed everyone, made the team easily, and was named captain.

The Pan Am team also featured Rick Robey, Johnny Davis, Tree Rollins, Leon Douglas, and Otis Birdsong. After tryouts, the team traveled through Canada and then went to Mexico City and won the gold medal. "Robert was the same throughout everything. He didn't talk much. He was very easygoing," Robey said.

The other All-Star team played in Europe, and that was where Parish first encountered Dave Gavitt, who led the team. The team played the Yugoslavs, Soviets, Italians, and Greeks over a three-week period. Gavitt got to know Parish on and off the court and is still amazed that Parish is running the floor at age thirty-nine.

"Never, in my wildest dreams, did I ever think he'd be playing in the NBA seventeen years later," Gavitt said. "When he ran, it looked like his legs were going to fall apart. He ran with his knees, I thought. But he got up and down the floor."

Parish got the nickname "Senator" on that trip. Toward the end of the trip, the team was invited to dinner by the Greek division of the company that makes Tupperware. It was a fancy-schmantzy affair at a yacht club overlooking the Aegean Sea, and Gavitt asked the usually silent Parish to thank the hosts on behalf of the team. Parish wanted no part of that. Gavitt persisted, finally telling him, "Senator, you've been nominated." Parish reluctantly rose and came off like Winston Churchill at the podium.

Dean Smith, who would coach the 1976 Olympic team, joined

them for part of the trip. It was his responsibility to atone for the debacle in Munich in 1972. Parish was high on everyone's list for the team, but he decided not to try out, as did Leon Douglas. Tree Rollins, whom Smith wanted, was not chosen by the selection committee, so the team went to Montreal with only Mitch Kupchak and Tom LaGarde as centers, but won the gold medal anyway.

Parish said that Peyton Moore, by now his agent, advised him against trying out for the Olympics because of fear of injury. But Moore said that while the advice was correct, it came not from him, but from the NBA teams that were looking to draft Parish. Several first-rounders that year, however, including three chosen ahead of Parish (Scott May, Adrian Dantley, and Quinn Buckner), were members of the 1976 Olympic team. Kupchak was also selected in the first round that year, after Parish. Several players chosen in the 1977 draft (Kenny Carr, Walt Davis, and LaGarde) were also on the squad.

"Atlanta [which had the first pick and was considering Parish] told him it did not want him in the Olympics. Neither did any team which was thinking of drafting him," Moore said. "And I think he hadn't been all that thrilled the year before with the Pan Am team and the other team. He had made up his mind by the time he came to see me. He got a lot of criticism for not trying out and I felt it was very unfair. I wrote an article in the local paper defending Robert's decision. He was convinced it would adversely affect his drafting position. Or that he might get hurt." Regarding Parish's financial situation, Moore said, "He had nothing in his icebox at home. Right or wrong, he was worried. I'd have wanted him to go. But I supported his decision."

Parish stayed home, was drafted by the Warriors, and bought his family a new house in a tonier but still all-black subdivision of Shreveport. His father, however, headed back to the old neighborhood every morning to meet his friends and drive to work. Some things never change.

The Celtics had no business owning the number one pick in the 1980 draft. They had the best record in the NBA the year before, not the worst. But they had it, thanks to a series of events that began in the summer of 1979, when they signed M. L. Carr, a free agent from Detroit.

Carr was an overachieving, likable, chatterbox whose specialty was defense. He was among the better players on an otherwise unimpressive Pistons team. The Celtics had shown interest in Carr years before, in 1973, when they had him in for a brief tryout. He had already been cut by the Kansas City Kings, and after the work-out in Boston he decided to play in Israel for two years. He then returned to the United States and played for the ABA St. Louis Spirits, where he was second in Rookie of the Year balloting to David Thompson.

When the ABA and NBA merged in 1976, Carr signed a three-year deal with the Pistons. The contract, which called for annual salaries of $60,000, $70,000, and $75,000, ended up being more important for what it did not contain, however.

Carr was in his third year with the Pistons when he and the team began to negotiate a longer, richer deal. His value was not in question. He also wanted to stay in Detroit. And the money—which eventually grew to $1.35 million over five years—also wasn't a problem. But there was a snag.

After Carr's first season with the Pistons, he received a surprise $40,000 thank-you bonus. The Pistons promised, though not in writing, to reward him appropriately in each of the final two years of the deal. The following year, the bonus was only $30,000. When Carr asked for an explanation, he was told that the Pistons simply wanted to make him a $100,000-a-year player. Still, it was found money and he wasn't complaining. He again was told there would be a third bonus if he continued to play well. He promptly went out, was third in the league in minutes played, and made the second All-Defensive team.

When the two sides starting talking about a new contract, Carr made it known from the outset that the third bonus had to be paid before he would agree to any new deal. With the money he was going to get shortly, the amount meant little to him, but the Pistons had promised him a bonus and he wanted it. Detroit agreed to pay the sum, but wanted it included as part of the new deal.

Then, in June 1979, coach Dick Vitale wrote a letter to Carr expressing his hope that the two would again be back on the Pistons bench. "I think you know where you stand in the eyes of Dick Vitale, super, super tall and super, super high. [Yes, he talked like that even back then.] Sometimes, a few dollars here or there isn't what it is all about in happiness. Remember, M.L., you are sincerely wanted by Dick Vitale and the Detroit Pistons."

Eleven days later Vitale sent another letter to Carr. The Pistons, meanwhile, through general counsel Oscar Feldman, continued to pitch the bonus as part of a bigger deal. Carr was equally adamant about settling old debts before signing a new deal. At one point, things got so wild that Carr even offered to return the money as soon as he received it, just to satisfy himself that the Pistons had met their end of the unwritten agreement. Detroit asked Carr to give the team the right of first refusal in any free agent offering as a show of sincerity to the franchise. Carr refused.

Carr, meanwhile, was doing what all free agents should do—talking with potential employers. The Knicks and Celtics were both better teams than the Pistons. Then Detroit offered him a deal for five years instead of four. Carr was looking at a seven-figure deal, all guaranteed, but he still wanted his bonus first. The Knicks then offered him $2 million over five years, and Carr was so confident and elated after the meeting that he tipped a New York cabbie $5.

A final flurry from the Celtics, however, tipped the scales in Boston's favor and the deal was done. Red Auerbach had cited the unending litany of Celtics' advantages and mentioned that there was this new kid, Bird, coming along too. Carr was convinced and, still miffed at the Pistons, made the switch.

"We're losing the hearts and guts of our team," sighed Vitale.

Then the fun began. The Celtics called a news conference for July 24 to announce the signing. The Pistons were not informed, which was a violation of league policy. Feldman demanded an apology. A contrite Auerbach responded, "I goofed." That was just the first of many disagreements between the teams over the next month.

In those days, free agency was dangerous for both the team that signed the player and the team that lost the player. Everyone agreed that the former team should be compensated, but only rarely did the two teams involved agree on the nature of the compensation. If there was no agreement, the issue fell into the hands of the commissioner Larry O'Brien, who decided the compensation as a final, absolute arbiter. His decisions invariably upset both teams.

The Celtics expected to take a hit. Their job was to minimize the damage, through either negotiation or arbitration. But they also were coming off a 29–53 season and their roster reflected that record. As Vitale noted, "They didn't have many players that made you get excited." Bird had yet to play a game, but even at that point, the Pistons allowed that "it would be in the best interest of the NBA for him to play in Boston." In other words, they would not ask for Bird as compensation, even though Carr had a proven NBA track record and Bird did not. Dave Cowens and Nate Archibald were at the ends of their respective Hall of Fame careers and out of the picture. Cedric Maxwell was intriguing, but the Pistons coaching staff, in a memorandum, submitted that he would not be adequate compensation for Carr "because he lacked the defensive and leadership capabilities" of Carr. Maxwell's "reputation for hustle, team play and attitude is certainly open to question," the memo said, and he would not be viewed as "an equal replacement."

Auerbach publicly stated that the one player the Pistons couldn't expect to receive was Bob McAdoo. It was a typical Auerbachian ploy. The man he really wanted to unload—and quickly—was McAdoo. The Celtics had acquired McAdoo in 1979 in a ridiculous deal that sent three first-round picks to the Knicks. The trade was the handiwork of then owner John Y. Brown, who was acting at the behest of his fiancée, Phyllis George. Auerbach was never consulted. Now Auerbach wanted McAdoo out, but he wanted something in return. He was only hanging on to him as bait, hoping that a guard could be found. Either way, McAdoo was history.

"The way we got McAdoo was a travesty," said Auerbach. "I got mad at McAdoo. He came in and the coach didn't start him, so he got sick. Meanwhile, he's out and around. He didn't want to play part-time because it might affect his average. So I said, 'Let's get rid of this guy.' "

And, despite his sorry performance in Boston, where, it should be pointed out, McAdoo walked into an ongoing disaster, the onetime

MVP (1974–75) and scoring machine still had value around the league.

Bob McAdoo was a big name. And to Detroit, which was struggling at the gate (and would continue to do so for years), that meant something. The Pistons also had one of McAdoo's former teammates from Buffalo, John Shumate, and Vitale was confident that Big Mac could make it in the Motor City. They had him rated as the third-best player on the Boston roster after Bird and Cowens. Maxwell was fourth.

In their brief to O'Brien, submitted August 30, 1979, the Pistons acknowledged that even a faltering McAdoo was still more valuable than Carr and conceded that McAdoo alone would be excessive compensation. They proposed adding two number one draft picks, one in 1980 and one in 1982. The proposal sounded more than reasonable. Auerbach rejected it. The Celtics had no first-round pick of their own in 1980, having traded it to Indiana for Earl Tatum, a move that was also engineered by Brown. Auerbach wanted two picks in 1980 because he didn't have his own and because he didn't want to wait until 1982 to get Complete McAdoo Gratification. He thus sent back a proposal to Detroit he knew had no chance: Curtis Rowe for Carr.

Feldman shot back a rocket. He called the Rowe offering "either a facetious one or an insult to my intelligence. Or both. I am appalled." Auerbach wondered if Leon Douglas might be thrown into the deal. The Pistons said no chance. Detroit came back with a request for Rick Robey, Jeff Judkins, and a number one draft pick. Auerbach said Judkins alone would be excessive. The Pistons said that reply "labors on absurdity."

Detroit's final proposal was for Maxwell (on whom the Pistons apparently had softened throughout all this) and a 1981 number one draft pick or $100,000 in cash. Again the Celtics said no. On August 7, O'Brien gave the teams two more weeks to try to work out a deal. The pressure, Vitale felt, was squarely on the Pistons.

"You have to remember what it was like back then," he said. "We were afraid of getting nothing. We felt Red had all this power and could intimidate the commissioner. Who were we?"

While all this was going on, Jan Volk, then the Celtics' general counsel, uncovered the proverbial smoking gun while going over previous arbitration awards by the commissioner. If the name Marvin Roberts doesn't ring a bell, don't be surprised. But had it not been for Marvin Roberts, there might not have ever been a Big Three.

Roberts was the Pistons' third-round draft pick in 1971 out of Utah State, but he never signed with the team. He spent five years playing in the ABA, and when the merger arrived he was declared a free agent, with the Pistons holding his NBA rights.

The Phoenix Suns apparently saw something in Roberts, though not much, and signed him to a contract in September 1976. This contract would not kick in until the 1977–78 season, and the Suns and Pistons started to converse about compensation. Detroit asked to be rewarded, but could not present any clear evidence to support its case, other than the fact that it had drafted Roberts. It had made no effort to sign him.

O'Brien then was given the case, and he ruled that because Detroit had suffered no damage, nor had it made any reasonable effort to sign Roberts, the Pistons would get nothing. And it was that ruling which Volk zeroed in on, alarming the Pistons with the possibility that perhaps they could get similarly shaken in the Carr compensation.

The Celtics' brief pointed out that Detroit had not paid the final installment of the bonus to Carr, as the team had promised. How badly could the Pistons want Carr if they didn't make that small showing of good faith? The brief pointed to Detroit's signing of junior eligible Earl Evans and Phil Hubbard, both forwards, as evidence that Carr was not in the Pistons' future plans. If the commissioner decided that any compensation was due Detroit—and Boston suggested that the Pistons deserved none—then someone like Rowe or Archibald would be more than fair.

O'Brien never had to make a decision. Three days after seeing the Boston brief, Detroit made the fateful proposal that changed the course of NBA history. The Pistons had two first-round picks in 1980, their own and one they had received from Washington as

compensation for the Bullets' signing of Kevin Porter. They would
send them both to Boston in exchange for McAdoo. The Celtics
agreed, and the deal was announced on September 9.

No one at the time could have had the remotest inkling of just
how imbalanced that deal would turn out to be. McAdoo lasted less
than two years in Detroit. He was constantly injured and was, basically, a bust. In his second season, he played only six games for
the Pistons, who finally got so fed up with him that they waived
him—getting nothing in return.

The Celtics closely monitored the Pistons throughout the 1979–80
season and hoped for the worst. They did their part, winning all six
games between the teams (Bird averaged 23 points and 12 rebounds
against Detroit). Vitale lasted only twelve games before being fired.
To this day he thinks Auerbach owes him a championship ring for
his role in the McAdoo trade.

The Pistons finished with a horrible record of 16–66, by far the
worst in the Eastern Conference. (New Jersey, at 34–48, was next.)
The Pistons went through seventeen players and had losing streaks
of fourteen, thirteen, eight, and seven games. They were 3–38 on
the road, dropped their final fourteen games, and, in midseason,
traded Bob Lanier to Milwaukee. Utah and Golden State had the
worst records in the West, 24–58, but, in a blind draw held at the
end of the season, the Jazz logo was picked out of an envelope by
O'Brien and Utah earned the chance to get the top pick in the draft.

Back then, the number one pick was determined by a simple coin
flip in the commissioner's New York office. But who would make
the call? O'Brien decided to have a preliminary coin flip to determine who would make the call on the biggie. Neither Auerbach,
who was in O'Brien's office, nor Utah GM Frank Layden, who
remained in Salt Lake City to save money for the cash-strapped
Jazz, would yield to the other. So O'Brien assigned heads to the
Celtics and tails to the Jazz and the coin came up tails. Utah would
make the choice.

The Jazz had run contests, talked to palm readers, and done just
about everything imaginable to solicit a consensus on what to call in
the coin flip. Layden said he was inclined to call tails, having read
somewhere that it came up more often than heads. However, as he

left for work that morning, his daughter, Katie, told him to pick heads. And blood being thicker than palm readers, he selected heads.

Of course, the coin, an 1883 silver dollar, came up tails.

Auerbach let out a congratulatory whoop and pounded a nearby table in triumph. Layden could only hear the celebration on the other end of the phone line. "There was such an empty feeling," he recalled.

Now the Celtics had the number one pick in the draft. The question was, what were they going to do with it? They wanted to get bigger, and two names from the senior class surfaced: Joe Barry Carroll, an enigmatic but undeniably gifted seven-footer, and Kevin McHale, a gangly forward with an enormous reach and shot-blocking potential who had dazzled scouts in postseason performances at the Pizza Hut Classic in Las Vegas and the Aloha Classic in Hawaii. Another option in the draft was Louisville guard Darrell Griffith, and while he could help the team's perimeter play, and was an Auerbach favorite, he was not going to line up in the trenches against the Philly behemoths.

Auerbach, however, had other ideas. Four days after winning the coin toss, he went to work. His target was Ralph Sampson, who had just completed his freshman year at the University of Virginia. In everyone's mind, he was the Next Great Center. He was 7-4. He was nimble, coordinated, and, as the Celtics discovered, loyal and not easily swayed.

Sampson had entered the University of Virginia and made an initial promise to stay for at least two years. The team then went out and won the National Invitational Tournament in his first season, beating Minnesota (and McHale) in the finals. Auerbach has always been a believer in "big, bigger, biggest" in basketball and Sampson apparently was one of those rare jewels who surface once a decade. And with the Celtics starting a new era under Fitch and Bird, Auerbach figured they wouldn't be in a position to draft a great one for years.

"Did we want him? Absolutely," Auerbach said. "Would we have taken him with the first pick? Absolutely. No question about it."

Auerbach wanted to meet Sampson and make his pitch in person, but the freshman initially was unwilling. It was hard for the Celtics to even make contact with Sampson.

Instead, a meeting was arranged in Harrisonburg, Virginia, Sampson's hometown, between Auerbach and Sampson's parents, his high school coach and adviser, Roger Bergey, and his college coach, Terry Holland. The issue seemed to be a no-brainer to Auerbach. The kid was committed to only two years anyway. And why risk going to a genuine loser next year, like expansion Dallas, when he could join the exalted Celtics and play with Dave Cowens, Nate Archibald, and Larry Bird?

The Celtics were also buoyed when Sampson made two statements that indicated that turning pro was not completely out of the question, despite his earlier remarks about staying at least two years. In one interview, Sampson had stated that had Utah won the coin flip, he wouldn't even consider making the jump. The Celtics took that to mean that because Boston won the flip, he might consider it. The other was that he was determined to be "set up for life" by whoever drafted him, something the Celtics clearly were prepared to do.

What they were not prepared for, however, was Sampson's decision. He did not attend the meeting in Harrisonburg, something that miffed Auerbach even though he had known ahead of time that Sampson would be in Charlottesville, on campus, seventy miles away. Then, a week after the meeting, Sampson released a statement through the University of Virginia sports information office stating that he was flattered by all the attention but was remaining in school. Auerbach and owner Harry Mangurian made one final personal appeal in April, offering Sampson a huge deal, but were turned down.

The reaction in Boston was predictable. Auerbach went ballistic. Not only was he unaccustomed to being spurned, he could not understand the reasoning behind the decision. This bordered on embarrassment. And it was so public.

"Maybe Ralph Sampson and his parents will come to their senses and realize they are being hoodwinked by a few glad-handers," Auerbach said. "I just don't know how they can sleep at night. It's ridiculous. If he were an intellectual genius and was planning on being a surgeon, you could see him wanting to go to school for four, five, six years. Then, I'd buy it. But he has said all along that he would only stay in school for two years. In this situation, how could anyone advise him to stay in school? They are taking away earning potential he'll never get back. And they're forgetting that if he gets hit by a car, it's the end of the line.''

Fitch said he was not surprised by the decision. He did eventually get to coach Sampson in Houston four years down the road. But he also knew the Celtics needed more than just a skinny 7-4 sophomore-to-be to stay competitive in the league. And he figured Auerbach had no chance going in, so he was not stunned when the rejection came.

"I'll tell you how serious I thought it all was," he said. "It was so serious that I didn't even go down there. I wasn't interested. Everyone knew that Ralph was going to stay. And I hadn't even seen him play. I guess I was one of the few who hadn't. But the Celtics did what they had to do. It didn't hurt to rap on the door because if someone says no, it's still better to hear that than to not knock on the door and find out years later he would have said yes. But I never thought they had a Chinaman's chance.''

Sampson didn't come out the next year either, when the Dallas Mavericks had the number one pick. Or the year after that, when the Lakers had the first pick. He stayed at Virginia for four years, got his degree, then ended up with the Houston Rockets.

Had the Celtics been able to lure Sampson away from Virginia, there's no telling how it might have turned out. But the Big Three certainly wouldn't have played together. And Larry Bird might have been condemned to the NBA equivalent of Ernie Banks's career—distinguished, successful, admired, but lacking the greatest achievement of all, a world championship.

If Sampson ever regretted his decision to stay in school, he never said so. He is the only two-time winner of the John Wooden Award, given annually to the best player in college. But despite being named Player of the Year in three of his four years at Virginia, he never could deliver the NCAA title to Charlottesville, which had almost seemed to be his *raison d'être*. The closest the Cavaliers got was the Final Four in 1981, Sampson's sophomore year, but North

Carolina eliminated them before losing to Indiana in the final. Sampson's final college game resulted in a heartbreaking defeat to eventual champion North Carolina State. Ironically, the team made the Final Four in 1984, a year after Sampson left.

"The fact that he didn't turn out to be great," Auerbach said, "is something you can't determine. Based on his college record and his potential, he should have been one of the greats in the NBA. And he was the Rookie of the Year [1983–84]. You couldn't foresee he was going to get hurt, his attitude, his mental toughness, his motivation. All those things you just can't tell."

Added Volk, "There's no telling what Ralph Sampson would have been in this environment. I really don't doubt that Ralph Sampson's career would have been different if he had come here and played with Larry Bird. Were the injuries inevitable? I don't know. And it's a debatable issue as to Sampson . . . as to where it would have gone. It's not a debatable issue with Joe Barry Carroll."

With Sampson out of the picture, the Celtics turned in another direction. They were in unfamiliar territory, never before owning the number one draft pick in the so-called modern era. Even Bill Russell wasn't the first overall pick.

Carroll, McHale, and Griffith were the top three choices in everyone's mind. The Bulls had the fourth pick and had already told McHale that he wouldn't get by them.

Things began to get serious when Fitch and Golden State executive Pete Newell got together in Lexington, Kentucky, for the U.S. Olympic trials. The Celtics, by virtue of the trade with Detroit, had the first and thirteenth picks in the draft. Golden State had the third pick. Newell and Fitch tossed names around but nothing was finalized or announced.

At the time, the Celtics' position was simple and consistent with Auerbach's machinations through the years—say something with gusto and sincerity even though it's the farthest thing from the truth. Just as he had said there was "no way" he was going to let the Pistons take Bob McAdoo as compensation for M. L. Carr, Auerbach let it be known that he really wanted Joe Barry Carroll. He didn't want Carroll. He didn't like Carroll.

"We were never going to take him," Fitch said. "But we let the whole world think that we were."

Auerbach and Mangurian had watched tapes of Carroll, including one game against Minnesota in which he was swallowed up by McHale. Fitch had heard positive things about McHale from his coaching chums in Minnesota, one of his college coaching stops along the way to the NBA. He also liked McHale from what he saw on tape.

"The thing I liked about Kevin was that he had that great fade-away from the baseline. And he had the long arms, and the shot-blocking ability and the rebounding ability. Kevin was easy to like," he said.

What makes a trade work, of course, is that both sides see the need for change. The Celtics needed to get bigger. The Warriors felt they had seen all that they needed of Parish. But there were other concerns as well, namely money and the possibility of losing Parish at the end of the 1981 season via free agency. Coach Al Attles saw a shake-up coming and he didn't like it.

"We'd hold meetings," he recalled, "and one of the points that always was raised was, Can this team win or do we have to go another way? I do remember saying that if you put the right people around Robert, we got a chance. If we can just get his low-post game going, that was the overriding theory. But it wasn't any one person's decision. They honestly thought at the time that the player they were getting would take them to that next level."

Economics weighed in heavily, too. Golden State was in difficult financial straits—hardly an uncommon position for an NBA team in those days—and Parish's original five-year contract, which now paid him in the $200,000-per-year range, was about to expire. The marketplace was changing rapidly—James Edwards had just signed a huge contract with Cleveland, and public menace Ted Stepien, who owned the Cavs, was throwing dollars around to shake things up—and Parish was due for a big hit. Numerically, his statistics showed him to be a better-than-average center. That would mean more money.

In addition, the threat of free agency was lurking—again—and the Warriors had already been burned repeatedly by those who had left. They were understandably hesitant about the prospect of another something-for-nothing exchange. In the previous years, they had lost Gus Williams, Jamaal (formerly Keith) Wilkes, Cazzie Russell, and Rick Barry. Wilkes, who had been the league's Rookie of the Year and a member of the 1975 title team, had signed with the Lakers. Golden State's compensation? A number one pick and $250,000. The Warriors received a scant $100,000 for losing Williams, who then led Seattle to two straight NBA finals and the championship in 1979. They got John Lucas and $100,000 for losing Rick Barry.

Parish's contract would expire in 1981, and by then the NBA would have a different form of free agency. It was called "right of first refusal," and it basically removed the compensation card from the hands of the commissioner. Instead, a club that had a free agent signed by another team would have the opportunity to match the deal. If that couldn't happen, the two sides could make a deal (as Houston did with Philadelphia over the signing of Moses Malone).

The danger with right of first refusal was that there was no guarantee you would get the player you wanted. On the other hand, there was no risk on the part of the attacking team of losing one of its own in compensation. The new rules were untested but at the time seemed more attractive than the compensation situation, even though, under the old system, the signing team knew it had the player once the contract was dry.

For the Warriors, the threat of losing Parish to a more affluent team was real. If someone signed him to a huge deal, doubling his current salary or more, how could they match it? Parish feels he was traded to Boston not so much out of displeasure over his performance, or out of an infatuation with Carroll (public statements to the contrary), but because of an inability to pay him the market rate.

"I was told they didn't have the finances," he said. "I would have been up for a big hit and they didn't know whether they'd be able to meet my contractual demands and be competitive with other teams. So they traded me to get something for me while they had a chance to do that. It's understandable. It was a business decision."

The Warriors' thinking was that if Parish did leave via free agency, they would never receive anything close to the number one overall pick in return. With right of first refusal, they would either get poor or conceivably get nothing. But, luckily for them, another center was waiting for them in Carroll. And the money would be less, too. The Warriors thought getting the number one pick for Parish was a risk well worth taking. They weren't going anywhere with him anyhow.

Once the Warriors realized they had a shot at Carroll, they never really considered taking McHale. He was seen as a forward, albeit a big and possibly gifted one. But if they were going to trade a center, they wanted one in return. And Carroll was younger, had a more developed and consistent low-post game, and might be an improvement over what they had.

"I went to Hawaii to see Kevin," Attles said. "I heard people saying, 'Bill Walton, Bill Walton.' But the thinking was that he wasn't a center. And the mentality at the time was center, center, center. We had lost all those free agents. And Robert was coming up soon. What if we draft McHale and then lose Robert? This was the first pick that very next year. The thing we never got away from was thinking that you only have one guy who can get it done for you."

As the draft approached, trade rumors were furiously swirling through Boston. The Celtics' stated objective of getting a big man had offers coming out of the woodwork. There was also talk of the Warriors parting with John Lucas, for the Boston backcourt (Nate Archibald and Chris Ford) wasn't getting any younger. And there was some talk, mostly initiated by Auerbach, of somehow getting Darrell Griffith in a deal or in the draft.

"That's how it was run down to me," Griffith said. "Boston needed a big guard and a center. They got the center in Parish. And they figured Utah would take a big guy, McHale. Unfortunately, it didn't turn out that way. But that's the way it was laid out to me."

But the Celtics had made up their mind. If there was to be a trade, fine. If not, then they were going to take McHale with the first pick. They also realized at the time that it might be a tough sell, given McHale's lack of notoriety (he had not even been an All-American) and the appeal of, say, Griffith.

"The reason you had to make the trade," Fitch said, "was because I knew I wasn't strong enough to say McHale was what we needed. It would have been hard. I remember seeing Billy Packer and we told him we were going to take McHale. He said that Joe Barry Carroll was the aircraft carrier in the draft. And with Griffith's team winning the NCAAs, there was all this hype.

"The biggest problem we have as coaches is convincing owners that newspaper guys don't always know what they're talking about. But I honestly think in those days that me, Red, and Harry [Mangurian] would have gotten mauled if we'd taken McHale number one. I had McHale first and Griffith second. Red liked Griffith, too. We were not going to take Joe Barry."

The reasons? Questions about his attitude, determination, and competitive drive, to name three. In many ways, they were the same questions that dogged Parish in his years at Golden State.

"I probably would have thought at the time that Joe Barry would make the better pro than Kevin," said Jerry Sichting, a teammate of Carroll's at Purdue. "He was bigger. He had that hook shot that few guys had. He made himself a pretty good player. But there was always that question of just how much he wanted it."

The actual deal came down a day before the draft. The Warriors agreed to part with Parish and the third pick. Boston would send Golden State the first pick overall and the thirteenth. That gave the Celtics the big man they wanted, though at the time he was seen as no more than a better-than-average backup who would spell Dave Cowens. And with the third pick, they figured McHale would still be around. Even if he wasn't, Griffith would be. Auerbach even called Layden and wondered how the team could possibly take Griffith over McHale.

"Frank, never pass up a center," Auerbach told Layden.

Maybe it was reverse persuasion. Auerbach has always been a proponent of choosing big men on draft day. And the Celtics never had to face the McHale/Griffith choice. In reality, however, how could they lose with either one?

The answer, of course, was that they couldn't. In fact, a few days after the draft, Pat Williams, then the general manager of the Philadelphia 76ers, said, "The general reaction of Boston's Eastern Conference opponents is a sigh of relief that we won't have to be facing a Bird/Griffith combination for the next ten years."

McHale arrived in New York the day before the draft, a common practice then and now for players projected to be among the top picks. He went to New York thinking he'd be a Warrior and not really caring one way or another. The Celtics meant little to him, and they had not contacted him (though Auerbach had made a visit to Minnesota to watch McHale play). McHale had never seen a professional basketball game.

Parish, meanwhile, was at his home in Hayward, California, already involved with the Warriors in contract extension talks, although he sensed the talks were fruitless. During the conversations, the team insisted that it was serious about keeping him and that it also would be able to get such players as McHale and possibly Truck Robinson. Then the phone rang and Warriors' GM Scotty Stirling was on the line. Parish was now a Celtic.

"We were in the midst of negotiations for a new contract, although I never thought they'd be able to pay me because they didn't have the finances to make a competitive offer," Parish said. "But they told me they were going to draft Kevin and trade for Truck Robinson and get a point guard. They told me it was time to put the right personnel around me, that I was their first priority and then they'd get Kevin and the other personnel. They told me that all these things were in the works, but that it was time to start on the right thing by me. Then I got the call. After that, I learned not to get my hopes up until I saw it in writing."

Golden State, as projected, took Carroll with the first pick. That left the choice up to Utah, which had publicly lusted after Griffith and, Boston felt, was not playing possum. Layden had even gone on the radio before the trade and said, with uncharacteristic bravado, "Boston can do what they want. We're going to take Griffith." Fitch could only think, "Let's hope they don't change their minds."

In many ways, Griffith was a logical choice. Utah was a small-market franchise which had arrived from New Orleans the year before. Griffith was coming off an All-Everything year, which included an NCAA championship. He was a player that fans would know, come to see, and identify with. McHale? There simply was no comparison in terms of visibility, marketability, and recognition.

There was, however, some sentiment in Utah for McHale. It came from the person who would most directly be affected by the pick, the coach, Tom Nissalke. He had experience with big men, having coached Moses Malone both in the ABA with the Utah Stars and, after the merger, with the Houston Rockets. And the Jazz had little quality up front—Ben Poquette and Allan Bristow were their best big men at the time.

Layden said there was no discussion about the number one pick, which the Jazz would have had if the coin toss had gone the other way. "If we had won the coin toss and had the first pick, we would have taken Joe Barry Carroll," Layden said.

Now they were faced with the choice of Griffith, a known commodity, or McHale, an unknown. Griffith had been interviewed, checked, and rechecked. McHale had undergone no such scrutiny.

It was hard not to like Griffith, the aptly named Dr. Dunkenstein. He was the MVP of the NCAA championship game in 1980, in which Louisville had defeated UCLA. He was College Player of the Year, *The Sporting News*'s Player of the Year, and winner of the Wooden Award. He was 6-4; he had excellent shooting range and a vertical leap that almost defied physics.

Nissalke, Layden, and Jazz owner Sam Battistone met to decide and Nissalke made his pitch for McHale. He had even gone to see McHale in high school and, at the request of University of Utah coach Jerry Pimm, had written McHale a letter extolling the virtues of the Ute program. Utah had been the only school to actively recruit McHale.

When McHale decided to attend Minnesota, Nissalke didn't forget about the gangly forward. He kept track of the Gophers, with an eye on McHale. Little did he anticipate he'd have a chance to draft him.

The Jazz had a history of making, well, strange deals. They had used a seventh-round pick in 1977 to draft Lucy Harris of Delta State. They had used a tenth-rounder in 1975 to draft Alexander Belov of the Soviet Union. And their number one pick from 1979, Larry Knight of Loyola, never played a game for them. They also had made the suicidal Goodrich deal, which enabled the Lakers to draft Magic Johnson.

"Some of their decisions," Nissalke said, "bordered on lunacy. So many of their deals were just stupid. And I think at that time they felt they had to take a proven quantity. I liked Griff all right. I mean, he didn't have any hands and he wasn't a good passer. He basically was a one-dimensional player. Great guy, but one-dimensional. I liked McHale. I thought he'd get nothing but better and better. We would have used him as a center. He could face the basket and he could play with his back to the basket. It was an ideal situation for me. And I knew that he was a terrific competitor. Sometimes big guys aren't because they've had it easy and they don't work hard. They don't develop. That wasn't the case with Kevin."

What about selling McHale, a relative unknown, to a Utah fan base that was, at best, fragile?

"That would not have been a problem," Nissalke said. "I mean, look at Bernard King. We had to trade him away [King was involved in some rather unsavory episodes in Utah], and when he came back with Golden State he got a standing ovation. No, I don't think that would have been a problem."

Nissalke and Layden had seen McHale dominate the Aloha Classic and came away impressed. "I was stuck on the guy," Nissalke said. "I thought he was a terrific prospect and wanted very badly to take him." But he soon discovered that Battistone wanted to pay the bills, and that meant putting people into seats. And that meant making the decision to take Griffith.

"I felt it was a terrible mistake, but I also had to sympathize with what the owner was going through," Nissalke said. "It wasn't a stupid mistake like some of the others. Griffith was the Rookie of the Year. I just had felt that McHale could have made us a pretty good team. We had Adrian Dantley at the time and he was just coming into his own. That would have given us a pretty good one-two scoring punch."

Layden announced the pick and no one in Salt Lake City was upset about it. Layden had called McHale just before the selection, letting him know what Utah was planning to do. "I always appreciated that," McHale said. "Frank didn't have to do that, but he did. Then, I hung up the phone and said to myself, 'Damn. Well, maybe I'll go to Boston.' But I still hadn't heard anything from them. Nothing at all.''

The Jazz got just about everything imaginable out of Griffith. He played ten seasons for them, gave the team an outside scorer, and was a fixture in the backcourt in the 1980s. He was there in the lean years, and he was there when the team got exponentially stronger with the drafting of Karl Malone, Thurl Bailey, and John Stockton. When he left, he was the franchise's all-time leader in games and minutes played and was second in scoring to Dantley. Nissalke, however, said Griffith left the game the same way he arrived—as pretty much a shooter/scorer and little else.

"I think after the first two years or so he just didn't come along," said Nissalke. "He never got to be a good defensive player. Or a good passer or ball handler. He still pretty much was one-dimensional.''

"We never regretted taking Darrell Griffith," Layden said. "We just didn't.''

And what about McHale? Could he have prospered in Utah? Nissalke thinks so. Layden isn't as sure.

"We had a tendency to burn out players," Layden said. "I'm not sure Kevin would have progressed in Utah like he did in Boston.''

Nissalke thought otherwise.

"He was exactly the kind of player I wanted. I was in a state of mini-shock when we didn't get him. But I knew what kind of player he was going to be. He would have been All-NBA with one of the weaker teams," he said.

Carroll and Griffith were now spoken for and McHale now had a pretty good idea where he was going to wind up. He found out for sure when the Celtics' representative at the draft that year, ticket director Steve Riley, walked over and told McHale that he was now a Boston Celtic. The Celtics made the announcement in Boston.

The selection marked the end of an eventful, hectic twenty-four hours for the twenty-two-year-old McHale. When he had left his Hibbing, Minnesota, home the day before, carrying just an overnight Val-Pac, he was certain he'd be a Golden State Warrior. He hooked up with his agent, Ron Simon, in Minneapolis and the two flew to New York. In his room at the Sheraton Center on Seventh Avenue, McHale finally got to relax before the auctioning began. Then, Simon brought him news of the trade.

When the Celtics made the pick shortly after noon, all of Hibbing knew. The town already was wired for cable. And any pedestrians or motorists on Howard Street could read the news on magnetic letters on the Security State Bank sign. McHale offered a few sound bites for the New York media and then placed a quick telephone call back to Hibbing, where he chatted briefly with his fiancée, Lynn Spearman. He then was prepared to head home, but received a summons from Boston: Mr. Auerbach and Mr. Fitch want you up for a quick visit. So he caught the 2:00 P.M. shuttle and saw Boston for the first time.

The day already was one extended joyride. He had been playing basketball almost nonstop for the last two years, with summer appearances at the Pan Am Games, the World University Games, and All-Star tournaments for seniors. He had spent so much time on basketball that he did not get his degree. He was tired. His older brother, John, had everyone and everything ready for a fishing trip to Red Sand Lake in Canada the following day.

At the obligatory press briefing, McHale unknowingly summed up the impact of the day's maneuvers by Fitch and Auerbach. "I've got to admire Boston," he said. "They got two players with one pick. When they go about something, they do it right. That's impressive." And, he added, "it'll be nice playing with the Bird."

He then got on a plane back to Hibbing, where a welcoming committee met him at the local airfield. When he returned home, he found shamrocks taped to the front door and to his car, which already had 140,000 miles on it. All the way back, McHale could only think of the craziness of the day and what would lie ahead. "I kept thinking, 'I'm actually going to be paid to play basketball. What a deal!' And it ended up being the absolute best thing that ever happened to me."

Parish, at the time, didn't know what to think. Years later, as his fortieth birthday approached and he still was drawing a substantial NBA paycheck, he credited the deal with saving his career.

"I'd be retired. No question in my mind, I'd be all done," he said.

The final chapter came later in the round, when the Warriors went to the table with the thirteenth pick. This was the second of the two Detroit picks the Celtics had sent to Golden State. The Warriors' selection did not surprise Boston, for the Celtics had considered taking the same player if they did not make the trade. He was Rickey Brown, a 6-10 monster from Mississippi State. When the Warriors selected him, that completed the deal: McHale and Parish for Carroll and Brown.

Brown didn't even last three seasons with the Warriors. He played in every game in his second season, then, just before the trading deadline in 1983, he was shipped to Atlanta for a second-round draft pick in 1984. His chief claim to fame in two-plus seasons in Atlanta was getting into a shoving match on the bench with coach Mike Fratello the night Bird scored his career-high 60 points in New Orleans. Brown never played in the NBA after that season.

In the space of two years, the Celtics had revamped their front line and brought together three players from disparate backgrounds, two of whom, Parish and McHale, had spent the bulk of their college careers on probation. And because they had, the Celtics were ready to make a run at an NBA championship.

CHAPTER 3

Kevin and the First Title

The Big Three's first year together, 1980–81, almost never came to pass. As unlikely as it sounds today, the Celtics almost lost McHale to an Italian team before he ever played a game in Boston.

As training camp opened, the Big Three were anything but. Parish was starting anew three thousand miles away from Golden State, and even further away philosophically. And McHale, upset with what he perceived to be the Celtics' lowball tactics during contract negotiations, decided to investigate an offer from a team in Milan.

In 1980, the appeal of the NBA was not close to what it is today. The money the Celtics were offering (around $200,000) would have been more than adequate for most impressionable twenty-two-year-olds, but McHale wanted only to be treated fairly. And, at the start, he didn't feel the Celtics were doing that.

McHale, who had spent three of his four years playing at a school on probation and had decided to remain there with a subpar team when opportunities elsewhere were endless and promising, simply wasn't going to fall for a snow job. The Celtics, of course, contend they never had any intention of mistreating McHale. Unlike Bird, McHale had a passing knowledge of the history and traditions of the Celtics, but he did not feel that the Celtic Mystique meant he could be shortchanged.

"They didn't know me," McHale said. "It was a matter of principle. I was the third pick. I thought I should get somewhere between what the second pick and what the fourth pick got. But I was getting offered what they were giving the ninth pick and I said to myself, 'Well, that's just not fair. I'm not going to do that.' "

The team in Milan was sponsored by a soft drink company and already had one American, Mike D'Antoni, then beginning his third year there after a five-year career in both the NBA and ABA. McHale and Simon flew over and began talks with the team two days after the Celtics opened training camp. They made sure in the process that everyone in Boston knew about the trip and the potential ramifications. The Celtics were not in jeopardy of losing McHale's rights at the time; they simply were in jeopardy of losing his services. Had he played in Italy for ten years, his NBA rights would have remained with the Celtics throughout.

Back in Boston, Fitch was apprised of the situation and offered a Marie Antoinette response: "Let him eat spaghetti." He knew what most seasoned NBA observers did: that Europe was a great place to play once your NBA career had come to an end, sort of like baseball in Japan. He also was hoping that his flippant remark, like cooked spaghetti, would stick to the wall and not bounce back and hit him in the face.

But Europe was not—and still isn't—a place where a highly promising rookie should go. Duke's Danny Ferry was the first legitimate high-profile collegian to begin his career in Italy. He got very rich, but his game never developed. (Some would argue he was vastly overrated from the outset.) Brian Shaw played in Italy after his rookie season with Boston, on the same team with Ferry. He came back and actually played well in Boston, but then got hurt and was never the same player. Eventually, he was traded.

Fitch loved McHale. But he also had a roster that included Parish, Dave Cowens, Larry Bird, Rick Robey, Cedric Maxwell, and M. L. Carr. McHale would have to earn his minutes, although Fitch never thought that would be a problem. If need be, he'd find them.

After one practice in Milan, D'Antoni told McHale that the team would win the European Cup if McHale stayed. McHale liked that. He also liked D'Antoni's brief description of *la dolce vita*, basketball style: the life was sweet and the living was good. Back home, Fitch kept shaking his head, knowing McHale would never last in Italy. "Kevin is a simple, hometown boy. He needs three meals a day, basketball, and someone he can talk to all the time,'' Fitch said.

But the money problem remained. Jan Volk, the Celtics' counsel at the time, cracked that Auerbach was willing to pay McHale ''oh, about what the third pick made fourteen years ago. No, it wasn't that bad. But we did have a lot of big guys. And we had no idea how good Kevin was going to be.'' Auerbach seemed unfazed by McHale's intransigence. ''Good luck to him. We'll get along without him. We've got along without him for thirty-five years. What's he going to do after that?''

McHale remained adamant. ''To me, everything is a trade-off,'' he said. ''You treat me fair, I'll treat you fair. But I got some numbers and I decided I wasn't going to play for anything less. I told the people in Italy that if I didn't hear anything from Boston in twenty-four hours, I would sign with them. Boston came up to what I said would make me comfortable and it all worked out. But it was kind of a rude awakening to the NBA.''

He felt bad to have to break the news to his gracious Italian hosts. He and Simon were negotiating with Boston via transatlantic phone call while the Milan folks were waiting to take them to lunch and celebrate the signing. But the Celtics moved and McHale signed with Boston instead. How did the Milan people take it? ''They just said, 'Something new happens in every business every day,' '' McHale said. He then said *arrivederci* and boarded a plane for Boston.

''It might have been interesting. I don't know if it would have been interesting for six months,'' McHale said of Italy. ''But I liked the attitude there. Everyone was so mellow. I think I might have enjoyed it there.''

Once the deal was struck, Simon placed a call to Fitch in Boston. The two were close friends from their Minnesota days. Knowing that it had to be Simon who was waking him up with a 4:00 A.M. call, Fitch picked up the phone and said, ''*Pronto, pronto*,'' not even bothering to ask how soon McHale might be available. He wanted him yesterday.

When McHale returned to Boston, Auerbach met him at the airport and took him on a wild drive over to the Celtics' practice site

at Hellenic College. While Auerbach spoke of how much he enjoyed the ice cream at the University of Minnesota concessions,
McHale tried to avoid gagging on cigar smoke. But that was mild
compared to what Fitch had planned.

McHale was in for a brutal stretch, but it was nothing compared
to what Parish endured. He was in for a life transformation from the
journeyman slug most everyone thought he was to a seven-footer
who could run the floor like a cheetah. And run some more.

In one exhibition game against the Bulls in Evansville, Indiana,
Fitch deliberately left Parish in the game as Parish accumulated foul
after foul. Fitch was merciless and unforgiving. He had been the one
who had demanded the trade and he wanted to make it work. Parish
was truly miserable for the entire month. There was no Clifford Ray
to listen to him vent.

"It was awful," Parish said. "I was Bill's whipping boy. Me and
Max [Cedric Maxwell]. I did a lot, but it never seemed to please
him."

"Bill was relentless with Robert," Rick Robey said. "Robert had
never run the floor particularly well and here he was having to do it
every day against me and Dave [Cowens]. Soon he realized he had
the speed and quickness and his game mushroomed."

If Parish ran fast, Fitch wanted him to run faster. There were
three speeds: fast, faster, and Fitch. Eventually, the work started to
show dividends. Parish, too, saw the results, although he has always
made the distinction between Fitch the coach and Fitch the individual. He respected the first. He detested the second.

"First of all, I definitely didn't care for him as a person," Parish
said of Fitch. "But as a coach, he was a great coach, one of the best
coaches I ever had. As far as preparation, knowledge of the game,
having everybody prepared, mentally and physically ready to play,
he was the best. Not to mention that he was the first coach that ever
got me in the best physical shape of my life. That was the best
physical condition I've ever been in in my life and I think it was one
of the main reasons that I was able to play consistently at a high
level—because of the conditioning.

"A lot of people say he made me a better player," Parish said.

"He didn't make me a better player. He didn't make one shot, so how could he make me a better player? I think physically he got me ready to be a better player. He definitely believed in being in better condition, and I think that's one of the main reasons the Celtics have been so successful over the years. We always would get off to strong starts, and that was because of the conditioning. Other teams are still trying to get it together at that point."

McHale also was feeling the Fitch treatment. First, he was a rookie. Second, he had had the temerity to miss some sessions of training camp while trying to get the best financial deal for himself. Fitch recognized instantly that McHale was not in shape and needed an introduction to Fitch's version of life in the NBA.

"We were putting it to him pretty good at practice," Fitch recalled. "Kevin was never in totally great shape. Then we'd have a rest period and I'd tell everyone to sit down. And when Kevin got back up, there would be a pool of blood under him from his hemorrhoids. But he never said a word and he never missed a game. I'll never forget that."

McHale also left an indelible impression on his teammates after the very first practice. Chris Ford simply remembered the long arms and the blocked shots. "He did it with both hands. We weren't ready for that, any more than we were ready for what Larry did the year before." The kid could play and showed that he was no simple rookie.

And he played hurt. He broke his nose in an exhibition game at Indiana. He mentioned something to Fitch about it during the game, but the coach told him not to worry. Everything looked fine. McHale wasn't so sure.

"I got back to the hotel and looked in the mirror and the nose was all over my face. I said to myself, 'That's not right.' So I called Ray [Melchiorre, the trainer], and I'm scared to death. I mean, I had broken my nose in college before, but nothing like this. This looked really nasty."

Melchiorre and McHale went to see a local doctor, who used liquid cocaine to numb the pain. "I kept telling the doc, 'It still hurts, it still hurts,' " McHale cracked. "Then he took these two chopsticklike things, stuck them up into my sinus and my nose cracked like a peanut. That was my first week in the NBA. I had no clothes. No money. No nothing. And one broken nose.''

After hearing about the treatment, Fitch went up to McHale and asked how he was. Then he said, "Don't ever tell anyone about the coke or guys will be lining up with broken noses all over the place.'' The nose didn't deter McHale or affect him. He kept right on playing, even though his face took on a raccoonlike appearance when the swelling started. He wanted to play and Fitch wanted him to play, and Fitch quickly discovered that the more McHale played, the better he became. It just never seemed to be enough to Fitch, though.

"Kevin never had to live up to what Bird did. Bird was one of those 'When is it going to happen?' guys," Fitch said. "And when it did, everyone shut up. You could get Kevin to do some of those things, but you had to jump on him or snap at him. I don't think he really realized that. If he got twenty-four, there was thirty there. Because he was around Bird and Parish, he'll never be recognized for being as good as he was. He's much better than he'll ever get credit for being. And in his younger days, I think he was good enough to carry a team. But he had to be prodded and rode because he had that quality.''

But he had another quality that Fitch deeply admired, one rooted in his upbringing. Where McHale comes from, life and sustenance were found in the ground, in the iron ore and taconite that lie along several ridges of the Mesabi Iron Range. Mining shaped his life. And the tough, long hours the job demanded and the toll it exacted on those who worked in the mines—particularly his father, Paul—shaped his personality and gave him an unwavering work ethic that only intensified throughout his NBA career.

McHale was born and raised in Hibbing, Minnesota, a mining community 180 miles north of Minneapolis. It is one of several small towns located on the Mesabi Iron Range, along with Eveleth, Virginia, Chisholm, and Buhl. Lake Superior is seventy-five miles to the east and Canada is one hundred miles to the north.

A few miles north of what is now downtown Hibbing is what used to be downtown Hibbing. The former Hibbing is part of a hole in the ground covering more than fifteen hundred acres. The Hull-Rust-Mahoning Mine, as the hole is known, is a spectacular site, a Grand Canyon of strip mining. It is three and a half miles long and one and a half miles wide, and has been called the largest open-pit mine in the world. It required more movement of earth than the Panama Canal. It is the town's *raison d'être*.

Hibbing and mining are like Bermuda and tourism or Saudi Arabia and oil—inseparable and indivisible. Mining made Hibbing and still supports it, though not as well as it once did now that much of the valuable red ore has been depleted. The mining company built hotels and roads and sidewalks. The mining company built the town's magnificent high school in 1920 for a then astounding $4 million. The high school was, and still is, a striking five-story structure, shaped like a massive letter *E* a few blocks off the main drag of Howard Street. It is listed in the National Register of Historic Landmarks.

The high school classroom doors are made of oak. The library has a mural depicting the entire mining process, from removal of the ore to its arrival in the steel mills of Pittsburgh. The mural contains sixteen life-sized figures, each representing a certain nationality. The auditorium was modeled after New York City's Capitol Theater, complete with cut-glass chandeliers imported from Belgium, two private boxes, a Broadway stage, a marble clock, and a massive Barton pipe organ. The school now has two Olympic-sized swimming pools, but, strangely, does not have a gym that can accommodate the number of people who want to watch high school men's basketball games. Even when an addition to the school was built in 1991, the new gym still did not have enough sideline space to accommodate bleachers. A vote to provide funds to alleviate the oversight failed. Hence, the Hibbing High School Blue Jackets (a name derived from the blue jackets that servicemen used to wear) still play their games at Lincoln Junior High School, the same place McHale played. It has room for bleachers. However, when the time came for a new, portable floor for the Hibbing Memorial Building, a hockey rink/basketball arena in town that can host state tournaments, McHale kicked in $10,000 toward the $42,500 bill.

Mining gave employment to Paul McHale for forty-two and a half years. Milan Knezovich, one of McHale's high school coaches, went to work at the mines at the age of fourteen—he was two years underage—because it was the thing to do. Kevin McHale worked there two summers, though not in very labor-intensive jobs.

"Most of the people simply went to work at the mines after high school. That was the way it was," Paul McHale says. "Oh, there were a few doctors and things like that. But most just went to the mine. That was the life here."

The first ore from the Mesabi Range was shipped in 1892, and soon thereafter miners converged on Hibbing from all over the world. Mining and timber removal accounted for an incredible confluence of ethnic types—almost forty different groups—although most who live in Hibbing today have ancestors from Yugoslavia or Scandinavia. Paul McHale and his ten siblings trace their ancestry to Ireland; Kevin's mother, who was born Josephine Starcevich, was one of four daughters of a man born in Yugoslavia.

Over the many decades of active strip mining, some 680 million tons of valuable iron ore were extracted. Mining made for poor aesthetics—from almost any viewpoint in Hibbing there is nothing to see but dirt, water, and sky in every direction—but reasonably good wages. And it served a national purpose. The ore was loaded onto trains at Proctor (whose high school teams are called the Rails) and shipped to the Lake Superior port of Duluth. From there, it headed south to the great steel mill cities, where it was turned into armaments and everything else that iron could make.

There is no longer active iron ore mining under way, but an offshoot of strip mining has revived the industry. Now, a lower-grade substance known as taconite can produce acceptable iron ore after it has been crushed and sifted. And there is plenty of taconite on the range, enough to have kept Paul McHale employed until 1982 and many others like him to this day.

The original town of Hibbing, which surfaced in the 1880s as a lumber village before the mining boom, was built on the site of a rich iron ore deposit. At first, that did not seem to be a problem because other sites along the range satisfied the steel barons and their charges. In fact, in 1912, the president of the Oliver Mining Company had to defuse rumors of imminent resettlement by saying that nothing would happen for at least fifteen years, if at all. What he didn't anticipate, however, was Serbian Gavrilo Princip firing a bullet into Archduke Francis Ferdinand, setting in motion a chain of events that led to the start of World War I. When the United States finally and reluctantly entered the war in 1917, the demand for ore intensified exponentially and the call went out to the iron ranges of northern Minnesota.

Frank Hibbing, for whom the town was named (he, fittingly, was also an immigrant, born in Germany in 1856 with the impressive but quotidian name of Franz Dietrich von Ahlen) had warned that the town might have to be moved. In December of 1891, he had emerged from a tent on a piece of land he had leased and said, prophetically, "I believe there is iron under me—my bones feel rusty and chilly."

On the edge of the present-day mine, there are still street signs to denote what used to be the thoroughfares of Hibbing I. A few buildings were moved in 1912, and by 1918 the fifteen thousand residents were told to move. The new location was two miles away, in a town previously known as Alice. From 1919 to 1923, the local mining company spent up to $20 million on new buildings, public works, sidewalks, and transportation improvements. This would be the new Hibbing.

Those unfortunate enough to own their homes were paid $1 for the land, but had to foot the bill for the moving. Some 188 buildings were relocated, ranging from homes to hotels. Some obstinate folks held out until as late as 1934, but finally gave in. The last building was resettled in 1958. The natural ore gave out a decade later.

Hibbing ore production reached its peak in the 1940s, as one fourth of the iron ore produced in the country came from the Hull-Rust-Mahoning Mine. The range had produced 17 million tons of ore during World War I and 40 million tons during World War II. There are huge cliffs around Hibbing, looking every bit as if Mother Nature put them there. Closer inspection, however, reveals that they are not cliffs at all, but enormous amounts of what the locals call overburden. That is the earth that has been moved to find the ore.

The task of getting the miners to and from their work also gave birth to another American institution: the Greyhound bus. In 1914, a Swedish immigrant named Carl Æric Wickman moved to Hibbing after hearing about a number of Swedes who had moved there for work, primarily clearing trees. Using a 1914 Hupmobile, a seven-passenger vehicle, he set up a taxi service, taking passengers from Alice to Hibbing. Soon, however, he tired of the bumpy roads and passengers who sometimes wouldn't pay. He sold the business to two other Swedes, Andrew Anderson and Charles Wenberg. They charged fifteen cents for the trip from Hibbing to Alice and twenty-five cents round-trip. That eventually led to the formation of the Mesaba Transportation Company and, eventually, to bus lines around the country. Wickman, who reentered the scene when he saw the profitability therein, centralized everything in 1930 and called his company the Greyhound Corporation.

The city of Hibbing itself boasts an amazing number of famous alumni for a town of its size (eighteen thousand) and location (the boondocks). McHale, Bob Dylan, Manson Family prosecutor Vincent Bugliosi (who left at age seventeen for Hollywood, but not before winning the state high school tennis championship), baseball great Roger Maris (who was born there but raised in Fargo, North Dakota), and even Gus Hall, the founder of the American Communist party, are all Hibbing natives. Dylan's father owned an appliance store. Bugliosi's father worked in the mines, later ran a grocery store, then worked for the railroad.

Paul McHale's family moved to Hibbing from Michigan. The Starcevich family came north from Illinois and settled in one of many mining communities. In the early days, these outposts were no more than collections of huts and shacks within walking distance of the mines. Paul McHale was seven years older than Josephine Starcevich. The two met when Josephine was working as a bookkeeper at a local lodge and Paul would visit her on the pretense of seeing his older brother Harold, who also worked there.

They were married when Paul was thirty-four years old, and three years later they welcomed their second son, Kevin Edward, into the world. The birth came two days after the family moved into the house they still own today, a small, single-story, three-bedroom home whose only concessions to the years of children are a Plexiglas kitchen door to prevent broken windows from pickup basketball games and a satellite dish in the backyard that allowed the family to watch their famous son when he played for the Celtics.

McHale has nothing but fond memories of his childhood. His father was, and is, an inspiration. Once, Paul McHale came home from work with a severely burned hand, courtesy of a mining accident. He missed one day of work, he thinks, then took vacation time (Sick leave? What was that?) to allow the wound to heal. The father of Hibbing high school teachers Dan and Matt Bergin, who also worked in the mine, had a month's vacation. After two days at home he went back to work, for free. That was the mentality that shaped the miners and, by extension, shaped McHale.

There are four McHale children, two boys and two girls, but there is only one giant. Somewhere in his mother's genealogical past there was a huge Croatian, and McHale got those genes.

"I gave him his height," his mother said proudly. "The McHales are the shorties. He has the good Yugoslavian blood."

"I had two great role models," McHale said. "My mother is a hot-blooded Croatian. She'd scream and yell and kill first. It was better to kill your son and then find out what he did wrong. That was her theory."

"He may say that, but I was the one who made sure he was home by curfew," his mother said. "He was an easy kid. Oh, there were times he'd make me mad. Real angry. Then, a few minutes after that, he'd be smiling again and he'd have me laughing."

Paul McHale was always at the mines, or so it seemed. He retired in 1982. Sometimes his workday would have him gone when the kids woke up and not back until the kids were in bed. He spent the last nineteen years before his retirement working in Virginia, Minnesota, a seventy-mile drive round-trip. He never considered leaving Hibbing.

John McHale was sixteen months older than Kevin, and for years that amounted to an unbridgeable gap, both mentally and physically. The sibling rivalry in the McHale house was both natural and, for the younger brother, critical in his development. Kevin McHale looks back to the many fights, disputes, and brotherly spats and sees them as an invaluable learning experience.

"The reason I am in the NBA is because I had a brother as competitive as he was. In everything we did. We fought over everything, and I mean everything," he said. "You learned how to lose and get better as opposed to losing and quitting. I know, because I lost all the time. Then I started to grow and get better. But I had learned a lot of lessons growing up, about not having success but going back the next day and trying harder.

"If there's anything about me that I'm the proudest of, it's that when I've had down times I always bounce back. I refuse to quit. If it means working two extra hours, I'll do it. Or five hours. I'm gonna get something accomplished. I'm going to get there. I think that stems from being brought up in a small town, with a great work ethic, with an older brother who pushed me mentally, physically, and every way you could push a person. When we were younger, we were not good friends. We fought all the time. Then, I got old enough and big enough to beat him up. So we became friends."

In junior high school, when it became apparent that McHale was sprouting into something beyond the normal child, basketball started to become more of a priority for him. Prior to that, McHale had played both basketball and hockey. Hibbing is hockey country now—it hasn't always been so—and the Iron Range has produced more than its share of hockey players, including the scrappiest members of the gold-medal-winning 1980 U.S. Olympic hockey team. It had, however, produced one NBA player, Dick Garmaker, who played for the Minneapolis Lakers and the New York Knicks. After leaving Hibbing High, Garmaker honed his game at the local community college and then went on to the University of Minnesota. He had a six-year NBA career. Garmaker has been memorialized in a perverse way in Hibbing: the exhausting wind sprints in which a player goes from the end line to the free-throw line, the end line to midcourt, and then the end line to the other free-throw line are known there as Garmakers.

McHale's decision to abandon hockey and settle on basketball was based as much on his growing body as anything else. And he came under the eye of Milan Knezovich, Hibbing alum who had gone to Drake, briefly thought of a pro career before injuries cut him down, did service in Korea, and returned home to teach and bring along another generation of Hibbing hoopsters.

"Kevin was a grade school kid then. It was 1966 [McHale was nine] and I raised about thirty-five hundred dollars or so to get the basketball program going," Knezovich said. "Kevin was part of that. We made it fun, but hockey had such a grip that basketball was on its way out. When I played, basketball was king. Anyway, we would meet every Saturday at eight A.M. with the coaches, and the teams would come in for organized practices. I was a center myself. So I'd take the gangly, diamond-in-the-rough kids. Kevin was one of those. I saw something special in him."

Knezovich saw a blossoming center in the gangly McHale, so he began drilling him in the finer points of playing the pivot long before he reached high school. His first rule for McHale was to hold the ball high, and it was a painful and often humiliating learning process.

"I'll never forget," Knezovich said. "He would get the rebound and bring it down. Always. I wasn't his coach then, but as the high school coach I would drop by because it was good for the kids to see the coach, and they loved to be watched. Well, I'd see Kevin get a rebound and bring the ball down and look to see who to throw it to. I told the coach something. I told him that every time Kevin brings that ball down, I want the other kids to collapse and smack him on the wrist. One time, he cried. They really hurt him. We did the same thing when he came to me [tenth grade]. I told him, 'Whatever you do, hold it up.'"

McHale learned that lesson well. If there was one signature to his game in the NBA, it was that he *never* brought the ball down after a rebound.

By the time McHale reached high school, he was one of four solid sophomores, and Knezovich sensed that he had a state champion in the making, especially if they remained intact. Another of the sophomores was forward John Retica whose father, Mario Retica, was the school's athletic director and, arguably, the father of Hibbing basketball. McHale always measured himself against John Retica, who scored 1,000 points in his Hibbing career, despite missing most of his senior year with a broken wrist. McHale never matched that mark, and it remains a sore spot among some of his loyalists in town. The two other sophomores were Chris Liesmaki and Steve Knezovich, Milan's son.

Eventually, the four sophomores were promoted to the varsity after a scandal of sorts: Milan Knezovich ran into disciplinary problems with four upperclassmen and was forced to remove them from the varsity. Once the tenth-graders joined the team, Hibbing went 13–6, losing to Duluth Central in the regional finals.

But Knezovich started getting heat from the parents of the four players he had dismissed, and things got ugly. His son started getting friction too, and Knezovich eventually resigned. He stayed on to coach cross-country (he convinced McHale to come out one year, for conditioning purposes only), but he clearly was wounded by the whole episode. He has never coached basketball since then, though he remains a Hibbing diehard, attending high school games regularly.

"That was probably the worst time in my life as a coach," he said. "I didn't want to break up that crew, but it caused a rift. Things got back to Steve and it was a terrible experience. But this team was big. I had moved Kevin in to center, was playing him as a sophomore, three quarters a game. Maybe more. He was progressing real well. He didn't look all that good to begin with, but as time went on you could tell there was going to be something there. And he was coachable."

Knezovich was replaced by a young, energetic, and enthusiastic newcomer named Gary Addington. He had spent three years in high school coaching before coming to Hibbing, turning a 1–19 team from a small town called Wanamingo into a 19–1 club in that stretch.

He had played football and basketball at Winona High School in Minnesota, gone to the University of Minnesota, and then transferred to Augustana in Sioux Falls, South Dakota, a Division II school. After his three years at Wanamingo, he heard about the opening in Hibbing and got the job. He had no idea what he was getting himself into.

Addington and Knezovich could not have been more different in their styles or approaches to the game. Knezovich was an old-time hard-liner who worshiped at the altar of the dominant big man and post player. That is why he lusted for the chance to stay with McHale. Addington believed in making things more open, in moving the ball, in playing what now is known, more or less, as the passing game.

"Everyone said Addington's style was five passes before you shoot," Liesmaki said. "But we still won games. And we had fun. Addington also was a little more structured. But he allowed Kevin to play his tricks. I think he was teaching things to Kevin without Kevin ever knowing it."

For one road game, Addington noticed that McHale was not around with the other varsity players to watch the junior varsity game, a definite no-no. When it came time for the team to dress, there still was no McHale. Addington had no clue as to where he might be; he knew McHale had made the trip. McHale then came stumbling in, apologizing profusely. He had gone with the bus driver for what he thought would be a quick hamburger run. Instead, the bus driver had stayed at the restaurant for dinner.

"I can just imagine what was going through Kevin's mind as he sat there and watched the bus driver eat his dinner, slowly enjoying each bite as the clock ticked away," Addington said. "But it was an honest mistake. I think I even started him that night."

Regardless of whom McHale played for, or how he was utilized, he never took the game too seriously, and he always made sure that he had fun. Unlike Bird, who lived and died for basketball, McHale saw it as a game first and foremost.

"I looked at basketball differently, I guess," he said. "I mean, I never equated victories with hard work. I expected everyone to work hard. I never expected someone to go out and *not* work hard. Why play? Success is not always related to how hard you work. If that was the case, you could get twelve plumbers out there who work fourteen hours a day and they'd dive all over the floor. But they wouldn't get it done. It's how much talent you have."

That approach stayed with him through college and into the pros and remains with him to this day. He has always had other interests, be they friends, family, golf clubs, or beer.

"He wanted to have fun more than anything else, even when

playing basketball," Liesmaki said. "He never lost sight of what was fun in life. I think that was pretty neat. He hasn't changed one bit, and that's remarkable."

His junior high coach, Terry Maciej, summed it up this way: "Kevin was the leader in everything, especially the pranks. He knew when to draw the line. He got the fun and work out of everything."

After one of his first practices, Addington heard the players talking about the usual stuff—girls, dates, and drive-ins. His wife was there with their two-year-old son; she was a frequent visitor to the high school, usually arriving as practice was winding down. "I told the kids that when I was in high school, basketball was my life and I never thought about girls," Addington said, knowing at the time that his words were probably being dismissed as soon as they came out of his mouth. "Then, as my wife comes over, Kevin piped up, 'Yeah, so you took the first one that came along and married her."

Fun in Hibbing meant hanging out at the drive-in, or getting something to eat at Rudi's Pizza, or going to a local hangout called "the dump." Smoking cigarettes was a daring enterprise; driving through yards somewhat more risky. Rat hunting was a big favorite, too. McHale would come home well after his curfew and his mother would be waiting, ready to lower the verbal boom. "But Mom, I had to be out now. That's when the rats come out," he would say sheepishly. "How could I argue with that?" Josephine McHale asked.

For vacations, the family would pile into Paul's blue Chrysler and drive to the Black Hills in the middle of summer. No air-conditioning. "I can't imagine to this day why he did that," McHale said of his father. "By the end of the trip, he'd want to kill us. Maybe before the end of the trip, sometimes."

The love of the outdoors was instilled in McHale early. He loves to fish, hunt, and play golf. He often would deliver a *Field and Stream* analogy on cue when reporters would request one after a game. He had utter contempt for those who thought hunting barbaric. "How do you think that steak got onto your plate? Do you think it climbed up there all by itself?" But he also was known to ruin a hunting trip for his brother by deliberately rustling the leaves

The Big Three: Kevin McHale, Robert Parish, and Larry Bird. ¹

Larry Bird, dubbed college basketball's secret weapon by *Sports Illustrated*, led Indiana State to an NCAA final against Magic Johnson's Michigan State team.

2

3

Robert Parish surprised most observers by staying at Centenary College for four full years, even though the NCAA refused to officially acknowledge his accomplishments.

After four respectable but uninspiring seasons with Golden State, Parish found new basketball life after coming to Boston in The Trade.

4

5

Another player involved in The Trade, Kevin McHale—a gangly kid from Minnesota—became the Celtics' sixth man and helped the Big Three capture their first NBA title.

Larry Bird and Red Auerbach share a victory cigar after the Celtics captured the 1981 NBA championship. In just two short seasons, Bird proved that Red knew what he was doing when he drafted Bird early and waited for him to finish his college career.

The longtime Boston-Philadelphia rivalry was renewed in the early 1980s, highlighted by the performances of Larry Bird and Julius Erving.

In his prime, Kevin McHale worked the post game to perfection, practically becoming an automatic basket every time he got the ball.

The 1986 championship team—the best ever—celebrates the Big Three's
third NBA title together.

The Big Three battled the
Lakers in three championship
series and helped make the NBA
the success it is today, but
Magic Johnson's last-second
hook shot gave Los Angeles the
1987 title.

Larry Bird adds an exclamation point to the legendary shoot-out with Dominique Wilkins in Game 7 of the 1988 Boston-Atlanta playoff series by burying a three-pointer in front of the Hawks' bench.

During their final years together, the Big Three often spent more time on the bench than on the floor because of injuries.

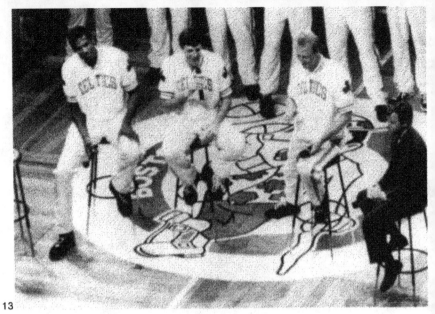

13

Bird had his number retired and raised to the rafters of Boston Garden while being honored by his teammates and fans after his 1992 retirement. McHale (who retired after the 1992–93 season) and Parish will be similarly honored.

14

Parish, the oldest player in the NBA and the last of the Big Three, is still running the floor with today's stars.

as the prey came into target range. And he once jokingly threatened to feed his younger sister to a python.

"The only time we never had to worry about getting Kevin up in the morning was when he was going fishing," his father said.

Otherwise, it was a battle each day. "He always was the last one up, the last one dressed, the last one out of the house," his mother said. "And he never had his shoes tied." Untied shoes came into vogue in the 1980s—maybe he was making a future fashion statement? "Maybe," his mother said. "But I don't think so."

Hibbing High reached the state tournament in McHale's junior year, but lost in the quarterfinals to Little Falls, the eventual state champion. Hibbing fell behind early, 20–8, and never recovered. The defeat capped a 16–4 season, but the nucleus of the team would be back and big things were expected of the Blue Jackets, particularly McHale, who had shot up to 6-9 by then.

"I kept yelling at my mother that she was shrinking my jeans," he said. "I mean, I had been average height for so long. But in high school, I just sprouted."

Even with Retica, Hibbing's top scorer, unable to play because of his wrist injury, the Blue Jackets plowed through the competition in McHale's senior year. They were 19–1 in regular-season play; their average margin of victory was nearly 19 points. They won one game by 53 points, another by 41, and two others by 32. McHale was named Mr. Basketball in Minnesota, and letters of inquiry started arriving at the McHale house on Outer Drive.

But only one college actively recruited McHale: the University of Utah. It was a strange courtship. Assistant coach Jim Marsh found out about the Mucker, as McHale was affectionately known, from relatives in Duluth. ("Mucker was an extension of the "Mc" in McHale's name. As in MuckHale.) Beginning in the spring of McHale's junior year, Marsh started to court McHale. The courting intensified the following year, to the point where Marsh would be a regular visitor to the town and to the McHales' house. He still recalls fondly a walnut bread that Mrs. McHale made.

He would take a flight to Minneapolis early in the week, rent a car, and make the drive to Hibbing, arriving in time to see the game on Tuesday. The folks who ran the Thrifty Scot, one of the few hotels in Hibbing, had a room ready for Marsh every week. Addington even introduced him once as a visiting professor. The University of Utah spent $8,000 of its recruiting budget on McHale.

"I would have given my heart, my soul, and my firstborn for Kevin," said Marsh. "A lot of coaches came to see Kevin, but Utah was the only one that really recruited him. Joe Cipriano [of Nebraska] came up, Bob Weltlich [an Indiana assistant] came to see him, and they'd all say, 'Look at those legs, the way they bend inwards. Look at that chest. I don't know if he can hack it in the Big Ten.' When I tell people now that no one recruited Kevin, they don't believe it. It's not like I was a genius or anything. No one wanted to make the trek up there. And it was a trek."

McHale figured out during his senior year that college was likely to be a freebie and he, like most everyone on the Range, had his heart set on Minnesota—or, as it is called there, the U. He had followed the exploits of Minnesota stars Corky Taylor, Ron Behagen, and Jim Brewer with envy, apparently either not knowing or overlooking the fact that the school was on probation for egregious and widespread shenanigans under the reign of Bill Musselman. How widespread? The NCAA press release that described the situation listed thirty-three different categories of infractions, and there were several violations in many of the categories. The infractions included ticket scalping, giving lodging to recruits, giving the mother of a player some personalized envelopes, and flying players to and from home. "You would have had difficulty turning a page in the recruiting manual and not finding violations," said the NCAA's David Berst.

The school had been placed on probation for three years, starting with the 1976–77 season, and was prohibited from postseason play for the first two years. In addition, the coach who had replaced Musselman, a former head coach at Eastern Michigan named Jim Dutcher, was limited to three scholarships. (Normally, a school has six.)

Marsh knew McHale was leaning toward Minnesota, but he also knew that the Gophers had just the three scholarships. It would have been interesting to see how McHale's career would have turned out had he gone there. Utah already had a successful team in the late 1970s, primarily due to the arrival of Tom Chambers and Danny Vranes in 1977. Led by those two players, Utah twice came within a game of reaching the regional finals. Also, the Jazz might have been more inclined to draft him instead of Darrell Griffith, since he'd have been a local boy.

Marsh got McHale to make his one and only recruiting visit and Utah went all out, from the helicopter ride over beautiful Salt Lake City to the meeting with the school president to the pickup games with the current players.

"He spent the whole weekend playing with my daughter, who was a baby then," Marsh said. "I thought we had a chance. He left Sunday. I got on a Western Air Lines flight Monday, and when I arrived I called home. My wife was crying. I then called Kevin and got the news. He was going to sign with Minnesota."

If fate played a big role in delivering McHale to the Celtics—and it did—it also played an equally big role in delivering him to Minnesota. Because if McHale's team hadn't made the state tournament that year, Minnesota would not have recruited him and instead would have spent its third scholarship on a seven-footer from Colorado it was considering. McHale might still have wanted to go to Minnesota, but he would not have received a scholarship. And given the economics of the times, and the fact that his parents might not have been able to afford to pay for his college education, he would have likely felt compelled to take a scholarship elsewhere.

But Hibbing made the state tournament, easily, and the team arrived in St. Paul with lofty expectations. There was a caravan down to the state capital, an estimated seven hundred people in all, unified in their belief that the Blue Jackets would finally claim a state title. They had been runners-up in 1953 to Hopkins. This time, they felt, things would be different.

The team crushed Minneapolis North, 64–41, in the quarterfinals, with McHale totaling 21 points, 12 rebounds, and 6 blocked shots. North was the only one of the eight schools in the tournament with so much as a single black player—it had nine black players, as well as a black head coach. The next game was a rematch against Little Falls, and Hibbing won, 41–39, after trailing by 11 in the third quarter. That set up a final against Bloomington Jefferson, the team that had beaten Hibbing the previous year in the consolation finals.

The Bloomington Jefferson Jaguars were undefeated, 26–0, and were led by 6-7 center Steve Lingenfelter. The year before, he had outscored McHale 15–5 and outmuscled him down low, prompting McHale to say afterward, "I felt like I came out of a football game." This time, McHale scored 16 points, and Hibbing led 32–25 at the half before collapsing. Lingenfelter scored 14 points in the fourth quarter and Jefferson won going away, 60–51. Hibbing had had more turnovers (9) than points (6) in an abysmal third quarter.

The day after, the Hibbing *Daily Tribune* had a picture of McHale and Lingenfelter going at it. Directly underneath was a photo of an agonized Hibbing cheerleader named Lynn Spearman, who later would marry Kevin McHale.

The defeat still rankles many in Hibbing, including Knezovich. Why didn't Addington pound the ball inside to McHale in the second half and let him work with the lead? Instead, films of the game show McHale in the high post and Lingenfelter going crazy inside. The mere mention of that game still makes Knezovich sick, years after the fact.

"If I had him, there's no way we would have lost the state. With a big lead? I would have jammed that ball into Kevin like you can't believe. He would have had fifty points," Knezovich says. "And I would have told the kids that this is what's going to win it, we've got to do it and that's it. A four-foot shot is better than fifteen or eighteen. Kevin averaged fifteen for me as a sophomore. I told Gary, 'You got big kids. You gotta post him. Feed the big boy.' But Addington was not a post-man coach. He believed in that perimeter stuff."

Addington stayed in Hibbing for eleven more years, taking the 1979 team to the regional finals, where it lost to Duluth Central. He then took a job as the athletic director of the Rochester, Minnesota, school system, but the urge to coach is still with him. Does he remember that Bloomington Jefferson game? "Only every day," he says.

While the tournament loss was a crushing one to McHale, the University of Minnesota's coaches were on hand, and they liked what they saw. But there was this scholarship problem, and Dutcher had an unwritten but generally ironclad rule about Minnesota kids: let them walk on. Then, when full scholarships were restored, the kids would get them.

That's how Lingenfelter got to Minnesota, but he left after two unfulfilling years, playing only fourteen games in each of his first two seasons. He then transferred to South Dakota State, where, in his senior year, he averaged 26.7 points and 10.6 rebounds a game. It was good enough for the Washington Bullets to draft him in the second round in 1981, forty-first overall, but he had a limited NBA career (ten games in two years). John Retica, who had been McHale's yardstick all through high school, got a golf scholarship to Minnesota but later transferred to Minnesota–Duluth, where he played basketball and made All-Conference.

And McHale? "Our assistant [Terry Kunze] came back to me early in his senior year and said he was not a Big Ten prospect," Dutcher said. "So we put him on the inactive list. Had Hibbing not made the high school tournament, we would not have recruited Kevin. I hadn't even seen Kevin until then. You could jump in your car after practice and go see Lingenfelter. He was around the corner. But to see Kevin would have meant missing a day of practice. Not many roads go through Hibbing."

The night before he made his decision, McHale came into his parents' bedroom, sat on the edge of their bed, and told his mother, "I want to go to the U." The McHales had been careful not to steer their son anywhere. Paul McHale had been trying for years to keep his wife quiet because she sensed Kevin would be something special. "It was his decision," she said.

At the eleventh hour, Kentucky and Louisville made futile pitches, but McHale needed a scholarship, so he called Dutcher. McHale had the leverage; Utah was willing to give him a scholarship, and he was willing to go there if need be. Dutcher said that if it took a scholarship, he would relinquish that third one he was hoarding and give it to McHale.

The hardest part was giving the word to Marsh. By the time Marsh arrived in Hibbing, he already knew, although there had been no official announcement. He then went to the high school and saw

McHale and Kunze playing pickup hoops. That was when it hit home.

"That was the first time I had to tell someone no, and it really hurt," McHale said.

"I thanked everybody, then went out and shot myself to death," Marsh said. But that wasn't the end of his forgettable day. He then flew to Kohler, Wisconsin, where he was also recruiting Jeff Wolf. When he got there, he saw Dean Smith leaving the house and knew that Wolf, too, was a lost cause. "I shot myself again," he said. He then flew back to Utah with no recruits and two mythical bullet holes in his body.

Minnesota and McHale were a perfect basketball fit, although it was a gigantic leap culturally. Minneapolis was everything Hibbing was not. During his years at the U, McHale lived in a state of blissful ignorance of the world around him, typified by his meeting with celebrated Vikings running back Chuck Foreman. Introduced to the Vikings star, McHale looked him squarely in the eye and said, "Nice to meet you, Mr. Foreman. What do you do for a living?"

On the court, he came into an ideal learning situation. Minnesota was a veteran team paced by future number one pick Mychal Thompson, Ray Williams, Flip Saunders, and Osborne Lockhart, who went on to play for the Harlem Globetrotters. The team wasn't going anywhere because of the probation, but it was good, with six players returning from a 16–10 team. McHale improved dramatically; he had not faced anything resembling this kind of competition in high school. And he was inserted into the starting lineup by the third game of the season, although by then he had already given Dutcher an early preview of what Addington and Knezovich already knew.

"We're on an early road trip to Nebraska," Dutcher said, "and we won fairly easily [66–58] and we're getting on the bus and everyone is there except McHale. Finally, out he comes, wearing a big red cowboy hat with a big *N* on it and a smile just as big. His shoes were untied. I met him at the bus door, but what could I say? I turned to my assistant and said, 'This is going to be a long four years.' But with Kevin, it was all self-inflicted. He never affected anyone else."

Minnesota went 24–3 that season. All of the Gophers' defeats were in Big Ten games: they lost twice to Michigan and once to Purdue. By the end of the season, they were ranked as high as third in national publications. And McHale was a steady, if not spectacular, contributor.

"He was outgoing, personable, friendly, and he had that cockiness. He was the first Christian Laettner, but he had a right to be that way," Mychal Thompson said. "He was long, lanky. He looked like Herman Munster on campus. He wasn't that accomplished a player, but I knew he was going to be good. Not *that* good, but good. And he'd never do anything to draw attention. He got along with everyone—blacks, whites. He didn't act like a star or come off and be a star. He even invited me to Hibbing once, but he said I'd be the first black there. I told him I'd wait till he came back to Minneapolis."

Probation killed the Gophers the next two years. NCAA rules now allowed transfers immediate eligibility at their new schools, and so several players left. McHale chose to stay. There were many opportunities to transfer. "From a basketball standpoint," he said, "I should have transferred. All [my classmates on the team] did. My junior year, there was no one left but me; we started four freshmen. My senior year, there was no one to complement my game. I just kinda played. If I had gone to any of the fifteen or twenty schools that called, it would have been different. They had senior guards who got you the ball. But it goes back to the whole loyalty thing. I wasn't going to leave. The thought of quitting just didn't enter my mind. I thought it would be a cop-out. It's easy not to play when you're hurt. It's easy to leave. It's hard to stick it out. I had role models who stuck it out. And so did I."

McHale averaged 15.8 points a game over four years. The team was 16–10 in his sophomore year, 11–16 in his junior year, and 17–11 in his senior year. Things got so crazy at the dormitory that year that he moved into an apartment with some football players and a wrestler, the latter of whom knew nothing about basketball. One day Jerry West, the Lakers' general manager, called to speak to McHale. The wrestler took the message, not having any idea who West was.

By that time, McHale's basketball prowess was known through the Big Ten, if not to the rest of the country, or to all his roommates. The summer between his junior and senior years, he went to Puerto Rico and played on the gold-medal-winning Pan American team for Bobby Knight. After a couple of weeks off, he went to Mexico City and played for the gold-medal-winning U.S. team in the World University Games, coached by Ken Anderson, who was the head man at NAIA power Wisconsin–Eau Claire. His enduring memories of those two international forays? The wisdom of Bobby Knight and the tequila-drinking ability of Jeff Ruland, one of his teammates in Mexico City.

Knight and McHale, surprisingly, dovetailed well. McHale respected Knight's expertise, but also wasn't overly awed by the tempestuous coach. "I really wasn't intimidated by him because he wasn't my coach," McHale said. "And I think he liked me because he knew he wouldn't have to deal with me all the time. We went fishing together. I really enjoyed the guy. I thought he was hilarious. And he really knew the game. He would say, 'Stop, stop, stop' after a play and he would run over the last five or six sequences and tell everyone what they did wrong. I'm thinking to myself, 'Whoa, this guy knows the game.' "

"I loved the guy," Knight said. "I really liked him. I bet if I asked him to do anything for me, he'd do it. I remember I came up to him before a game the next season and I said to him, 'You son of a bitch. Don't you dare use any of the stuff I taught you.' I just enjoyed having him around. And I really think he enjoyed playing for me."

The 17–11 Minnesota team in McHale's senior year received an invitation to the National Invitational Tournament, the undercard of the NCAA. Minnesota made it all the way to the finals, losing 58–55 to Virginia (and Ralph Sampson). McHale played terribly. Dutcher recalled getting a call from Knicks scout Dick McGuire in which he said that McHale would be perfect for New York, which had the twelfth pick. The postseason tournaments would soon make up for McHale's NIT finals performance, though, and elevate McHale into exclusive company among potential draftees.

There was one more thing for McHale to consider before turning pro: the Olympics. The 1980 coach was Dave Gavitt, who years later would be united with McHale in Boston. McHale had already determined that he was good enough to make the team, having been awakened to his blossoming talents by the Pan Am trials. He called the trials "my awakening as a basketball player." He came away from them believing that either he was better than he thought or the others weren't as good. Either way, he was among the best. He hadn't even considered the NBA until he had been shown a story in which he was ranked among the top forwards in the country.

"Kevin would have played on the team had the games not been boycotted [by the U.S.]," Gavitt said. "He clearly wanted to play and he would have made the team. But then Carter announced the boycott about two weeks before the Olympic trials and Kevin and some other guys—Sampson too—decided not to go. I didn't know him back then, but Knight had told me, 'You watch this kid. He is tougher than hell.' They had these breakdown drills for big men and he had this incredible reach. I do remember that. And the big, square shoulders.''

McHale has been a lifelong Democrat, which often leads to interesting discussions at home because his wife is a Republican. "That doesn't mean I don't love her," he says. (And it also didn't stop his father-in-law from noting that McHale was his son-in-law on some campaign literature while running for local office in Hibbing.) But he was incensed by Carter's decision. Even before the boycott, he wondered why he needed to go to Moscow to play against professional teams when he would be doing it in the fall for some NBA team. "We had just come off Vietnam and here we are, seeing what is happening in Afghanistan, and we're saying, 'We'll show you. We won't go.' What a joke! 'We'll show them.' That was so bogus.''

So he didn't try out. And, to his regret, he also left Minnesota without a degree. He had taken the spring quarter off in his junior year to try out for and compete in the Pan American Games, so by the spring of 1980 he was two quarters shy of the credits he needed for a degree. He went back to Minnesota after his first season with the Celtics, but was waylaid by a friend who suggested a trip to the lake and a boatful of beer. That sounded eminently preferable to the classroom, and McHale accepted.

"That was the end of my degree talk," McHale said. "For a couple summers after that, I said to myself, 'I'm going to do it this summer, I'm going to do it.' And then there was that part of me that said, 'What will it do for you?' I never liked summer school. Here you are, twenty-two, twenty-three, and you gotta go to school in the summer? But I should get it. To be that close . . . All the people I knew at Minnesota were on the five-year plan. That's what would have happened to me. I'd have gone back, gotten my degree in the winter, and become a working stiff."

On October 1, 1980, the roles of Parish and McHale for the upcoming Celtics season changed radically. On that day, while the Celtics were in Terre Haute to play an exhibition game, Dave Cowens got on the team bus and informed his teammates that he was retiring. Injuries (and the inexorable drive of Fitch) had pushed him to the brink. Now Parish, who had been acquired as an experienced backup and as an eventual replacement for Cowens, was, by process of elimination, the starting center. And McHale moved another notch up the ladder as well.

Cowens didn't feel he was abandoning the team and leaving it with a huge hole. He was convinced that Parish would be able to play the pivot well and for a long period of time. He told his teammates so. And although he had seen McHale for only a couple of weeks, he was so impressed with the gangly youngster that he offered him his uniform number. "I would rather watch someone I enjoy seeing play wear the number than have it hang from the rafters." His number, 18, was soon retired, however, and McHale wore number 32.

Cowens wasn't the only missing body from the 1979–80 team. Pete Maravich, a midseason pickup, also retired. And one of the keys from the year before, M. L. Carr, fractured a bone in his foot in October and was limited to forty-one games, although he returned for the playoffs. But everyone else was back from the 61–21 team and expectations were high, as they should have been. Parish moved into the starting center spot and remained there into the 1990s; he started all eighty-two games and earned a spot on the Eastern Conference All-Star team.

McHale was brought along slowly by Fitch, something that might be harder to do today, given the enormous sums being paid to rookies and the attendant expectations. Maxwell and Bird were the starting forwards. Parish was the center. Fitch did a masterful job of rotating his leviathans all season.

In his first NBA season, McHale played only 20.1 minutes a game—and just 17.4 per game in the playoffs. But he made the most of his time on the floor at both ends, averaging 10 points, 4.4 rebounds, and 1.8 blocked shots a game, and was named to the All-Rookie first team. He blocked shots by Mike Mitchell and Bill Robinzine, both veterans, in his first NBA game and in his twelfth game, set a franchise record with six blocked shots. (Parish broke the record a month later, however.)

Fitch instantly recognized McHale's value as a game-changing weapon off the bench. McHale could play two positions, but he also had the capability to tilt the playing field simply by his presence on the floor. Fitch rarely started McHale in the three years they were together; he thought McHale was the best reserve in the game and figured, Why tinker?

Red Auerbach is credited with developing and popularizing the sixth man concept, the belief being that the first player off the bench should, essentially, be every bit as good as or even better than the player he is replacing. The sixth man was expected to be equal parts spark plug, generator, and life support. He should be able to produce offensively, as McHale and Ricky Pierce did, or defensively, as McHale and Bobby Jones did. Or he should simply be an overall commanding presence at both ends, as Bill Walton was.

"Kevin was so good at being the sixth man," said Fitch, "that if the quality of the team had remained the same over the years, he'd have had a ring on his hand every year. He could play forty minutes a game if he had to. He had the ability to come in and, without even throwing a warm-up pitch, throw a hundred-mile-an-hour fastball. All things considered, Kevin should go down in history as the absolutely ideal sixth man. He could play any position up front. He could give you inside scoring, outside scoring. He blocked shots. That's such a luxury for a coach. You tell him, 'Tonight, Kevin, we need shot blocking.' Or, 'Tonight, Kevin, we need scoring.' And that's harmful to the other team.

"It's like [Dennis] Eckersley now. The same thing. You told him, 'Your role is to change the game.' And you had to sell it to him. When that first season ended, I was as happy as hell with him. It's just that I had to coach him mad half the time because I wanted him to be better. He'd do it his way. But Kevin is likable. He can piss you off and you want to kill him. Five minutes later, he'd come back with a smile and give you the last five dollars in his pocket."

The 1980–81 season was, like the season before, an eighty-two-game horse race with the 76ers. And, for most of the season, the Celtics played Alydar to the Sixers' Affirmed. The team won fifteen of its first twenty-two games, but after a 107–105 defeat in Milwaukee on November 30, the Celtics were still an astonishing four games out of first place as the Sixers broke from the blocks at 19–3. Still, the special quality of this team may have been defined on November 21, when they came from 21 points down in the third quarter and beat Golden State, 108–106, for their sixth straight win. They later would put together streaks of twelve and thirteen victories but were all alone in first place for only two games all year.

Philadelphia, meanwhile, had improved its team with the addition of a first-round pick named Andrew Toney, who, for a short time, was as much of a Celtics killer as anyone in the franchise's history. He could torment Boston as no one else did—not even Magic Johnson—in the early 1980s.

After falling four games in arrears, Boston regrouped and then won fifteen of its next sixteen games, including the twelve straight, to close to within two games of the Sixers by New Year's Day. Bird picked right up where he left off after his rookie season, continuing to lead the team in points, rebounds, steals, and minutes played. This year, however, Parish was able to provide additional scoring punch inside and from the perimeter. In Bird's first year, he had averaged nearly 5 points a game more than the next highest scorer (Maxwell). Parish changed that. He averaged 18.9 points a game and led the team in scoring in twenty-five games. In one memorable stretch in the first week of December, he averaged 26.3 points and 15.3 rebounds in games against Atlanta, Dallas, and Washington.

McHale, too, was quick out of the box, and he was also developing a reputation as a fourth-quarter assassin. A month after

McHale had 6 blocked shots in a game against the Bucks, the Celtics were playing the Bullets and trailed by 14 in the third quarter. McHale was inserted and almost single-handedly turned the game around. As the Celtics battled back, McHale tossed in a jump hook over Elvin Hayes to tie the game; blocked a shot by Kevin Grevey, starting a Celtics fast break; and hit two turnarounds over Wes Unseld, the second with ten ticks left on the clock, to put Boston up by 4. The Celtics won, 101–99.

He was even more incredible seventeen days later in Atlanta, scoring 17 points in the fourth quarter as the Celtics rallied to win, 112–107. Johnny Most, the longtime Celtics play-by-play voice, shrieked, "Sir Kevin the Fourth," as McHale made basket after basket. The unfortunate lad victimized by this onslaught, Dan Roundfield, uttered prophetic words after that torch job: "He is going to be a great player. He does all the things a great player is supposed to do. I tried every trick I knew."

On a team with less talent and even lesser expectations, such as Utah or Golden State, McHale would have been given carte blanche, not to mention more minutes. But things were different on the Celtics and always have been. John Havlicek waited seven years before starting. The NBA was never exposed to Maximum Strength McHale until Maxwell got hurt during the 1984–85 season and was subsequently traded, clearing the way for McHale to start.

The Celtics went west during the holidays, and in their third game on a four-game swing Bird did something he would not do in any of his other 897 regular-season or 164 playoff games: he did not score a point, in what has come to be known as the "eight bricks and a block" outing. The performance actually was a continuation from the game before in San Diego, in which he had gone 4 for 17, missing his last 9 shots of that game. A slump? How does no baskets in eighty-six-plus minutes sound? Bird talked of being drained after the San Diego game and wanted to rest up for the Warriors tilt. "I felt better. I thought I had a better release. I just didn't have the touch I usually have." He figured that the last time he had gone scoreless was in a junior high game. He had gone 1 for 15 in a game against New Jersey as a rookie, but no points in thirty-seven minutes? Not even a free throw? It may have been the single most noxious moment of the season. Not surprisingly, the Celtics' winning streak of twelve, their longest in sixteen years, came to a crashing halt.

The team headed up to Portland, and the following night Bird and Robey made the most of the nightlife in the Rose City. "I guess his reasoning was that he had rested so much before the last game, and look what good it did him," Robey said. "We figured we'd try the other approach. I guess it worked." It sure did. Bird came out against the Trail Blazers and made three baskets in the first sixty-eight seconds. He hit his first six shots before launching an air ball. He had 22 points in the first half, 33 in the game, and punctuated the performance with a three-pointer to seal a 120–111 victory.

From December 1, through January 31, the Celtics were 28–2. And still they could not overtake the Sixers. As the two teams raced to the end, both figured the regular season was one long warm-up for an inevitable collision in the conference finals. Home-court advantage was the sole carrot, but it could be a spurious advantage, too, as Boston had learned the year before. Twice the Celtics sneaked into first place, but each time only for a game until the Sixers wrestled the division lead back in a classic case of one-upmanship. Bird delivered a virtuoso performance in Los Angeles on Valentine's Day weekend, with 36 points, 21 rebounds, 5 assists, 5 steals, and 5 blocks. Parish had everyone's jaw dropping in San Antonio a week later with a 40-point game, including 15 in the first quarter and 10 more in a stretch of less than four minutes when the Spurs made a run. All of the Spurs, accustomed to the Parish of old, marveled at this new creature. "He now has teammates who can get him the ball where he can be effective," said Stan Albeck, the Spurs' coach.

The schedule maker had decreed that the two titans meet to close the regular season in Boston. And the stakes could not have been higher for a regular-season game.

The Celtics trailed Philadelphia by a game (they had lost a meaningless home game to Detroit two days earlier), but a victory would give them the division title: it would tie the standings at 62–20, it would tie the season series at 3–3, and it would tie the conference record, but the Celtics would win the title because they had a better division record. That's how close these teams were—a third tie-breaker had to be used. But the title also carried with it an extra bonus: a bye in the first round of the playoffs. The loser would have to host Indiana two days later. The winner got at least a week off.

Philadelphia fell behind early and never recovered. The Boston lead peaked at 22 in the third quarter. McHale played only thirteen minutes and scored 3 points, but he had two huge blocks; the second, against Julius Erving, led to a Carr basket at the halftime buzzer and a momentum-sustaining 11-point lead at the half. Andrew Toney, who would come to be known as the Boston Strangler, sent a message to the Celtics faithful: he had 35 points in thirty-three minutes. The last 3 came at the buzzer, a reminder that the two teams would meet again. Still, the Celtics rejoiced. They had never had more than a half-game lead all season—and they had that only twice—and now they were the division champs. Bird celebrated by throwing the ball to the rafters as the game ended, and the team waited for the identity of its playoff opponent.

The first round, in everyone's opinion, was simply a warm-up for the eventual, unavoidable rematch with the Sixers. The Chicago Bulls happened to be the Celtics' hors d'oeuvre and lasted the minimum, four games. McHale played a long stretch at center in Game 1 and responded with 21 points in relief. Boston won the first two games easily and then Bird went wire-to-wire in Game 3 and submitted a triple double (24/17/10) as the Celtics hung on to win.

The team had a free Saturday in Chicago before Game 4 on Sunday, and Bird and Robey decided to enjoy themselves. After having dinner, they found a tavern and had a few beers. They also discovered that some of the Chicago Bulls cheerleaders were at the bar, and soon more beers began to arrive at Bird and Robey's table, courtesy of the cheerleaders.

"We drank into the wee hours, and I mean wee hours," Robey said. "I think it was four thirty when we left. And we had a nine thirty bus. We just had forgotten about the time. Then Larry promised the cabdriver a fifty-dollar bill if he could get us back to the hotel in five minutes." That, in itself, is a stunning revelation, given that Bird would dive on the floor to pick up a nickel.

The following morning, Bird fell asleep on the trainer's table while getting taped. Bill Fitch blamed Robey. "He'd never blame Larry," Robey said. When the game started, Bird threw up an air ball for his first shot. Fitch again looked at Robey with executioner eyes. Then Parish picked up three quick fouls and Robey was summoned to play the final nineteen-plus minutes of the first half. He played well. Bird ended up with 35 points, 11 rebounds, and 5 assists in forty-five minutes. And the Celtics won the game, 109–103.

"And the kicker," Robey said, "was that we're leaving the floor when the game is over and Larry sees the cheerleaders. He goes up to them and says, 'Thanks for all the beers. We sure had a good time.' "

The Sixers had to go seven against the Bucks, but they prevailed and then headed up to Boston for yet another playoff meeting. Philadelphia was upset with the schedule; the first two games were back-to-back so that CBS could have Game 4 for a Sunday broadcast. Billy Cunningham, Philly's perpetually joyless head coach, moaned about having to play three playoff games in four days. The Celtics had had another week off and were ready, rested, and eager. They believed they were a much improved team from the year before, and figured they would not fall into a hole as they had in 1980 when they lost the opener. But Toney made two free throws in the closing seconds of the first game and the Sixers took a 105–104 victory. Bird missed his last nine shots of the game (he went the full forty-eight minutes) and McHale fouled out in nineteen minutes.

The Celtics came back the next night and squared the series with an authoritative 19-point victory. McHale did his usual fourth-quarter dance, scoring 14 down the stretch. Bird had 34 and had to quiet a standing ovation when he was pulled with four minutes left. He clearly didn't like the idea of acknowledging the ovation, saying, "I don't think we should show any feeling until the series is over and we win it. Then, I'll show it." Fitch made him wave, which, of course, set off more cheers.

Bird had yet to win a game in the Spectrum—the Celtics had gone 0–8 there in his pro years—and they would be 0–10 when they returned for Game 5. Parish disappeared in both games—his playoff stats rarely match his regular-season totals—and Bobby Jones saved Game 4 for the Sixers with a steal of a Nate Archibald pass.

The situation looked bleak, and the parallels to the year before were frightening. A repeat seemed even more likely when the Sixers took control in Game 5. Philadelphia led by 6 and had possession of the ball with ninety-six seconds to play. Standing in the runway, Sixers general manager Pat Williams started to accept congratulations from the fans who decided to beat the traffic.

"They were wishing us good luck in the finals. We were thinking we had knocked them out in five again," he said. "I mean, it had happened. We had done it. Then, it all came unglued."

Boy, did it ever. The usually reliable Bobby Jones blew four plays down the stretch. Had he blown three, the Sixers would have won. Parish, trying to redeem himself after his Philly performances, blocked two shots, which led to a three-point play by Archibald and a Bird basket. Carr then made two free throws and the Celtics somehow won the game. The series was already a classic. And the final two games only increased the excitement.

Game 6 had just about everything. The Celtics rallied from a 17-point hole in the first half. Maxwell went into the stands after an abusive fan. (He was later fined $2,500 for the transgression.) Play had to be stopped in the fourth quarter when a fan threw a cup of Coke at Maxwell. (McHale mopped it up.) Again, the Sixers had the game won and let it slip away. Then it was McHale's turn to put his stamp on the series. Thrown into the breach when Parish fouled out, he made the most memorable play of the evening by blocking a Toney drive with fourteen seconds left and Boston leading 98–97. And, even more critical, he controlled the block and got the ball to his point guard. After the victory, McHale danced off the floor, arms raised, index fingers erect. Why not, he reasoned? It was time for some payback.

But there was still one more game. The Celtics specialized in Game 7 victories, having lost only two of the fifteen Game 7's in the team's history. Scalpers were out in force well before the game started, asking, and receiving, more than $100 for tickets. It may have been a bargain.

By this time, both teams knew they were likely playing for the

NBA championship. The Houston Rockets, who were 40–42 in the regular season, had emerged from the Western Conference playoffs, beating an equally mediocre Kansas City team in five. The winner in Game 7 of the Eastern Conference finals had every reason to expect a championship; the Rockets could not match up against either team.

The game had an eerie flow for the Sixers. Again, they took the lead and held it. With 5:24 left, an Erving floater made it 89–82, Sixers. But the Sixers scored only 1 point in their last ten possessions (there were unspeakable crimes committed by the Celtics which went unnoticed) and Boston rallied to win, 91–90, on a Bird bank shot. Bird had made three steals in those five fateful minutes. These were the days before the illegal defense rules were strictly enforced, and he roamed inside, pouncing on passes intended for someone else. And when he got the rebound of a Philly miss, he himself took it up the court to make the winning shot. ''I just knew that I wanted the ball in my hands. I wanted it there more than anyplace else in the world,'' he said. The Celtics held on for another minute (Mo Cheeks missed a tying free throw) and the Boston Garden turned into a jubilant party.

The comeback had been historic. The Celtics became only the fourth team to rally from a 3–1 deficit in a playoff series, and no team has done it since.

The finals were really an anticlimax. CBS thought so much of the series that it showed the weekday games on tape delay. The Rockets wore T-shirts saying, ''Not Ready for Prime Time.''

The Celtics came out flat in Game 1, which began just forty-eight hours after the emotionally wrenching seventh game against the Sixers, and were down by 14 points before they finally got rolling. They staggered to the end, but won, 98–95. The game was an obvious letdown for the Celtics. It was highlighted, however, by one spectacular sequence by Bird. He took a shot from the right side and instantly knew it was off. He also instantly gauged where the rebound would come. He ran to the spot, but because he was nearly out of bounds he took the rebound in flight, switched the ball from his right hand to his left hand, and made a short lefty push shot.

After their weary performance in Game 1, the Celtics blew Game

2, 92–90, another downer. In retrospect, CBS may have known exactly what it was doing.

The teams split in Houston. The Rockets sunk to unthinkable depths by scoring only 71 points in Game 3 and making just 24 field goals. "That was good old-fashioned defense," said Chris Ford. Del Harris, the Rockets' coach, saw the game differently: he thought the Rockets looked like a collection of twelve-year-old Robert Parishes. "It looked like we had never seen a basketball before," he said. Houston then played only six players in Game 4 and won, after which Moses Malone, heretofore relatively silent on and off the court, opined that he had high regard for the Celtics who had won thirteen world titles but "I don't think much of this club." He then suggested that four buddies back in Petersburg, Virginia, could join him and beat the Celtics. "I don't think they're all that good. They just get a lot of publicity because they're in the East."

Game 5 featured a sublime performance from Maxwell, who had 28 points and 15 rebounds, and the Celtics responded to Moses's comments, routing the Rockets, 109–80. The Celtics led 34–19 after one quarter and were never threatened. They then went down and closed the door on Houston's season, winning 102–91 in Game 6 at the Summit. Bird staved off a Houston rally with two hoops, then fed Maxwell for a bucket and drilled a three-pointer to seal the win. At the victory celebration afterward, Bird lit a cigar, and everyone partied while chanting "Go right at 'em, go right at 'em," their unofficial theme of the season.

Bird had not shot well in the series (41.9 percent) and Robert Reid was falsely proclaimed to be the one and only Bird stopper. Later, others—Paul Pressey for one—would be similarly misidentified. But Bird's poor shooting and adequate scoring (he averaged 15.3 points) overshadowed his yeoman work on the boards (15.3, including back-to-back 21-rebound games) and Maxwell was named the series MVP. It wasn't a robbery; Max had averaged 17.7 points and had the big game in Game 5. Parish stood up to Malone, and McHale played only 13.8 minutes a game.

The Celtics celebrated their world championship late into the night. For many, including Bird and McHale, it was their first championship of any kind. For others, like Rick Robey, it was merely another notch in the belt. Robey had won a high school title, an NIT championship, an NCAA championship, and now an NBA title as well. The Celtics rented a ballroom in the Stouffer Hotel in Houston and champagne flowed freely. Well into the wee hours, only Bird and Robey were still around the ballroom, but Robey had fallen asleep on the couch.

Bird wasn't about to sleep, nor did he want to try. He reminisced about his first NIT game in this same city, four years earlier, a game Indiana State lost to Houston, 83–82, despite his 44 points and 14 rebounds. Bird thought he was fouled at the buzzer, but the referees wouldn't give him the call. That night, he recounted the play from beginning to end. Then he turned toward the prostrate Robey and said, "This is how it would have gone," and he tossed a cheese ball through the air and into Robey's open mouth.

McHale, meanwhile, was finding champagne to be much tougher on him than Moses Malone or Billy Paultz had been in the six-game title series. The following morning, he boarded the Celtics' plane for Boston and was still feeling the effects from the night before. "Jeez, Red," McHale said to Auerbach, "I never knew winning hurt so much." Auerbach laughed as McHale stumbled to his seat.

"I almost died that night," McHale said. "It was my first extensive experience with champagne. It's not exactly the drink of choice in northern Minnesota, you know. You drink that stuff, they beat the tar out of you."

Shortly after the NBA finals, Maxwell was in New York to receive his MVP award. Unfortunately for him, this was to be the year the winner received a watch instead of a car. At the award ceremony in New York, Max was told the watch cost $7,500. "Can I have the cash instead?" he said.

CHAPTER 4

Falling and Rising Again

When the Celtics gathered in the fall of 1981, there was every reason to believe that another championship was well within reach. The franchise has always maintained high expectations for itself, and its measure of greatness is inflexible. An NBA title, and nothing else, is all that matters. The Charlotte Hornets may hold a parade and celebration for a team that wins a single playoff series, but such standards are unthinkable in Boston, or, for that matter, in any city where the goals are high, unwavering, and not easily attainable.

Fitch had lost no one of any importance from the world champions of the year before. The starting five was back. Parish had signed a four-year contract, never thinking about testing the free-agent market (although under the rules at the time, the Celtics would have been able to match any offer). The bench was intact. Before the season ended, the team added a rookie who would take a few years to blossom: Danny Ainge.

But there also was the matter of the Curse. The Russell Curse. No NBA team had repeated as champion since 1969, the last year Bill Russell played. In fact, in the intervening years only two teams, the Lakers (1972 and 1973) and the Bullets (1978 and 1979), had even made the NBA finals after winning the year before. And the Celtics hoped to change that.

The Celtics got off to a strong start, something that was an automatic throughout the early and mid-1980s. They won thirteen of their first fifteen games, one of the losses being a 106–104 home defeat by the Rockets in Houston's first visit since the NBA finals from the year before. Moses Malone made the most of his visit, scoring 37. Late in November, the Celtics reached a settlement with the Toronto Blue Jays that allowed Danny Ainge to leave baseball and join the defending world champions. The agreement ended more than four months of litigation, negotiation, and name-calling. Red Auerbach had taken Ainge with a second-round choice, almost as an afterthought. Ainge, the Player of the Year in college basketball, already was well on his way to a baseball career and had made it clear he would not abandon that sport for pro basketball. Auerbach decided it was worth a chance.

The matter ended up in court, with the Blue Jays prevailing, but eventually Toronto accepted the settlement because it did not want an unhappy distraction, which was what Ainge had come to be. And Ainge had hit only .211 in his short baseball career.

The Celtics and Sixers played tug-of-war for the third straight season. The Sixers held first for most of the first half of the season, while the Celtics stayed on their heels. From November 6 to January 8, the margin between the teams was never more than one game.

"All you thought about was Boston. That was all you concerned yourself about. Where's Boston? I think that's what made the rivalry," Bobby Jones said. "But I don't think there was any sense of urgency until we got to the playoffs. And you knew they'd be there."

Bird had a spectacular January, highlighted by a 40-point, 16-rebound game in Hartford against the Pistons, and he was named Player of the Month. He then went to the All-Star game in early February and was named the game's Most Valuable Player. Parish was the runner-up.

Immediately after the All-Star break, the Celtics held a slim lead and headed west. When they returned eleven days later, after a 3–3 trip, they were in second place, one and a half games behind the Sixers. The trip had ended with a tough 103–100 defeat to Seattle, despite a 34-point, 13-rebound performance from Parish. Another loss on the trip was a 112–110 setback in Phoenix.

After a two-day hiatus, the Celtics welcomed Utah into Boston Garden and won convincingly, 132–90, with Bird scoring 27. Two

days later, San Diego arrived and was similarly thrashed, as Cedric
Maxwell took scoring honors with 31. But in the next home game,
a 106–102 victory over Milwaukee, Bird caught an elbow from
Harvey Catchings that fractured his zygomatic arch—that is, his
cheekbone. The injury snapped a consecutive-game streak of 219.

Boston headed to Texas without Bird for the first time since he'd
become a Celtic. Already the Celtics were without Nate Archibald,
who was sidelined with a wrist injury. But M. L. Carr was coming
back from an early-season knee injury, and Boston continued to
roll, sweeping the Lone Star State with victories in Dallas, San
Antonio, and Houston. Parish got the trip rolling with a 27-point,
14-rebound game against the Mavericks and Maxwell led the scoring in the next two games. Bird was still unavailable when the
Celtics returned to Boston, but Parish had another strong game (28
points, 12 rebounds) as the Celtics edged the Knicks.

With seven straight victories under their belt, the Celtics didn't
lose again for three more weeks. Even a trip to Philadelphia didn't
deter them: Bird scored 29, Parish dominated the boards with 21 rebounds, and Boston won easily, 123–111. However, a week later the
Sixers came to Boston and ended the Celtics' streak with a 116–98
rout. Andrew Toney led Philly with 23. But the streak had covered
eighteen games, the third longest in NBA history. And, coach Bill
Fitch was told afterward, no team that had won eighteen straight
games in a single season had failed to win the NBA title that year.

The streak also effectively ended the Boston-Philadelphia battle
for the Atlantic Division crown. The Celtics had upped their lead to
six games during their eighteen-game romp and then won eight of
their last twelve, taking the division by five games.

The 1981–82 team might have been the best of the four that Fitch
coached. The team won sixty-three games, the third most in team
history, and became the first team to have three straight sixty-win
seasons since the 1971–74 Milwaukee Bucks.

Parish had stepped forward and delivered a year that would land
him on the All-NBA team as the second-team center. It remains the
one and only time he has made either the first- or second-team
All-NBA squad. Parish averaged a career-high 19.9 points per
game. He cut down significantly on his one acknowledged weak-

ness, foul trouble, reducing his disqualifications by half. His rebound haul that season was exceeded only once in his Boston years
(1988–89). McHale, too, had continued to improve and was rewarded with more time, going from twenty to twenty-eight minutes
a game. He finished sixth in the league in blocked shots. He was one
of the most effective and frightening weapons in Fitch's arsenal,
incapable of being decoded or deprogrammed, and again showed his
durability, playing in all eighty-two games.

Bird averaged 22.9 points a game and started a five-year streak in
which he did not foul out of a single game. He shot better than 50
percent for the first time in his career and, also for the first time, was
honored for his defensive prowess with a spot on the second All-
Defense team, a unit selected by the head coaches. The only blight
on his year was the five-game absence; Bird has always been a believer in playing every game and as many minutes as humanly possible.

Winning the division again gave the Celtics a first-round bye.
They then came back from the welcome respite and won a tough
five-game series over the Bullets, who unveiled the bruising two-
some of Jeff Ruland and Ricky Mahorn. The Sixers dispatched the
Bucks again, this time in six games, and the stage was again set for
the third straight Eastern Conference final matchup between Bird's
Celtics and Erving's Sixers.

Each team had much more, of course, but they were identified by
their superstar forwards. At times Bird and Erving even guarded
each other, although Bobby Jones often would be summoned to
silence Bird and Maxwell generally had the tough assignment of
containing Doc. The Sixers, with the Jones boys (Bobby and Caldwell) and the indefatigable Maurice Cheeks, had developed into a
defensive team par excellence. The series again was highly anticipated and, with the Lakers on a roll in the West, the first Bird-Magic
matchup in the finals seemed a distinct possibility.

The Celtics had taken the regular-season series with the Sixers,
4–2, winning twice in the Spectrum. Philadelphia's second victory,
however, was insignificant, in that Boston already had clinched the
division title and Parish, who was Boston's leading scorer (21.4)

and rebounder (14.4) against the Sixers, didn't even play. He was resting up for the playoffs.

Games between the Celtics and the Sixers in those days had an intensity all their own. "It was the most intense of all," Parish said. "We saw them six times a year and then in the playoffs. I think the rivalry grew with each game, each year. The better Doc got, the better Larry got. The better Philly got, and the more that they won, the better we got. They'd go on a streak and win eight or nine in a row and we'd do the same thing. Then we'd meet and the media hype would be so big, and I used to love that. We'd feed off it."

In the two short years since Bird had entered the league, Boston and Philly had twice met for the Eastern Conference crown and each had a victory. But the rivalry existed long before things heated up between Larry and Doc.

There really isn't anything close to Boston-Philadelphia in terms of a legitimate, historical, hate-filled professional basketball rivalry. Boston-L.A. is fierce, but comparatively genteel. New York–Boston never sustained itself. Detroit-Boston was fun because of the animosities involved, but it was short lived.

In the 1960s, there were two spring constants in Boston: taxes and the Celtics-Sixers. Bill Russell and Wilt Chamberlain drove the rivalry back then. Chamberlain won all the individual awards. Russell won all the championships (eleven in thirteen years). In 1965, John Havlicek stole an inbounds pass to preserve Boston's win in Game 7, a play memorialized as "Havlicek stole the ball!" There were fights in the 1960s, including one in which Sam Jones wielded a photographer's stool to fend off the menacing Chamberlain. Red Auerbach even got into the act long after his coaching days, running out of the stands in a 1983 exhibition game to challenge Moses Malone. Auerbach was upset that Malone had come to the defense of teammate Marc Iavaroni, who was jostling Bird. Auerbach also tore coach Billy Cunningham's sport jacket in the process.

Among the personalities involved in those memorable clashes were a slew of Hall of Famers. Those contests exposed a raw nerve that was left undisturbed until Bird and Erving clashed in the 1980s.

"The Bird-Ewing era was a special one, no question about it," said former 76ers general manager Pat Williams. "It was as hot a rivalry as those guys ever played through. There's no question that it was different every time we played Boston. And it was the same for them, too. There was a fever and an electricity there and it was rekindling the Philly-Boston rivalry from the Russell-Chamberlain era. It was starting to get ferocious again in the late 1970s, when we got Julius, then it died a bit. But Bird arrived to revive the whole thing. It needed another spark."

In the early 1980s, the two teams knew going in that one of them was going to the finals—and that unless one of them stumbled along the way, they would meet to determine which team would make it.

In those days, there was a distinct sense of one-upmanship between the teams. The 1980 blockbuster deal in which the Celtics got Parish and McHale was prompted by their inability to match up with the 76ers' front line. Philly countered that same year by drafting Andrew Toney, and there wasn't a Celtic who wasn't petrified by him. In 1982, the Sixers added Moses Malone to the mix. In 1983, the Celtics traded for Dennis Johnson in part because they needed an Andrew Toney/Magic Johnson stopper. In 1984, the Sixers drafted Charles Barkley. In 1985, the Celtics added Bill Walton, although by that time they also were engaged in brinkmanship with the Lakers as well.

"It got progressively harder as Bird came along. Then came Robert and Kevin. We had difficulty stopping all three guys," Bobby Jones said. "They had size and ability. I remember one game, they are on a fast break and both Bird and McHale arrive at the low post at the same time. McHale said to Bird, 'You take it.' Bird said, 'No, you take it. I had it the last time.' On most teams, you couldn't blast guys out with a stick of dynamite. Here, they are taking turns."

There is no better example of how these teams tried to build to stop each other than another pick in the 1984 draft. The Sixers picked a guard from Lamar named Tom Sewell. Did they need him? No. Did they want him? No. Did he have a chance to make the team? No. He was drafted because the Sixers' intelligence reports indicated that Sewell was high on Boston's list. (He was.) They drafted Sewell for the express purpose of keeping him out of Boston. Before the day ended, the Sixers had shipped Sewell to Washington and the Celtics ended up with Michael Young, who never made the team.

The Sixers arrived in Boston to open the 1982 conference finals on Mother's Day. They had flown in from Milwaukee; they'd had to go there because they blew a chance to clinch the semifinal series at home in five games. (After their el foldo the year before, the Philly press was speculating on yet another collapse after the Sixers built a 3–1 lead.) The Celtics had three days' rest, which they needed after their grueling Bullets series. Game 5 had been a 131–126 double-overtime Celtics victory. Game 4, also a Boston win, had gone into overtime as well.

Boston, having lost Game 1 of the conference finals at home in each of the last two years, was determined to avoid a threepeat. The Sixers were without Lionel Hollins (although he would later play in the series), and Darryl Dawkins had a bad leg. The Celtics took full advantage and established a franchise record for largest victory margin with a 121–81 rout. The game was summed up best by the Sixers' Earl Cureton: "Mama said there'd be days like this, but not on Mother's Day."

Philadelphia managed only 5 field goals in the third quarter and scored only 11 points. Bird, who had felt as if he was playing in a Skinner box against the bump-and-grind Bullets, responded to his newfound freedom with a triple double (24/15/10). "It feels good to be running again," he said. Cedric Maxwell suggested the Celtics could not be beaten, at least not when they played like that, and rookie Charles Bradley put the exclamation point on a joyous afternoon with a rafter-shattering dunk.

Cunningham, frustrated by the events, immediately yelled out "Showboat!" and called time with sixty-six seconds left. He was actually looking ahead to the start of Game 2, three days hence. The Sixers then headed back to Philly, ignoring the newspaper headlines.

Game 2 was no blowout. The teams went back and forth until an unlikely hero emerged in the fourth quarter for Philadelphia: Caldwell Jones. He was a seven-footer whose many skills included re-bounding, defense, and shot blocking, but scoring points was not one of them. Like most of his teammates, Caldwell Jones had played horribly in Game 1—he had fouled out in twelve minutes. But with Game 2 on the line, Jones stepped out onto the perimeter and drained five straight jump shots, and Philadelphia won, 121–113. Jones scored 22 points with Parish giving him the green light, as he should have. Jones knocking down five straight jumpers seemed about as likely as the World Bank relocating to Haiti. The possibility defi-nitely was not one of the Celtics' concerns. "He made a believer out of me," Parish said. "It won't happen again." It didn't. But once had been enough.

Game 3 quickly took on ominous overtones for Boston when Nate Archibald dislocated his left shoulder in the first minute. He was diving to deflect a pass and came down hard on the Spectrum floor. Trainer Ray Melchiorre immediately got up and said, "Disloca-tion." He was right, and Archibald was lost for the series. The Sixers, with Bobby Jones coming up big in the third quarter, led by 14 points early in the fourth quarter and by 10 (97–87) with 3:26 left. But a late Boston rally cut the margin to 2 and Maxwell had three chances at the end of the game to tie the score. He missed the first shot, had the second blocked by Erving, and was stripped by Maurice Cheeks before he could attempt a third. The Sixers won, 99–97.

Game 4 was not as close. The Sixers came out smoking and scored 16 straight points en route to a 32–20 first-quarter lead. Boston, with Parish scoring 18, eventually tied the game, but Toney, who had 39, supplied the knockout punch in the second half. "Something has to be done," Chris Ford said. The Sixers led by 12 after three and then outscored Boston 34–21 in the fourth quarter to win easily, 119–94. More important, as had been the case the last two years, the Sixers led 3–1. It was the first time all season the Celtics had lost three in a row.

Boston returned home and prepared for a last stand. The game had to be shifted to a UHF TV outlet (Auerbach squeezed $35,000 out of the station in rights fees) because "Marco Polo" was on the VHF station that usually carried the Celtics' games and was too popular to be preempted. McHale and Parish dined on chicken and cauliflower at Parish's home before the game and the Chief responded with a fire-lighting, 15-point first quarter. "I've never had it before," McHale said of the pregame repast. "I'll make sure I have it again." The result was a 114–85 victory as the Sixers shot a frigid 33 percent and got no closer than 17 in the second half. Bird had 20 points and 20 rebounds; Parish added 26 points and 15 boards. The fans serenaded the Sixers with chants of "See you Sunday," the day of Game 7, which would be played in Boston if the Celtics won Game 6 in Philadelphia.

Now it was the Sixers' turn to go into the bunker. Before Game 6, new Philadelphia owner Harold Katz fielded questions about having to move the franchise if his team lost this game, for it was widely assumed that a Boston win at home in Game 7 would be a formality. The Sixers came out and built a 25–10 lead, but by the end of one quarter, after a 10–1 Celtics run, their lead was 26–20. The Celtics then took over the game in the second half, limiting Philadelphia to seven field goals, two of them on goaltending calls. Parish, playing with five fouls, had 7 of his 13 rebounds in the fourth quarter. He and Bird each had 14 points, while McHale had 17. And Philadelphia, an 88–75 loser, looked all but ruined. The series was squared and Maxwell said, "The confidence thing just isn't there for them now."

A crowd of four thousand greeted the Celtics when they landed in Boston. Fans stormed the van carrying the players and McHale lost his wallet. The culprit later returned it. The result of Game 7 seemed all but preordained, as the Sixers again appeared headed for a gut-wrenching crash. Before the game, Dawkins tried to lighten things up in a somber locker room by telling jokes. Cunningham felt like Jim Bowie at the Alamo. Only twelve people—maybe not even that many—gave the Sixers any chance. They walked onto the floor and saw a sign saying "Deja Vu" directly across from their bench. Five guys wearing sheets and dubbing themselves "the Ghosts of Celtics Past" paraded past the Philly bench. "I thought it was the Klan," Erving joked later.

The first half was close the entire way, with the Sixers taking a 52–49 lead into the locker room. But they had led by 6 at the half

in Game 6 before self-destructing. However, this time they opened
the second half with three straight baskets—two Cheeks hoops and
an Erving dunk. Their lead was now 9, and they never looked back.
Toney scored 18 of his 34 in the second half and Erving added 29,
as the Sixers won going away, 120–106. Bird finished with 20, but
he had no points in the final eighteen minutes. Parish chipped in 23
points and 14 rebounds, but it wasn't enough. McHale, curiously,
was the team's best player in the first half and then did not play
again until the fourth quarter. He had 20, too. It all made for a very
bizarre afternoon, capped by the Boston fans chanting, "Beat L.A.,
Beat L.A.," a classy gesture by a group heretofore presumed to be
ordinary, classless fans, just like their brethren around the league.
(The Sixers didn't beat L.A.; they lost in six.)

"We celebrated too soon," a chagrined Maxwell said.

"This hurts more than anything," Bird said.

Philadelphia's defeat by the Lakers prompted action in the off-
season. Katz, waving dollars everywhere, signed Moses Malone as
a free agent to a then record contract that paid him $13.2 million
over six years. The Celtics, meanwhile, also had something going
with the Bucks. Milwaukee coach Don Nelson, thinking he had his
team close to a title, wanted the services of his old friend Dave
Cowens. But the Celtics had retained Cowens's rights even after
retirement, and Red Auerbach wanted something in return. Years
earlier, the Cincinnati Royals had coaxed Bob Cousy out of a longer
retirement to be their player-coach. Auerbach got Bill Dinwiddie
from Cincinnati for the move. This time, he wanted and got Quinn
Buckner. It seemed like an unbelievable heist, for Buckner was a
seasoned pro with supposedly impeccable credentials and Cowens
had not played in two years.

But the Buckner move had another, undesired effect. It created a
logjam in the backcourt and started a season of pouting by Nate
Archibald, who was in the last year of his contract and didn't ap-
preciate the new company. Buckner fit into neither labeled position
in the backcourt, but he clearly was more of a point guard than a
shooting guard. However, the Celtics and Fitch soon realized that
Buckner was not as good as they thought or hoped. But the impact

was felt on Archibald, who missed sixteen games and averaged only 10.5 points a game, the fewest in his five years with Boston. His minutes declined as well, which also bothered him. Then, too, Boston had Danny Ainge; Fitch wasn't all that fond of Ainge but felt the need to play him, along with Gerald Henderson and Carr, who were also competing for backcourt minutes. None of the players was content with his playing time or role.

In 1982–83, the friction wasn't limited to the players. There was also growing disenchantment with Fitch. His autocratic style was exactly what the Celtics needed in 1979, but in 1982, most of the players felt they no longer needed to be disciplined. McHale, then in the final year of his contract, thought the excessive discipline and secrecy ridiculous. He compared it to child rearing: if you always yell at your kid, eventually he'll tune you out, but when you choose your spots, the kid will listen.

In 1982–83, Fitch did not choose his spots well, and several Celtics, including Parish, Maxwell, McHale, and Carr, did not listen. Fitch was a control freak, and anything that went awry, however minuscule, was blown out of proportion. By then, the players could discipline themselves, or so they felt. But Fitch could no more relinquish control than he could quit and move to Albania. On one occasion, Fitch let it slip, purposely of course, that Carr had a hand injury. Carr had no such injury, but the next day he showed up at practice with his hand bandaged in an enormous white wrap, publicly tweaking his coach.

There was one revealing moment in Atlanta. Fitch was an early and assiduous advocate of videotape, and before the game he had a tape playing on a VCR in the locker room. The table holding the equipment collapsed, and the television and VCR fell to the floor. Parish and Maxwell immediately erupted into paroxysms of laughter. It was almost as if Fitch himself had forgotten his lines or misstepped at an inopportune or embarrassing moment.

And it symbolized the growing rift on the team. Maxwell, one of the best talkers in the league, was upset about being mentioned in a paternity suit and chose that season to stay silent. His silence was as unnatural as it was bizarre. And, prior to the season, two respected players whose locker room presence equaled or outweighed their abilities on the court, Chris Ford and Eric Fernsten, were released. They were missed.

The Celtics still came out of the blocks strong, however, winning thirty-seven of their first forty-seven games and keeping pace with the Sixers. In that span, they also made another curious personnel move, trading for Cleveland sharpshooter Scott Wedman. There seemed to be no need for Wedman's presence on a front line that already included the Big Three, Maxwell, Rick Robey, and, in a pinch, Carr. Wedman wasn't a bad influence or a McAdoo presence on the team, but he was an All-Star and he wasn't going to see a lot of time. He had started every game in Cleveland. There would only be reserve minutes for him in Boston.

But after starting 37–10, the Celtics began a downward spiral that reflected not only their growing inner tension but also the fact that they were not going to catch the 76ers. They won only nineteen of their last thirty-five games. On March 30, they were humiliated in Indianapolis, 130–101, by a poor Pacers team. The next night, the teams played in Boston and Bird scored 53 points, setting a Celtics' single-game scoring record. It was one of the few highlights in a dreary finishing stretch that saw Boston go 13–11 in the last twenty-four games and lose seven of its last eleven road games.

Most teams would kill for a 56–26 record, but not the Celtics. They had finished poorly, and clearly something was wrong. Their road record of 23–18 was the team's worst since Bird arrived. And, for the first time, they would have to endure the dreaded first-round miniseries, as the Sixers easily won the division by nine games.

The Celtics needed the maximum three games to beat Atlanta in the miniseries, which was punctuated by an incident in which Tree Rollins bit Danny Ainge. (Somehow, the story has gotten a different spin over the years, as many feel Ainge was the one who bit Rollins.) And then it was the Celtics' turn to deal with Milwaukee, a team they had managed to avoid the three previous years, but one that now would become almost a yearly staple in the postseason.

The Celtics had the homecourt advantage, but lost it immediately, as the Bucks won the opener, 116–95. Fitch, fed up with the whole proceeding, embarrassed his starters by putting them back into the game late in the fourth quarter. The crowd booed. What made matters even worse was that Bird was sick with the flu. Bird gave it the proverbial college try, but was clearly impaired.

In Game 2, Ainge picked up the slack for a while; he had 24 points at the half and then missed his final nine shots, as he and the team ran out of gas. McHale basically wimped out when he had to challenge the burly Bob Lanier, and the Bucks won 95–91, leaving Boston not with a split, but with a sweep.

In Milwaukee, Nelson called Ainge a cheap-shot artist. Bucks fans read the remarks and got on Danny every time he touched the ball. He clearly was rattled by the experience. The Bucks won Game 3, 107–99, and Fitch was now blaming the media for creating and stoking controversy on his team.

Down 3–0, the Celtics stayed competitive for a while in Game 4, but the result was no surprise. The Bucks won, 107–93, becoming the first team ever to sweep the Celtics in a best-of-seven series. Fans gleefully raised brooms in the stands of the MECCA, an outmoded, outdated facility but a thoroughly fitting scene for the Celtics' demise.

The locker rooms in the MECCA look more like backstage at the Broadhurst Theatre. There are mirrors that extend from desks all the way to the ceiling. In the Bucks' celebration, owner Jim Fitzgerald asked rhetorically, ''Tell me, are we the better team? Are we the better team?'' After a 4–0 sweep, there wasn't much doubt.

The Celtics' locker room was quite another story. Bird, choosing his words between sniffles, said he had never felt worse as a basketball player, not even four years earlier in Salt Lake City, when his Indiana State team had lost in the finals of the NCAA tournament. This team was in near anarchy.

''That was the lowest I've ever been in basketball,'' he said. ''I've been defeated in big games before, but if you take one series, that was it. It was a bad year. The players didn't get along. They were mad at the coach. I rededicated myself to playing, and I played a lot that summer. I came back with a mission, and I did everything I wanted to do that next year.''

But at the time, however, Bird's promise seemed like an empty one. There was the Fitch Factor. When Fitch saw the handwriting on the wall and left shortly after the Milwaukee debacle, he had one public defender: Bird. Then there was the prospect of McHale's impending free agency, the first time a member of the Big Three was even eligible to think about going elsewhere. McHale had announced after Game 4 that he could "hold his head high," a remark that infuriated Bird.

"I was working hard," McHale maintained. "I can tell you, I've worked less hard and had a lot more successes when I was healthy than I did later when I was banged up. We were just so discombobulated. I thought we were working hard, but nothing was happening. The whole chemistry of the team had changed and something was really off. It was like running uphill in mud. They had a good defensive game plan and everything just went bad."

So you had a vivid contrast amidst all the rubble: Bird, upset, embarrassed, and promising to turn things around, and McHale, upset but far from humiliated, and satisfied that he had done the best he could. Never was there a more telling example of how the two players, at that stage of their career together, saw things. When the locker room was virtually empty, Bird said, "Kevin is a great player and I hope we re-sign him. But if we don't, I'm gonna knock him on his ass the first time I go up against him."

Parish was allied with McHale regarding the Fitch Factor. He would have driven the man to the airport had he been asked. But he sided with Bird when it came to whom he'd want in a foxhole when the mortar shells started flying.

"With all due respect to Kevin," Parish said, "the one thing that separates Larry from Kevin is heart. Larry just wanted it more. I think if Kevin wasn't so talented, maybe he would have pushed the club more. But he didn't. His talent level was so high and things came easy to him. He never really had to push himself all the time. He put the time in practicewise. I'm talking about games. Kevin was always so much better than the guys he was playing against. The only other player who could play the low post as well was Kareem. And I always felt that if no one ever fouled Kareem, he would go ten-for-ten or twelve-for-twelve every game. Same thing with Kevin. He's so talented and bigger than everyone else. If he had pushed himself, I'm telling you, it would have been interesting to see how good he would have been.''

This was one of the rare times that a rift occurred among the Big Three, and it was even rarer that it became public. Bird, clearly, was upset by McHale's attitude. McHale was simply being McHale, honest and open. He talked about his impending free agency that night, too, as if it was simply another step along the road.

''I genuinely like Larry. He's a good guy,'' McHale said. ''When he talks, it's what he's feeling at that exact moment. It's 'What you see is what you get.' He may say something to you and then feel entirely different the next day and say something entirely different. That's his personality. There's nothing wrong with that. Me? I'll say what I feel most of the time. But there are times that I'll be pissed off and I'll think, 'I could say something, but tomorrow the sun is going to come up and I don't want to have to answer questions about what I said yesterday because tomorrow I won't feel the same way.'

''I've only developed a few tight, long-lasting relationships in basketball with people I've played with, and I don't know why that is,'' McHale went on. ''Danny [Ainge]. Jerry [Sichting]. Bill [Walton]. And there were guys I loved playing with. You work in the office with people, but does that mean that you invite them over every weekend? But one of the things I can say about Larry and Robert is that we never had an argument that lasted. And if we ever yelled at one another, it was all over the next day. Nothing ever lasted.''

And that was the case with this argument, too. Bird went home to Indiana and his new house (complete with a full-length basketball court and glass backboards) and worked on his game as he never had before. And McHale was about to undergo the most momentous summer of his life since he joined the NBA.

Once the 1982–83 season ended with the Philadelphia 76ers finally winning the big one (in a four-game sweep of the Lakers), McHale's original three-year contract expired and he became a free agent. It was the one and only time that any of the Big Three became free agents while still in the prime of their careers. Bird always insisted on signing a new contract while his old one had a year remaining.

There was still no unrestricted free agency in the NBA, and even if there had been, McHale, who had played three years under one contract, would not have been eligible. Every free agent was subject to his current team's right of first refusal, which meant that free agents weren't really free at all. And it meant that the Celtics would lose McHale only if they really didn't want him back, or if an offer was so out of line that they felt disinclined to match it and instead tried to get something in value via a trade.

At the time, there still was considerable debate as to just how good McHale was or was going to be. His statistics had improved each year, as had his perceived value around the league. He had not missed a game in three years, and in 1982–83 he had averaged 14.3 points while playing almost twenty-nine minutes a game.

But his relationship with Fitch was deteriorating by the day and he did not want to go through another year like the one he had just experienced. He clearly was reluctant about reupping with the Celtics if Fitch stayed. He didn't have to worry for long. A month after the Celtics were eliminated, Fitch resigned and took the head job with the Houston Rockets. Soon thereafter, mild-mannered K. C. Jones, an assistant who was virtually ignored by Fitch, was elevated to the head job.

Early in his career, McHale had found Fitch entertaining. "I don't think we ever didn't get along," he said. "I wore on him, too. I'd bust him. He'd bust me. It wasn't malicious. There were times when I'd be in a goofy mood and he'd get pissed off. He was a demanding coach and person."

Fitch said of his relationship with McHale, "Bird got as mad at him as anyone. They'll look back on their relationship the same way that Kevin will look back on his relationship with me. It'll be a lasting friendship. It won't be one where we'll be old friends or close, but the longer they go on, they'll understand. If I looked back on things I did outside of basketball to help guys personally, Kevin would be at the top."

Soon after the playoffs ended, McHale and his agent, John Sandquist, made an opening offer to the Celtics, saw it rejected, and then headed to New York. The Knicks worshiped at the McHale altar and he wasn't adverse to listening to their sales pitch. Before a game in Madison Square Garden during the season, McHale joked with a writer about coming to the Knicks. He held a ball at the foul line and told the writer that he would stay in Boston if he made the shot. He then threw the ball over the backboard.

The courtship was very public and McHale was immediately portrayed by Auerbach as a potential traitor, louse, and ingrate. McHale's status as a Celtics legend is now ensured, but back then it was anything but. *The Boston Globe* ran a cartoon that showed a player with a pig's face in McHale's uniform, and called him greedy. More than 70 percent of fans polled thought the Celtics should trade him.

"I was talking to other teams like I was supposed to do, but the bottom line was that I wanted to come back and play in Boston, especially after they named K.C. as the head coach," McHale said. "But they were screwing with me."

Why didn't he make a public fuss?

"Not my personality," he said.

To make things crazier, Harry Mangurian was a lame-duck owner, having announced in June that he was placing the team up for sale. He knew the franchise was more valuable with McHale than without him, and he also knew that the Knicks would have difficulty making an offer to McHale that the Celtics would not immediately match.

Regardless of where McHale went, he was going to make big money. His first contract had been rendered obsolete by an exploding market and he was due for a huge, huge raise. At the time, no Celtic was earning $1 million a year, although Bird was about to sign a second contract putting him at $1.8 million. McHale was around $275,000 and thinking along the lines of seven figures.

"I never thought at that point," he said, "that you could actually get financial security in the league. You come out of college and make a couple hundred thousand dollars and that's a lot of money. But the average career is like four or five years. You can't retire on that. But this was a point where I thought, 'I can set myself and

Lynnie [his wife, then pregnant with their first child] up.' That's why I had a number in mind."

The Knicks were more than willing to pay it. But the salary cap was in effect at the time and they had to do some creative financing to meet McHale's terms. And even if they were able to do that, they also had some valuable free agents of their own whom they wanted to re-sign.

"The McHale thing," said Eddie Donovan, then a Knicks executive, "was a total fiasco. I don't ever think he really wanted to play there."

And, of course, he never did. The Celtics made doubly sure McHale wouldn't get a chance by making a preemptive strike against the Knicks, signing three of their valued free agents—Rory Sparrow, Sly Williams, and Marvin Webster—to offer sheets. The message was clear. If New York matched the salaries and kept the players, it would have no money available to sign McHale. The Celtics would, because a team was allowed to exceed its salary-cap figure to retain its own players.

It was a masterstroke, designed with one goal: to get the Knicks into a bind so they would risk losing three valued players and still be uncertain that they could sign McHale. In hindsight, however, the potential three-for-one exchange still seems totally tilted in Boston's favor.

The offer sheets came in June at the league meetings in New York. Jan Volk typed them out on a typewriter in the office of Larry Fleisher, the head of the players' association and also a player agent as well. (He represented Webster.)

"If the Knicks got to their cap number, they couldn't make a deal for Kevin," Volk said. "We didn't know when that was going to happen, so we decided to help the process along. It was strange. We gave them all offer sheets. We asked Rory Sparrow what he wanted, he told us, and we told him it wasn't enough. We told him we thought the Knicks surely could spring for a couple hundred thousand more."

The three deals represented roughly $1.5 million in yearly payouts and were signed in a hectic three-day stretch. The Knicks had fifteen days to decide what to do with all three offer sheets, which, in effect, gave them a fortnight to work hot and heavy on McHale. Inexplicably, the Knicks matched the Sparrow deal almost immediately. They waited the full fifteen days before acting on Webster and Williams (whom they then traded to Atlanta). During that fifteen-day span, three newspapers reported that McHale was on the verge of signing a big deal with the Knicks, and Auerbach reverted to form by ripping Sandquist for trying to make a name for himself rather than getting a good deal (read: what the Celtics were offering) for his client.

Once the Knicks matched the three offer sheets, however, the McHale–to–New York talk died a quick and painless death. He still wanted assurances from Boston that he would not be re-signed and then traded, and he sought contract language to prevent such a move. Auerbach wouldn't budge on this issue, but he told McHale the team had no intention of moving him. He would make the same pledge years later when McHale was rumored to be on the trading block.

Then, in mid-July, Volk flew out to Minneapolis and met with Sandquist and McHale in a bar at the airport. By then, the sides had agreed on terms—four years, $4 million—that gave McHale the security he wanted. The deal was signed and McHale was back in everyone's good graces again.

"I left a ton of money on the table in New York," McHale said. "The whole thing could have been changed and circumvented, but we were going through a coaching change and an ownership change. It should never have come to what it came to. I've never felt that what you're paid is a direct reflection of what kind of player you are. Some people say, 'I'm the best this or that and I gotta have more money.' If that's the case, then go out and show it. I got paid more money that year than I ever thought I would make in my entire life. And I don't think I jerked the Knicks around. They knew I wanted to play in Boston and that if things changed [that is, if Fitch left] I'd remain in Boston. And I told them that."

Said Volk, "We always wanted Kevin back. There just was a difference of opinion as to his value. We were talented and, at the time, underachieving. But we gave him a helluva contract. And you know what? Kevin then did something very interesting. Just like Larry and Robert, he got better."

How would McHale have fared elsewhere?

"Maybe he would have been motivated to go all out all the time," Parish said. "Like you say, you never know. You can always sit back and speculate. What would it have been like? But look at it like this: even though he coasts, look how great he is. Think about that for a second. The guy is a bitch of a player."

The Celtics would have a new coach, a newly signed McHale, and, even more critical, a new presence in the backcourt when they reported to camp in the fall of 1983. Tired of being tormented by the Andrew Toneys and Sidney Moncriefs, Auerbach pulled one of his master coups, getting Dennis Johnson from the Suns. The price, essentially, was Robey, who, with McHale's emergence, was becoming less and less of a necessity and more and more of a luxury. There were also draft choices involved, but the principals were Johnson and Robey. The deal seemed lopsided then, and three years later it looked even more ridiculous. Robey made no impact in Phoenix whatsoever.

The deal meant more playing time for McHale and less party time for Bird, which was good for both players. Bird and Robey had been incorrigible nightlifers on the road and, before the 1982–83 season, Bird reported for camp overweight, wearing bib overalls.

"I really gave it to him," Fitch said. "Larry wasn't a free spirit, but he'd always get hung up with Robey. And Robey was always there. Those two guys ran a lot together. When Robey left, it was probably a great thing for Larry's training habits."

And as the Celtics soon discovered, it was also a great thing for Larry's game—and, by extension, for the Celtics, too.

By the time the basketball season actually began in 1983, the Celtics were a model of tranquillity and stability, and they remained so over the course of the season. They had few injuries and went the entire year with the same twelve-man cast. That mood was in sharp contrast to the turbulent and tumultuous summer of 1983.

In addition to the McHale/Knicks melodrama and the departure of Fitch, there also was the sale of the team to three New York–based businessmen. In the 1960s and 1970s the Celtics had gone through owners the way most of us go through toothbrushes. Mangurian had seemed like the ideal boss, but he could not coexist with the owners of Boston Garden and he became exasperated in dealing with them.

The new owners paid $15 million and took on another $4 million in debt. The price seemed high at the time; three years later, they would sell 40 percent of the club for almost $50 million. One of their first acts was to make sure their meal ticket was well fed for some time. In late September, Bird signed a seven-year deal worth $12.3 million, making him the second-highest-paid player in the NBA after Moses Malone.

Bird's original five-year deal had another season to run, but he wanted to sign a new deal and have it done before training camp started in late September. He made it clear that once the season started, he would not negotiate.

This time around, there was none of the acrimony of the previous salary negotiations. Auerbach had modified his view that forwards could not turn around teams, having seen Bird do exactly that. And there was no debate as to Bird's place in the game—he was among the two or three best players.

Malone had won the MVP award in 1982–83, a year after he signed a huge offer sheet from Philadelphia ($13.2 million over six years but with incentives, which Auerbach never liked). Bird was willing to take less, for at the time he considered Malone to be the preeminent force in the game. Malone also had won the Most Valuable Player award the year before, his final season with the Rockets.

The talks went smoothly, except for one minor snag. There was a question over $30,000, a pittance given the overall value of the contract. But Auerbach was insistent. Bird, who by now was doing a lot of the talking and was tight with the Celtics' legendary czar, could not understand the holdup. Finally, Auerbach relented, but only to a degree: if Bird agreed to give up the $30,000 in question now, Auerbach would in turn write a check to Bird for $250,000 when he retired at the end of the contract, as Bird then expected would be the case.

Bird said to himself, "This makes no sense to me." But he also knew that $250,000 was worth a lot more than $30,000, even seven years down the road. So he agreed to Auerbach's trade-off and forfeited the $30,000 in question. When his contract expired in

1991, however, Bird did not retire. He signed a whopping $7.07 million deal, most of it ($4.87 million) in the form of a signing bonus. And Auerbach never had to write the $250,000 check he had said he would. Bird laughs about it now. Auerbach beat him for $30,000.

That signing came the day before camp opened. There was one more crisis, and it came about unexpectedly. Two weeks into training camp, Parish suddenly went AWOL when the team went on a weeklong exhibition trip out west. The reason: he was upset that he was making less than McHale, who was still a reserve.

Parish always felt that he was last on the Big Three priority list for contract signings, and while he was always well compensated, the timing sometimes made it hard to dispute him. In 1991, the team signed Bird and McHale to extensions while both players were coming off surgery, but waited on Parish, who was healthy. But there also were times when Parish was either uninformed or simply wrong in feeling that the team bent over backward for the other two while standing firm with him. In 1986, McHale signed an extension starting at $1.3 million and ending at $1.6 million in the fifth year. Those are the figures McHale came in asking for and those are the figures the Celtics had decided were fair and representative. There was no fight, no rancor, and no problem getting it done. Yet when Parish came to the will-call window, there was some give-and-take and he was led to believe, incorrectly, that the Celtics had caved in to McHale but were playing tough guy with him.

"I don't think we have ever undersold Robert," said Alan Cohen, one of three New York–based owners. "And I don't think he could ever say he was underpaid."

Parish was, however, more than upset in the fall of 1983 after both McHale and Bird had signed new deals. He was hot. Unfortunately for him, he was also under contract, earning about $650,000 on a deal that had two more years to run.

Before training camp began, Parish had sounded the alarm. "How can you pay a nonstarter more than a starter? That's an insult to me." But he showed up at camp on time and things quieted down. The Celtics and Parish, who by then had his third agent in as many years, began discussing an extension.

Things were moving smoothly, but apparently not quickly enough for Parish, who wanted the deal completed in a week. When a second week passed, he went public by refusing to make a team flight to Phoenix for a Celtics' exhibition game. He was now, officially and uncharacteristically, a holdout. The Celtics took all extension offers off the table and announced that they would in no way be threatened or intimidated.

The whole thing lasted only eight days, the duration of the Celtics' exhibition swing. During the trip, Bird noted that "if Robert doesn't want to be here, he doesn't want to be here. We've got enough talent on the bench. This will hurt, but we'll get by somehow." The problem was that the Celtics really didn't have a quality backup center. Robey had been traded. Rookie Greg Kite, their first-round pick, was in no way ready for regular NBA play. The Celtics most definitely would not have gotten by without Parish.

McHale, interestingly, was one of the few who would not criticize Parish or even comment on the holdout. All he would say was "Robert is doing what he feels is in his best interests." Not only was McHale the target of Parish's unhappiness, he also had to pay the price on the floor. He played center on the exhibition swing, and in one game he went 3 for 16 from the field. Fitch had said early in McHale's career that McHale would starve if he had to play center in the NBA. Maybe that was a harsh assessment, but clearly McHale preferred spot duty in the pivot, and he said as much when Parish eventually returned.

During the Celtics' trip, there were proposals and counterproposals, but the Celtics refused to renegotiate and were confined by the salary cap anyway. They threw some extension figures around, but Parish found them unacceptable.

"The negotiations dealt as much with a human sense as a financial sense," Volk recalled. "Because I think there was a perception there that Robert felt he wasn't respected or appreciated. And that was not the case. But it was resolved. We told him yes, there would be an extension, but not right now."

The Celtics got Parish more money by accelerating some of his deferred payments, once he returned to playing, with no strings attached. Eventually, they extended his contract as well.

"It was kind of like the Laimbeer thing," Parish said, referring to his unprovoked assault on the hated Bill Laimbeer in the 1987 Eastern Conference finals. "I just lost my composure. I don't regret doing it. [If I had it to do over again,] I would have handled it differently. First of all, I had a contract. And when I signed it, I agreed to live up to it. Maybe I would have still been as vocal, but not as demanding, about something being done."

The whole thing is atypical of Parish, given his general displeasure with publicity and his desire to remain in the background. He had never been shy about responding to perceived injustices, be they contractual matters, All-Star snubs (he was, however, really upset in 1992 when he saw that Malone, who had been out the entire season, was still ahead of him in the fan balloting), or sneaker deals (he always had to fight for one, going through several companies, while Bird and McHale were Converse lifers), but he rarely, if ever, did anything that could be construed as controversial or rocking the boat. The holdout was utterly incongruous. He had quickly sized up the situation in Boston when he arrived and was content to remain as anonymous and invisible as any black seven-footer could possibly be.

"I don't think I'm really going to be appreciated until I retire," he said. "Most people don't realize how good they've got it until they don't have it. Once I'm all retired and done with basketball, then people are going to realize the type of player I was and what I've meant to the Celtics as a player. For some people, it's very difficult to be overshadowed, overlooked, or even taken for granted. [That is what happened] all the years I've been here because of the system we had. And because of Larry, and all the exposure he had. And Kevin. Everything revolved around those two. Which is good for me. Having two legitimate stars took all the pressure and spotlight away.

"But," he went on, "if I was white, with the success I had, I'd be just as large as Kevin or Larry. Look at what happened when Bill [Walton] was here, and he was here one year. But you have to realize that Boston is a white town and Boston likes white heroes and that's understandable. I know that and I accept that. And besides, I prefer it the way it is. Because I know I have the respect of

my peers and my teammates and coaches, and that's more important
to me than all the outside endorsements and adulation I would get if
I was white. But there's no doubt about it, if I had been white, I
would have been large in Boston. Very large.''

But he was black and large and talented and, with the new ar-
rangement on his contract, happy again. The Celtics now had everyone on board and proceeded with a new coach, new ownership,
and the goal that had been a staple since Bird arrived: a championship.

Boston looked awful in its opener, a 127–121 road loss to the
Pistons. The Celtics then ripped off nine straight victories and were
off and running. They again played tag team with the Sixers for the
first two months, but moved into first place for good with an overtime victory over the Mavericks on December 30. Bird then erupted
on a February road trip, averaging 27 points, 13 assists, and 13
rebounds in three victories. The Celtics closed out the trip with a
win over the Suns and returned home in first place, nine games
ahead of the struggling Sixers.

The Celtics prepped for the playoffs by reeling off another nine-
game winning streak at the end of the season and then eliminated the
Bullets in four games. Their next opponent was the Knicks, a team
that had supplanted the Celtics as the Eastern power in the early
1970s and won two NBA titles in four years.

Boston–New York was not in the same category as Boston-
Philadelphia, but it was much more of a rivalry than, say, Boston-
Washington or Boston-Cleveland. The two teams had met three
times in the playoffs in the early 1970s when the Celtics were on the
rebound after Bill Russell's retirement and the Knicks were the
establishment. New York twice eliminated the Celtics, the most
painful series being the 1973 conference finals, when Boston, which
had won sixty-eight games that season, lost a seventh game at home
for the first time. The Celtics had been crippled by a shoulder injury
to John Havlicek, which they could not overcome. The following
year, Boston won in five and went on to defeat the Bucks for the
title.

In 1984, the Knicks had Bernard King, and he was at the absolute
peak of his game, despite having dislocated fingers on both hands.

He had averaged 42 points a game in the previous series against the Pistons, prompting Cedric Maxwell to predict, "No way he's going to get forty on us." Maxwell even imitated King's stride in the locker room. "No way a guy who walks like this is getting forty on me," he repeated. The rest of the Knicks were solid everyday players such as Bill Cartwright, Trent Tucker, Truck Robinson, and Rory Sparrow and unpredictable types such as Ray Williams. They were marvelously coached by Hubie Brown and had split the season series with Boston, 3–3.

New York was clearly spent from its Detroit ordeal and was hammered, 110–92, in Game 1. King was held to 26 points, and a killer 17–2 run decided things. K. C. Jones almost became a candidate for summary execution, however, when Bird, who had a gimpy ankle going in, limped off the floor with 3:30 remaining and the Celtics up by 20. What in the world was he doing out there, anyway? Jones took the heat, using his favorite word, "boo-boo," to describe his decision to leave Bird in the game, while Brown noted that his best players were on the bench in the fourth quarter, which is where all good players should be in an obvious blowout.

It didn't matter. Game 2 was three days later, and Bird was rested. He then went out and torched the Knicks for 37 in another pain-free Celtics win, 116–102. King was even worse—he was held to 13 points and he almost got into a fight with the taunting Maxwell. Before Game 1, Max had declared, "We're going to stop the bitch," and he looked like a prophet. McHale then added spice to the proceedings by saying the Knicks were in the grave, awaiting burial. Presumably, that would come sooner than later.

King & Co. made sure it was later. New York won both games in Madison Square Garden, taking Game 3 when the Celtics bricked six straight free throws and then winning Game 4 when King finally exploded, scoring 43. "They're back out of the grave and we're still holding the shovel," McHale lamented. The Celtics then regained the upper hand with another rout in Game 5, 121–99, as they made twenty-seven of their first forty-two shots and built a 23-point lead by halftime. Danny Ainge and Darrell Walker got into a fight and the Knicks cut the Celtics' lead to 8, but they ran out of steam. Boston returned to the Big Apple for the knockout punch, but King responded with 44 and the Knicks prevailed, 106–104. Bird had 35, but he missed a short banker to tie the game and Maxwell couldn't convert an even shorter rebound. It was back to Boston for a Sunday showdown. The Celtics had not played in a seventh game since the fabled Philly series in 1982 and had no intention of seeing their season slip away to Brown's desperadoes.

It was Mother's Day and it would again be a massacre with Bird playing the role of Genghis Khan. He came out and swished his first shot, a sixteen-footer, en route to a 15-point first quarter. On two occasions, King fouled Bird before Bird could shoot. Bird took the two shots, made them both and got the free throws. He had 28 at the half, 2 more than King scored in the game. And he put his trademark stamp on the affair with a three-pointer late in the third quarter that gave Boston a 21-point lead. The Celtics won, 121–104, capping a series in which Bird averaged 30.6 points, 10.6 rebounds, and 7.1 assists. But it was Game 7 that Brown remembers. Admitting that the crowd "really got to me for the first time," Bird finished with 39 points, 15 rebounds, 10 assists, and 3 steals.

"To lose a Game Seven in the second round against a great opponent," Brown said, "for a coach, in exhausting. But then when you underscore the fact that it was New York and Boston, it takes on a more tiring type of mental gymnastics. Because they always resurrect all of the relics of past games.

"When we lost and we had the press conference, it was hard to admit that the season was over. But you had to take a step back and realize that that was the day that Larry Bird stepped from the All-Star category into the category of being a legend. He was absolutely magnificent because they needed him, that day, to take the next step beyond being an All-Star player, and he did. He was just sensational. It was an incredible performance."

The Bucks were next. Revenge was in order. The Celtics had discovered the previous year that they simply could not push the "on" button when the playoffs started. Parish had even said that had the Celtics beaten Milwaukee that year, the next team waiting would have carved them up in similar fashion. This year would be different.

Boston opened with a subtle strategy change, double-teaming the soon-to-be-retiring Bob Lanier, the Bucks' center. He missed six of his first seven shots. The Celtics went on to an easy win, 119–96, and then came back two nights later and made it 2–0 with another comfy-cozy job, 125–110. In that game, Boston led by 23 in the second and 28 in the third. McHale erupted for 14 points in a 3:15 stretch and the Celtics were halfway there. They then took Game 3 in Milwaukee, 109–100, overcoming a 15-point deficit despite sub-par performances from Parish (10 points) and McHale. Bird, too, had 8 turnovers. Milwaukee avoided a sweep in Game 4, but Game 5 was back in Boston, where a heat wave had settled in. Bird, who led Boston in scoring in all five games, had 21 points as Boston led by 11 at the half and then ran off 13 unanswered points in the third quarter. The Celtics were back in the finals again. They knew they would open at home. They then waited to see who their opponent would be, and the marquee matchup that had been anticipated by everyone finally arrived when the Lakers closed out the Suns in six. For the first time as pros, Larry Bird and Magic Johnson would go at it.

The L.A.-Boston rivalry of the 1980s picked up from two de-cades earlier. The Lakers had the most impressive individual stars back then—Jerry West, Elgin Baylor, Wilt Chamberlain. The Cel-tics won all the championships. Boston and Los Angeles met in the NBA finals six times in the 1960s. The Celtics won them all. Boston survived a scary seven-gamer in 1962, winning the finale in over-time after Frank Selvy missed a chance to win it for Los Angeles at the buzzer. The Lakers led 2–0 in 1969, were within a favorable bounce of going up 3–1, led 3–2, and still lost. Owner Jack Kent Cooke had balloons placed at the top of the Forum for Game 7. They were to be released in conjunction with the Los Angeles cham-pionship. The balloons stayed where they were.

There was an interregnum in the 1970s. The Lakers won the title in 1972, thanks to a 69–13 regular-season record, which featured a thirty-three-game winning streak. The Celtics won in 1974 and 1976. But their paths would not cross again until 1984, when Bird and Magic Johnson were already ensconced as the game's dual saviors. History will always remember the 1980s as the Bird/Magic Era, but the Celtics were much more of a rival for Los Angeles than the Lakers were for Boston. Part of that was history; when the Lakers finally won a series from the Celtics in 1985, owner Jerry Buss proclaimed that one of the more odious statements in the English language—"The Lakers have never beaten the Celtics"—was now no longer true. Part of it was that the Celtics' biggest rivals were in the East—Philadelphia and, later, Detroit—while the Lakers had nothing comparable in the West. And the two teams played only twice during the regular season.

"The Lakers was more of a media hype than anything else," McHale said. "They were so far away. The eastern cities are all pretty much the same. L.A. is a whole different gig. It was Larry, the brooding bad boy, and the smiling Magic. And that's how the teams were perceived."

Nevertheless, when the Lakers landed in Boston, they would be harangued and harassed at the airport, bothered at the hotel, and jeered in Boston Garden. Said Magic, "We'd get off the plane and the baggage men at the airport would say, 'Larry's going to get you tonight. There'll be no Magic tonight.' It was a sense of real excitement." One unusual aspect of this rivalry and all Boston rivalries was the fact that the Celtics had a national constituency—the so-called Green People. They had a following everywhere and fans in every building. Two men in the Los Angeles area started a Celtics newsletter for West Coast fans. It sold. The Celtics were America's Team, if such a team existed.

Bird and Johnson entered the league in the same season, 1979–80, but waited four years before the Lakers and Celtics met in the NBA finals. That was truly a watershed year for pro basketball. A landmark labor agreement was in place, including a new wrinkle called a salary cap. The sport turned to a sharp young lawyer named David Stern to replace outgoing commissioner Larry O'Brien. And, in a stroke of luck, the new boss got a matchup in the finals that could attract even the casual fan. As it turned out, the series was a beauty. It had everything.

It started off with a rather improbable schedule. The Lakers had eliminated the Suns on Friday night, knowing that if they did, Game 1 would be Sunday in Boston. Network television was beginning to show its ugly head not only in the scheduling of the games, but in the timing of the starts—all night games, for instance, began at 9:00 P.M. in the East. The Lakers also knew, however, that Game 2 would not be until the following Thursday, another absurdity traced directly to the television folks and their witting accomplices in the league office. Stern did not want the finals on tape delay, as they had been in the early 1980s because CBS would not bump its prime-time lineup during the May sweeps, so Game 2 would be after the sweeps period ended. (In later years, the start of the season was moved back into November so the finals would come after the May sweeps and thus be deemed acceptable for prime time.)

The Lakers arrived in Boston too late for a real practice, but they drew out a practice floor at their Boston hotel on Saturday and went through plays and assignments. On Sunday, they discovered that Kareem Abdul-Jabbar was suffering from a migraine headache, a not unfamiliar experience for the towering center. The Garden crowd was in a festive mood. It could chant, "Beat L.A., Beat L.A.," and really mean it. But the Lakers looked anything but whipped, roaring out to a 20–6 lead in the first six minutes. They ran at every opportunity and dared the Boston guards, the team's suspected Achilles' heels, to beat them with outside jumpers. McHale watched the explosion from the bench and thought to himself, "If they're like this today, what in hell will they be like Thursday with all that rest?" Abdul-Jabbar, meanwhile, had 32 points and 8 rebounds in thirty-five minutes and looked not at all bothered by his migraine. "It's just like when your tires get out of line," he said. Parish, meanwhile, was horrible—he was constantly beaten by Abdul-Jabbar and was able to score only 13 points before fouling out. "What can I say about the man? It was one of those days. He was on fire," Parish said of Abdul-Jabbar.

Parish has always had an unabashed reverence for Abdul-Jabbar, dating back to the 1970s. When the teams met in 1984, Kareem was thirty-seven years old and still an enormous factor in the league. What no one knew at the time, of course, was that he would play for five more years.

"The older you get, the tougher and longer it takes you to get back to where you were the year before," Parish said. "Kareem showed great mental toughness to go through the rigors of an NBA season at that age. And to do it again and again until he's forty-two? That is amazing. He should be given a medal for just that. Forget about all the other things that he accomplished.''

The Lakers had won the battle of the pivots in Game 1. There was a subplot unfolding now that as time goes on seems more and more ludicrous. The Celtics opened—and stuck—with a game plan that called for Gerald Henderson to guard Magic Johnson. Henderson was 6-2. Magic was 6-9. The Celtics had acquired Dennis Johnson, a defensive demon, to help them against killer guards such as Andrew Toney and Magic. Even though D.J. was stronger, taller, and vastly more experienced than Henderson (he knew Magic from their wars in the West), the Celtics stuck with Henderson because Magic was guarding him, and that would enable Henderson to stay with Magic when the Lakers ran, which was all the time. It was a not-so-subtle admission of weakness by Boston. And it wasn't until the middle of the series that this obvious blunder was rectified.

Henderson was the hero in Game 2, but not for anything he did on Magic. Instead, he stole a sloppy crosscourt pass by James Worthy late in regulation and tied the game, just when the Lakers seemed destined to go up 2–0. The steal and basket (Havlicek, you may recall, simply stole the ball, and Bird, three years later, also made only a steal) came moments after McHale had missed two free throws with twenty seconds to play and the Lakers leading 113–111. Even after the play, Los Angeles still had thirteen seconds to win the game, but Magic, incredibly, dribbled out the clock and the Lakers did not get off a shot before time expired. In overtime, the Lakers led 121–120 when Scott Wedman drained a baseline jumper. Parish then made a big defensive play, stealing the ball from Bob McAdoo. The Chief got fouled and made both free throws, redeeming himself after his poor Game 1 performance. The Celtics, somehow, had squared the series. The Lakers went home, utterly convinced of their superiority but ruing the one that got away.

Game 3 was an unadulterated blowout. The Lakers got their vaunted running game going and destroyed Boston. Leading by 11 at the half, Los Angeles exploded for 47 points in the third quarter to boost the lead to 25. During one five-and-a-half-minute stretch, the Lakers scored 18 straight points while the Celtics missed ten shots and had five turnovers. The 137–104 final represented the largest playoff defeat in Celtics history. Bird was disgusted afterward and gave one of his best Churchillian "We shall fight on the beaches" addresses, while also admonishing his teammates. He said twelve heart transplants were first on the agenda. "Until we get our hearts where they belong, we're in trouble," he said. "We're a team that plays with heart and soul, and today the heart wasn't there. I can't believe a team like this would let L.A. come out and push us around like they did. We played like sissies."

The remarks signified a new Celtic approach for the remainder of the series. The Lakers were going to be challenged, not escorted, to the basket. Boston would start flexing its collective pecs and see how the Lakers responded. The Celtics had been totally outplayed for three games and were not on the brink of elimination only because of a lucky break at the end of Game 2.

"The dividing line in 1984," said Dave Wohl, who was then an L.A. assistant coach, "was that the Big Three would do anything. They were the aggressors. They would taunt you, elbow you, anything it took. Our guys had a certain hesitation to be the aggressors. There was a directive from the league that year, I remember, which in effect said, 'No mayhem.' The Lakers took it to heart. Boston said, 'Screw that.' We had the reputation of being Showtime, but none of us believed it. We thought we were physical and hardworking. We had one of the best defensive teams in the league. But Boston was always taunting us with words and deeds. Larry was as good as anyone. And Kevin would let loose a zinger now and then."

Prior to the start of Game 4, at the Celtics' shootaround, the team talked of getting tough. Until then, that's all there had been: talk.

"Kevin came in and said, 'We gotta start getting tough with these guys,' " recalled Danny Ainge. " 'We can't keep letting them dunk all over us and get all those lay-ups.' I looked at Kevin and said, 'Well, why don't you do something about it? I'm tired of getting booed all the time because I try to take a hard foul against Magic.' "

McHale did something. The Celtics trailed 76–70 in the third quarter of Game 4 and, as Kurt Rambis was about to complete a fast-break lay-up, McHale emerged to sideswipe him, taking Rambis down by the neck. Both benches emptied—and the series turned irrevocably in Boston's favor. There had been some early bumping and grinding before the Rambis incident—Bird had back-checked Michael Cooper into the press row while making an inbounds pass and had jawed with Abdul-Jabbar about errant elbows—but this was a real takedown.

McHale blames the incendiary tactics of M. L. Carr for starting the whole thing. On the bench, Carr had told McHale, "Kevin, we gotta take 'em out. They're running all over us. No more lay-ups."

"It was a bing-bang play," McHale said. "He wasn't going to get the lay-up. I just clotheslined him. I remember thinking, 'Uh-oh, I must have hurt him. Oh, Jeez. I may have killed the guy.' But he was OK. And we ended up winning the series, so it ended up being a pretty good play. But if I was going to thug someone, it would have been Magic or Kareem or Worthy. Kurt is a hardworking guy and he's not the guy I would have chosen to take out of the game."

That was one change in the series. Another was Bird's jousting with Michael Cooper, who, despite giving away three inches, gave Bird more trouble than any player he ever faced.

"We could play a lot of ways then," McHale said, "but we could not run with the Lakers. And Cooper bothered Larry. It was the first time I saw anyone bother him. So Larry started taking him down in the post and just beating him to death. Cooper was saying, 'Uh-oh.' Once that happened, the series changed. Larry couldn't come off picks or shoot jumpers around Cooper because the guy was too quick. So he took him down low and beat the living tar out of him."

After the Rambis takedown, the Celtics still needed some breaks to win the game. Incredibly, they trailed by 5 in the final minute of regulation, but Parish converted a three-point play on a follow-up and Bird then made two free throws with sixteen seconds left to tie the game. Parish then stole a Magic entry pass to Worthy and it was on to overtime. Magic missed two key free throws in the overtime and then Worthy, with two freebies that could have tied the game, missed one. Maxwell walked across the line and gave the choke sign. Bird felt better, but he still was not mollified as the Celtics escaped with a 129–125 victory. "We can play better," he said.

The Lakers were beside themselves. Through four games they had not trailed at the end of regulation, and the series was knotted at 2–2. They had lost the homecourt advantage. More important, they had lost control of the series. They no longer set the tone or established the pace. Their concentration was disrupted. Riley even tried some spin control, calling McHale a "thug." He knew what everyone else knew: things had changed.

Boston was in the middle of a brutal heat wave for Game 5. Temperatures were in the high nineties, with oppressive humidity. Had this been any other place in the NBA, the weather would not have been a problem, but the Boston Garden had no air-conditioning and it was a sweatshop. The Lakers placed oscillating fans in their locker room and tried to stay calm and cool. And they did, for a half. But the lingering image of that game is a pitiful Abdul-Jabbar (7 of 25) sucking oxygen as the Celtics pulled away in the second half. Bird played as if it was a typical summer night in Indiana, scoring 34 points and grabbing 17 rebounds in forty-two minutes. McHale and Parish also had double figures in points and rebounds as the Celtics cruised, 121–103. They now were within one victory of a world championship that a week earlier had seemed unthinkable.

The Lakers got good news as Game 6 rolled around: Kareem had another migraine. He vomited before the game and then interrupted Riley's pep talk to give one of his own. "I reminded the players that the Celtics weren't the only team with pride," he said. "We have athletes, too."

Boston continued to dominate, however, and had built an 11-point lead by the third quarter. The Lakers had tried some rough stuff early when Worthy slammed Maxwell from behind into a basket support. The Celtics shook it off and kept working. Abdul-Jabbar was on his way to another banner day (30 points, 10 rebounds), but the Lakers' real spark plug that afternoon was the heretofore MIA Byron Scott. The rookie guard, who had come in a deal for the popular Norm Nixon, had scored 13 points in the previous four games, but he scored 10 in this one and they all came in a critical stretch. Over the final fifteen-plus minutes, the Lakers went on a 36–12 tear and won going away, 119–108.

Bird was miffed. He had 28 points and 14 rebounds but was mad that he didn't get the ball more in the second half. He took only 11 shots, although he also attempted 13 free throws. "I wanted the ball in my hands, especially when the eleven-point lead was going down," he said. "I was making things happen when I had it. I didn't get it when we needed it."

Afterward, Riley talked of the chance to make history because the Celtics had never lost a world championship at home. And he also ordered up another migraine for his center for Game 7.

Game 7 belonged to Cedric Maxwell. Before the tip, while munching on fast-food french fries, he told his teammates to get on his back because he felt like a pack mule and was ready. Was he ever. He had 24 points (he was 14 of 17 from the line) along with 8 rebounds and 8 assists. The Celtics led by 6 at the half and then closed the third quarter with a 9–0 run to build the lead to 13 after three quarters. They led 99–85 with 7:58 left, but the Lakers had one final push. They cut the Celtics' lead to 5, and then to 105–102 when Worthy hit a jumper with seventy-two seconds left. And when Bird missed—the Celtics shot 39.5 percent, but compensated with a mind-boggling 52–33 advantage on the boards—the Lakers had a chance to get to within a point.

Parish, who had had big plays in Games 2 and 4, delivered again, smothering a Magic pass and stealing the ball. Dennis Johnson got fouled and made two. The rest was played for history. The Celtics had beaten the Lakers for the eighth time in as many meetings in the NBA finals.

And Bird was now even with Magic. They had each played four years and each had two rings. Bird, who averaged 27.2 points and 14 rebounds a game, was the unanimous choice as MVP. Shortly thereafter, wearing a bowling shirt, he accepted his first NBA Most Valuable Player trophy at the league meetings in Utah. He had promised to come back after the Milwaukee debacle, and he was true to his word.

"You gotta come back with a vengeance," he said. "At the time, I was the captain of the team. Guys respected me. But they never respected me more than when I came back and said what I said and then went out and got the job done. That's when I really got total respect. They were all dedicated to getting me the ball in the final minutes. And it seemed like they all knew who the man was at that point. That one year, I had everything clicking.''

The following year, the Celtics withstood the training camp absence of Maxwell (who was without a contract) and the trading of Henderson to Seattle (for a number one pick in 1986) and won fifteen of their first sixteen games. One of the victories was in their first meeting with the Sixers, who still had the same cast along with a brash new rookie named Charles Barkley. But the victory that night was quickly forgotten because of a fight between two improbable combatants: Bird and Julius Erving.

It was Erving's first fight. Bird had been in one with Allan Bristow early in his career. He had also had a fight with the Sixers' Marc Iavaroni in an exhibition game, and he would later belt Bill Laimbeer in the playoffs. But the mere thought that the two icons of the East would go at it was, and still is, unthinkable. "Larry you could sort of understand," Maxwell said. "But Doc? That's like the sun setting in the east.''

It was one of those nights when Bird had it going. He had 42 points (17 of 23 from the field) by the third quarter and Erving had only 6 (on 3 of 13). The Celtics were leading by 20 and, to make matters worse, referee Jack Madden had left the game with a knee injury, leaving things in the hands of Dick Bavetta.

Bird and Erving had traded elbows before everything came undone. Then Bird was called for an offensive foul, and as he and Erving came back up the court they traded more elbows, words, and, eventually, blows.

"Larry was saying things to Julius," Danny Ainge recalled. "Things like 'You better retire if that's the best you can do.' Or, 'Get someone else to guard me. You can't do it.' ''

Erving landed three punches. Bird was held from behind, first by Moses Malone and then by Barkley. Bobby Jones also got involved as both benches emptied.

"Julius had held him and Larry tried to slap him away and fell down. That had embarrassed him," Jones recalled. "I got in between them. Julius got him pretty good. Larry just kept saying, 'Get out of my way.' I just stood there. There was frustration on both ends, but everyone forgot about it. You've got a game the next night. To me, though, it was kinda funny. I mean, those two guys?''

But as long as Bird had his basketball game intact, which he obviously did, the Celtics would continue to prosper, despite lingering concerns about the team's depth, especially in the backcourt. The trade of Henderson had given Buckner the third guard job, but he proved to be too erratic. Finally, the team addressed the issue in February with the signing of free agent Ray Williams. No sooner had he come aboard, however, then Maxwell underwent arthroscopic knee surgery. It wasn't thought to be serious, but it effectively ended his season. On February 18 in Utah, McHale became a starter. He would remain so for the next three-plus seasons.

As for Bird, he simply outdid himself, which no one thought possible. He had back-to-back buzzer beaters against Portland and Detroit. He personified the ravenous nature of a team bent on winning every game. It won sixty-three, best in the NBA, and Bird, despite missing three games with elbow problems, led the league in minutes played. He also got an introduction to another American institution.

Early in the season, when the Celtics were in Dallas, Bird and Quinn Buckner were enjoying a beer in the atrium of the Hyatt Regency. Bird usually avoided such scenes for obvious reasons, but on this night he was just another patron in the bar as scores of people passed him by, unimpressed by his presence or simply unaware of his celebrity. These people were making the short walk over to Reunion Arena to see Bruce Springsteen, who by then was well into his "Born in the USA" tour. You'd have had to live under a rock to be unaware of Springsteen, but Bird had no idea who he was.

"Do you mean Rick Springfield?" he asked.

"No, Larry. Bruce Springsteen. He's the you of rock and roll," Bird was told.

That hit home. "Hm, must be pretty good then," Bird offered. "Where have I been?"

Bird, however, had heard of rock star John Cougar Mellencamp, who was a fellow Indianan, and attended one of his concerts in 1987 at Boston Garden. Two years earlier, he also perpetrated a hoax on the media and even his teammates by claiming that the two of them were tight. There was a story making the rounds in 1985 that Mellencamp was staying at Bird's house in between shows at Providence and Worcester. The *Globe* reported the story and Bird did nothing to disavow it. It never happened. But Sichting heard about it and, being a Mellencamp fan, got Bird to invite him back to the house after practice so he could meet Mellencamp. The two players walked through the front door and Bird yelled out, "Hey, Dinah, is John here?" Dinah Mattingly looked quizzically at her future husband and said, "John who?" Bird then looked at Sichting and broke up.

The 1984–85 season was best dramatized by one nine-day stretch in March that not only resulted in two Celtics' scoring records, but also revealed a great deal about the men who set them.

On the afternoon of March 3, 1985, with his nine-day-old son in attendance, McHale established a Celtics' scoring record of 56 points. The Celtics were playing the Detroit Pistons, one of his favorite opponents. The Pistons had no one who could bother McHale—he averaged 28 against them that year, shooting 61 percent from the field—and he was unstoppable that day, connecting on 22 of 28 from the field and 12 of 13 from the line. He also had 16 rebounds that day—10 offensive—which matched his career high.

Kent Benson (who got himself ejected) and Earl Cureton were McHale's principal victims that day, but the most interesting twist in the afternoon may have been Bird's role. In McHale's giant shadow, Bird merely put together a triple double of 30 points, 15 rebounds, and 10 assists. And it was his guiding hand down the stretch that set up McHale: Bird was directly responsible for McHale's last 9 points. What made it even more ironic was that Bird had the Celtics' single-game scoring record at the time, having poured in 53 against Indiana two years earlier. It was almost like Sebastian Coe being the pacesetter for Steve Ovett.

McHale was never one to glorify such games, but he did say that he might frame the box score, show it to his kids, and say, "Look what your old man did one day." Bird, however, threw out an aside in which he implied that, again, McHale could have gotten something more and was content to settle for something less. Somehow,

Bird homed in on the figure of 60 and chided McHale for not scoring 60 points.

"I told Kevin afterward that he should have gone for sixty," Bird said. "You don't give up. You do the best you can while you have the opportunity to do it. When he had opportunity, he should have went for as many as he could. What's the difference if you come out two minutes before the game is over? You've already played the whole game. You might as well finish it up and have your greatest game you can and not worry about it."

McHale, predictably, never understood Bird's reasoning then and still doesn't now. He felt he had done his job and the workday was over. "I just knew I had broken the record," he said. Two days later in New York, against the hopeless Knicks, McHale scored 42 on 15 of 21 from the field. Bird, again, had a triple double (20/19/10). McHale was so hot that Ray Williams, who was making his first return visit to New York, told him to try to break the 56-point record he had established forty-eight hours earlier. McHale's response: "What for?"

Of course, no one knew it at the time, but McHale's record would last only nine days. He was the Aleksandr Kerensky of Celtics' single-game scoring leaders. On March 12, in a college gym at the University of New Orleans (the Hawks played some home games there that year, lured by guarantees they could not refuse from Barry Mendelson, the former Jazz executive who had engineered the ruinous Gail Goodrich trade), Bird got his 60.

He was 22 of 36 from the field. He scored the Celtics' final 18 points over the final 5:11. His teammates deliberately fouled the Hawks to get the ball back. McHale played Bird's role from nine days earlier and had 5 assists, 1 shy of his career high. Bird had 37 points in the second half alone, and at the end of the game he was making such outrageous shots that even the players on the Atlanta bench could not restrain themselves. (Some were fined for their antics.) Mike Fratello, the Hawks' coach, got into a pushing match with Rickey Brown, the "other guy" in the 1980 trade involving McHale and Parish.

In the final month of the regular season, the Celtics pulled away from the Sixers and easily won the division. Bird had a couple of beauties left in him, though. He came off the bench against Milwaukee and scored 47 on alleged Bird-buster Paul Pressey. He then torched Robert Reid, another rumored stopper, for 48. In the first round of the playoffs, he missed a game against the Cavs because of elbow woes, but when the fans had the temerity to chant for Bird in Game 3, he couldn't resist. "They'll get me," he said before Game 4. "Both barrels." He then went out and scored 34 as the Celtics clinched the series.

Boston then eliminated the Pistons in six games. This wasn't anything like the emotional series the two would play a few years later. Detroit then lived on its offense, not defense. In Game 1, the Big Three outscored the Pistons' front line 74–38 and outrebounded them 38–10 in a 133–99 victory. "We'll have to grow taller," sighed the Pistons' coach, Chuck Daly.

The Celtics won Game 2 and then fell victim to a barrage by Terry Tyler in Game 3 (16 points in the fourth quarter) and Vinnie Johnson in Game 4 (22 in the fourth). Bird then came out in Game 5 and scored 43, his playoff best, and the Celtics won. They then closed out the Pistons and prepared, again, for the Sixers, who had swept the Bucks and were waiting.

The Sixers had added Barkley and had won fifty-eight games. However, they had also blown a golden chance to beef themselves up for the rest of the decade. They had had three first-round draft picks that year, but they made a poor pick at number ten (Leon Wood instead of, say, Kevin Willis, Jay Humphries, John Stockton, or Vern Fleming). They also then wasted a late first-rounder on Tom Sewell. The Sixers would do further damage to themselves after the 1985–86 season when, in a hideous deal, they traded Moses Malone to Washington instead of drafting Brad Daugherty. They had owned the number one pick in the 1986 draft, but they traded it to Cleveland for Ray Hinson and cash. They also dealt Malone to Washington for Jeff Ruland (others were involved), which, they felt, left them protected at center. As the decade came to an end, they had only Barkley left to lead them.

The Celtics won the series in five games. Parish totally outplayed Moses Malone in the four Boston victories and averaged 17.4 points and 13 rebounds a game. Julius Erving, meanwhile, showed signs of athletic senescence by shooting 32 percent from the field and averaging just 10.8 points. He did, however, volunteer that the Sixers were "four or five points better on both courts." Countered McHale, "Just where is that court?"

Boston took the first two at home and Barkley predicted that the Sixers would be headed for the Bahamas if they lost Game 3. The Celtics won that one, too, but the Sixers avoided a sweep and sent the series back to Boston. As the Celtics left the floor, a fan yelled to Bird, "See you Friday," which would have been the day for Game 6. "You have a better chance of seeing God," Bird shot back. Added Maxwell, who was in verbal if not basketball form, "It'll be a mercy killing. They're condemned."

Boston needed some heroics by Ainge and Bird at the end, but prevailed 102–100 and took the series. The lasting image of that series was Andrew Toney with the ball, surrounded by Bird, unable to hear his coach, Billy Cunningham, screaming for a time-out. Bird then stripped Toney to preserve the victory. Bird had not shot well in the series, and later stories surfaced that he may have injured his hand in a bar fight. He did shoot well in practice, however, and one day he accepted a bet from a writer that with his right hand fully taped he could make more free throws than the writer. He did. He made eighty-six out of one hundred. The writer, who lost $160 (his newspaper footed the bill) made fifty-four.

That series marked the end of the Philadelphia rivalry for the Big Three. Cunningham soon retired and the teams never met again in the playoffs while Bird, McHale, and Parish were still playing together. In fact, the Sixers' sweep of the Bucks prior to the Boston series represented a zenith of sorts. Eight years later, the team had yet to win another seven-game series.

Guess who was waiting for the Celtics? The Lakers had again steamrolled through the West and were anxious for revenge and redemption. They were tired of being humiliated; Carr called them the Fakers and regarded them as western wimps.

The Lakers had learned their lesson, though, and were now prepared to play physical with Boston, using Bob McAdoo and Mitch Kupchak as their bruiser relief corps.

Still, nothing seemed to have changed when the Celtics routed

Los Angeles 148–114 in Game 1. Boston led by 30 at halftime and Scott Wedman was 11 for 11 from the field. The Celtics preached caution, recalling the Mother's Day massacre of the Sixers three years earlier. The Lakers owned up to their pathetic performance and vowed it would not happen again. And it did not.

"All I did was bang in 1985," Kupchak said. "Especially after Game One, when we got walked all over. We could not afford to be passive. The Big Three had that rare combination of skill and being able to be physical. You usually only get one or the other. You get a big brute who isn't that skillful, or you get a skilled player who can't match up physically. Those three guys were both. You didn't see any ninety-eight-pound weaklings out there."

With Abdul-Jabbar, now thirty-eight, leading the way, the Lakers won Game 2 with a startling turnaround. Again he delivered a pep talk before the game, and then he went out and scored 30 points, grabbed 17 rebounds, and blocked 3 shots. The Lakers led by 18 at the half and weathered the anticipated Boston rally. Cooper was white hot from the outside (8 of 9) and the Lakers got their split. L.A. then routed Boston 136–111 in Game 3, which featured some phantom fisticuffs and the ejection of Ray Williams for trying to use Kurt Rambis as a bucking bronco. And, for the first time, the Lakers' new physical approach seemed to be taking its toll on the Celtics, who basically were playing five men. "I feel like Tommy Hearns," McHale moaned. "They're beating us on the boards. They're beating us up."

Dave Wohl compared the new Lakers to a child who'd been victimized by the neighborhood bully. "They keep stealing your lunch money and every day it's another quarter until you finally get fed up and whack him. Our guys are tired of having their lunch money taken away," he said. Bird said the two teams should meet in the Forum parking lot and have at it there. "I don't know if the league is up for that, but the Celtics are," he said.

Boston salvaged some pride with a huge win in Game 4, as Dennis Johnson made the game-winning basket at the buzzer. Under previous circumstances, the series would have then returned to Boston, but the NBA and CBS had conspired to institute a two-three-two format for the NBA finals. The league said it made the change to cut down on travel, which was, frankly, baloney. Neither team wanted it. It was done solely to help out television. CBS needed a series of at least six games to make a profit, and the chances of a six-game series were better with a two-three-two format. The Lakers took advantage of the schedule and won Game 5, 120–111, and the Celtics looked spent. Four of the five starters, including the Big Three, went at least forty-four minutes. Dennis Johnson went the full forty-eight. The Boston bench was all but nonexistent. Earlier in the season, when the Celtics were riding a bus to the Omni in Atlanta, Bird spied a sign that offered advertising space on a vacant bench; the sign said, ''Rent A Bench.'' ''Hey, K.C.,'' he said to the coach. ''We need bench help. Call that number, quick.'' It was funny then, but the bench was no laughing matter when the series returned to Boston.

In Game 6, the five starters accounted for all but 26 of the Celtics' 240 minutes. Only seven men played. Again, Boston wore down in the second half as series MVP Abdul-Jabbar delivered a 29-point performance and Magic had a triple double. Bird was 12 of 29; he shot 44 percent in the series, 42 percent after Game 1.

''In 1985, we had three, maybe four guys on Larry. We wanted to pressure him all the time. We wanted to deny him the ball, just make him work to even catch it. I think we were more relentless in that series, and in the last two games I think it caught up with them,'' said Wohl.

Redemption was more than sweet for the Lakers—it was ambrosia. After eight failures, the Lakers had finally beaten the Celtics in the NBA finals. ''They can no longer mock us,'' Riley said. ''Everybody likes to beat the bully on the block,'' Cooper said.

The Lakers were the champions. They then added Maurice Lucas to the mix the following year, won thirty-one of their first thirty-seven games, and finished 62–20. They never got a chance to defend, however, for they were upset by the Houston Rockets in the conference finals. It would not have made any difference, however, for no team was going to beat the Celtics in the 1986 playoffs.

CHAPTER 5

The Best Ever

The 1985–86 Celtics won sixty-seven games. It wasn't the best record in franchise history, let alone league history. They even lost three playoff games. But they dominated as no team has in recent history, winning their games by an average of 9.4 points, the best differential in fifteen years. By the final third of the season, the issue of who would win the game each night was decided early and emphatically. Then, other highlights, quests, and pursuits took top billing. The Celtics were as good as it gets, no matter what your yardstick. There certainly has never been a demonstrably superior team.

They were an astonishing 40–1 at home, which included three wins in Hartford. In one overpowering stretch, they beat visitors to Boston Garden by an average of 16 points over thirteen games. Their average margin of victory at home was 13 points. After an embarrassing Christmas Day defeat on national television to the Knicks, they won forty-six of their last fifty-four games, with winning streaks of fourteen, thirteen, and eight games. They lost no more than two games in a row, and that happened only twice. Seven of their defeats were by 4 or fewer points, and three came in overtime. Of the fifteen losses, only two, including a home-court flameout to Portland, were not tainted by giveaways, ejections, or injuries. Beating the Celtics was so rare that for the first five years of his NBA career, Joe Kleine listed the Sacramento Kings' February 1986 victory against the Celtics (in which Bird inexplicably missed two free throws down the stretch) as his favorite moment. They were 27–14 on the road.

They were spared from major injuries, too. Bird started the year with a bad back, but was better by January and did not miss a game. He never went wire to wire again. McHale missed fourteen games with an Achilles tendon problem, but Scott Wedman proved to be a more than capable short-term backup. The other seven members of the regular rotation missed a total of twelve games among them. Even when Wedman went down with a rib injury in the playoffs and missed all but two minutes of the finals, the Celtics didn't relent. They were loose, confident, carefree, and, above all, they were good and they knew it. And they wanted everyone else to know it, too.

"We had that arrogance, very cocky," Parish said. "When you win on that level—consistently sixty wins a year—and you win the way we won, well, there definitely is an arrogance. We were tough to beat in that stretch. Very tough."

"If I could, I would go back and play that year every year for the rest of my life," McHale said. "And I would never, ever get tired of that team. The people. The atmosphere. If every year God said you could do only one thing again, I'd assemble that team and go back and play it over again. Honest to God, if we could have stayed focused for the whole year, we would have won seventy-two or seventy-three games. But guys just weren't focused all the time. We had a lot of free spirits."

Danny Ainge recalled that year with equal fondness, but thought that the team's loosey-goosey attitude helped. "It allowed us to win a lot of games along the way and made us get through the season. You need to have fun to get through an NBA season. It was as loose a team as could possibly be."

And it was quite different from the team that had surrendered the title to the Lakers the previous year. Gone from the 1984–85 team were Cedric Maxwell (traded), M. L. Carr (retired), Quinn Buckner (traded), Ray Williams (not re-signed), and Carlos Clark (not re-signed). They all had one thing in common: not one of them played a minute in Game 6 of the 1985 finals. That's how much Jones thought of his bench.

The first sign that things would be different came at the annual
league meeting in late June. Trying unsuccessfully to avoid reporters, a large, lumbering, and conspicuous redhead named Bill Walton met with Celtics officials at the Hyatt Regency hotel in
downtown San Francisco. Walton had a clause in his contract en-
abling him to leave his current team, the Los Angeles Clippers, by
a certain date. He was interested in Boston, and vice versa.

Eventually, it came to pass. After much haggling, the Celtics and
Clippers agreed on a swap: Walton for Maxwell. This was an exchange of mutual headaches. Walton had never delivered for the
Clippers, and they were tired of him. And, unfortunately for Maxwell, he, too, had a bitter parting. The Celtics felt that Maxwell had
not devoted himself to rehabilitating his knee with the appropriate
seriousness. He became persona non grata in Boston, and only
ended his self-imposed exile for Larry Bird Night in February 1993.

Walton was one key addition. If he was healthy—always a question with him—he could drastically reduce Parish's time on the
floor. The Chief was all for the deal, and Walton paid huge dividends, playing in a career-high eighty games and winning the NBA
Sixth Man Award. The other key addition came from Indiana in the
form of shooting guard Jerry Sichting, whose reliable outside shot
prevented teams from collapsing on the Celtics' bigger players.

And then there was the established nucleus. The 1985–86 season
was a watershed of sorts for the Big Three, for it was the first time
they began the year as starters and finished it as starters. The game's
greatest frontcourt now was a nightly institution as well as something splendid to behold on the basketball court. They were at the
pinnacle of their collective games; never again would all three be
completely healthy and productive together for as much as a single
season.

The Celtics indisputably had the best starting five in the NBA.
They had a reliable, veteran three-man bench rotation of Walton,
Sichting, and Wedman. And they had four ''happy to be here'' guys
to round out the squad: Greg Kite, Rick Carlisle, Sam Vincent, and
David Thirdkill. Sly Williams had started the season with Boston,
but was released.

The one nagging question going into the season, and one that dominated the first third of it, was Bird's health. Like millions of Americans, he had come down with a bad back, exacerbated by shoveling gravel at his Indiana home over the summer. A month into the season, he summoned therapist Dan Dyrek to his house for help. Dyrek had worked miracles with Bird's elbow the year before. He now had an even bigger challenge.

Dyrek and Dr. Robert Leach, a local orthopedic surgeon who worked with the Boston players, visited Bird and were appalled by what they saw.

"He was on the floor of the family room," Dyrek recalled, "and he was in significant pain. We immediately set up an appointment for the next morning. I remember leaving the house and his back was what we call red hot. It was so inflamed I couldn't believe it. I told him that no way was this going to be an immediate cure. It took two months. But by December, we had it under control."

Bird was 5 for 15 in the season opener, and there would be similarly uncharacteristic numbers for him in the box scores until the new year. The Celtics blew a 19-point lead in that game and lost to the Nets in overtime. The usually reliable Dennis Johnson missed two free throws that would have clinched the game, and Walton submitted the hideous line of 5 fouls and 7 turnovers in 19 minutes in his Boston debut. "I was a disgrace to the team and to the sport of basketball," Walton said accurately.

The Celtics won their first game the next night in Cleveland, and through Christmas they were 21–7. But Bird's back was still bothering him and the offense had begun to calcify, resulting in four losses in eight games prior to their arrival in New York for a Christmas meeting with the Knicks. (McHale had not made the trip with the team, preferring instead to stay home Christmas morning, see his children open presents, and then hop the shuttle. "Who wants to wake up Christmas morning in the Summit Hotel?" he said. He was chastised for the snub, but it revealed a great deal about the man and his priorities.)

The Celtics led by 25 in the third quarter and then went to sleep. Behind Patrick Ewing, the Knicks rallied and won 113–104 in double overtime. Bird was 8 of 27, and there was genuine concern that he might not be able to shake the back pain. But as it turned out, that game served as a wake-up call for the team. They then put it into overdrive the rest of the way. Bird's back finally stopped hurting and he became unstoppable over the final three months.

Once Dyrek got Bird's back under control, the Celtics were truly magnificent. It was hard to believe, given what Bird had done the previous two years, but he seemed to be even better. It was as if Red Auerbach had taken all the qualities of previous Celtics greats, put them into a blender, and come up with Bird. He had Bill Russell's rebounding genes, John Havlicek's shooting genes, and Bob Cousy's passing genes. He was tough like Jim Loscutoff and could shoot free throws like Bill Sharman. Over the final fifty games, he averaged 27 points, 10 rebounds, and 7 assists and shot 52 percent. He tore up a locker room in Atlanta one night at halftime when the Celtics were getting mauled and taunted by the Hawks. He scored 17 in the third quarter and Boston rallied to win in overtime. In one stretch of eight games, he had five triple doubles. And he did something that year that made him even more legendary: he won the inaugural three-point shooting contest during All-Star weekend, the first of three straight victories.

It was his team. That was unquestioned. When Walton was excited about getting more offensive chances one night due to a rare start, Bird took him aside and told him, "I get the shots on this team. I know you think you will tonight, but your job is to rebound. So get over there and do it." After a game in Washington in which Scott Wedman played well and scored 24 points, a newspaper headline read, "Wedman Leads Celtics to 97–88 Victory." Bird saw the headline, turned to Wedman, and said, "That will never happen again. This is my team." As Walton pointed out, "If our running game wasn't working, or our post-up game wasn't working, we'd just give it to Larry and get out of the way. And he'd go make a three. The magic of Larry Bird was to create excitement everywhere he went." And the Celtics played to packed houses everywhere.

Bird would add a third consecutive Most Valuable Player award to his already impressive portfolio, a feat previously accomplished by only two players, Bill Russell and Wilt Chamberlain, both centers. He was, as *Time* magazine noted the year before, simply the best player in the game. He also was named the MVP of the playoffs, won the league's free-throw shooting title, and finished in the top ten in five different categories: scoring, rebounding, steals, free-throw percentage, and three-point shooting percentage. Only one other player, Cliff Hagan of the St. Louis Hawks in 1960, had managed such a feat since the league began in 1946.

With Bird healthy, the Celtics easily absorbed the loss of McHale, who missed fourteen games and came off the bench in four others while getting into shape. Wedman averaged 15 points a game when McHale was out. McHale accompanied the team on its western swing in February, but did not play in any of the games. He nevertheless served as toastmaster, tour guide, and general *bon vivant*. He then returned with a vengeance, leading the club in scoring in the NBA finals with a 25.8 average and making the first unit of the All-Defense team, which was selected by the coaches.

"What really made that team amazing," McHale said, "was that we'd lose a game and everyone would refocus. I remember telling K. C. [Jones] after a loss not to worry. We'd win the next ten to make up for it. And we did it. It was fun. There was so much give and take. Danny? You could give him grief all the time. Same with Bill [Walton]. Larry was in his absolute prime and I was hitting my stride. We had so many parts. And everyone complemented each other so well. It was like if we played well, we just knew we were going to win."

Walton proved to be a wonderful addition, both on and off the court. He became a human dartboard for Ainge, McHale, and Bird, who teased him about his past and his unconventional lifestyle. On a plane ride to Los Angeles in February, Walton asked Bird for his tickets to a Lakers game. Bird was taken aback.

"Doesn't your brother work for the Lakers?"

"Yes, he does," Walton said. "But we haven't spoken in years."

"Can you imagine that?" Bird said, shaking his head. "Only Bill."

Walton made the front line even stronger and occasionally was used in tandem with Parish. He submitted some signature performances, the most celebrated of which was an 11-point, 8-rebound, 7-block, 4-assist game in just sixteen minutes against the Lakers. There may not have been a more productive night, minute for

minute, by any player that season. And that it came against the
Lakers, a team he had also briefly considered joining, made it that
much more rewarding. He also had a 19-point, 13-rebound gem
against Philadelphia, all crammed into twenty-five minutes. No one
benefited more from Walton's presence than Parish, who punctuated
another typically steady season with a 25-rebound game in March
while gladly seeing his minutes drop. He again showed his durability, playing in eighty-one games, and was named to the Eastern
Conference's All-Star team for the sixth straight season.

The Celtics were in firm control of the season from January on.
They broke the NBA record for consecutive home victories in one
season (twenty-nine) with an early April victory over the Pistons.
They clinched the division title with thirteen games left, the conference title with eleven games to play, and the best record with six
games remaining.

They then prepared for the playoffs, fully expecting to meet the
Lakers in a third NBA final. No one expected anything different.
But first the Celtics had to get through the East, and their first
opponent was the Chicago Bulls, a team that had won only thirty
games that season.

But that number was a bit deceiving because the Bulls' superstar,
Michael Jordan, had missed sixty-four games with a broken bone in
his foot. Before the series began, Jordan had to convince a skeptical
Chicago management that he was healthy enough for the playoffs,
but once they had started, no one doubted his readiness.

In Game 1, Jordan hit the Celtics for 49 points, taking 35 of
Chicago's 86 shots. The Celtics won, 123–104, as Bird, Parish, and
Dennis Johnson combined for 106 points. The Bulls turned to Jordan again in Game 2 and he didn't disappoint. He scored an NBA
playoff record 63 points, but again it wasn't enough. He rimmed out
a jumper that would have won the game and the Celtics escaped in
double overtime with a 135–131 victory. Bird had 36 points and
Ainge 24.

Who knew what to expect in Game 3? Bird already had decided
that Jordan was, well, something else. ''I would never have called
him the greatest player if I didn't mean it. It's God disguised as
Michael Jordan.'' Whew. Over the years, Bird would always place

Jordan in some extraterrestrial category of one while sticking with Magic Johnson as his choice for the best all-around player.

In Game 3, the Celtics clamped down on Jordan like a human vise. The strategy worked. He had to give up the ball and scored only 19. Everyone went after Jordan. Big men. Small men. He eventually fouled out after a frustrating night and the Celtics, with McHale scoring 31, easily won, 122–104, sweeping the series. Their attention turned to Atlanta.

The Hawks were busy trying to make a name for themselves. They had won fifty games and their head coach, Mike Fratello, had been named Coach of the Year. They had the electrifying Dominique Wilkins, some muscle up front, and an icon named Spud Webb, but lacked the experience and intelligence to be taken seriously. They also liked to yak it up, as they showed in a midseason game against the Celtics in Atlanta.

That night, the Hawks were on a crusade to assert their legitimacy, which they felt would come only with a victory over Boston. The Omni was packed with the largest crowd in franchise history. The team had even imported the insufferable Dancing Barry from Los Angeles. (McHale simply looked at the mascot and said, "He wouldn't go over big in Hibbing, I can tell you that.") Atlanta came out hot, led by 23 in the first half, and began to yuk it up. Furious at the Celtics' play and Atlanta's trash-talking, Bird went berserk at halftime, throwing chairs around the locker room and screaming at his teammates. He then proceeded to score 17 of his 41 points in the third quarter. Bird even gave the choke sign to Wilkins when he missed a free throw late in regulation. Walton broke the game's final tie with a tip-in and then rejected an Eddie Johnson shot. Bird settled things with four free throws and the Celtics walked away with a 125–122 overtime victory.

Against that backdrop, the two teams met in the conference semifinals. Boston had won all six regular-season meetings with the Hawks, but they had all been competitive. Atlanta had not been much of a road team all year (16–25) and the Celtics won the first two games of the playoff series in Boston. They then won Game 3 in Atlanta, slipped up in Game 4 as Webb rallied the Hawks, and then returned to Boston to administer the last rites. The Celtics built a 66–55 lead at the half and then played arguably the finest quarter of playoff basketball in the franchise's history. Or in anyone's history. They ran off 24 unanswered points and outscored the Hawks by an astonishing 36–6, holding them without a point over the final 5:31. The Hawks managed two field goals and two free throws in the quarter and trailed by 41 with twelve minutes to play. "All you can do," said Fratello, "is call time-outs and make substitutions. The league doesn't let you make trades during games." The final was 132–99 and the Celtics found themselves facing the Bucks for the third time in four years.

This time, it was not even close. Boston had gone 5–0 against Milwaukee in the regular season and Milwaukee had struggled over seven games to eliminate the 76ers. Sidney Moncrief was ailing and Don Nelson sensed annihilation. Boston won the opener 128–96, the first time any Celtic team had won back-to-back playoff games by 30 or more points. Bird, with 26 points, outscored the Milwaukee front line of Randy Breuer, Alton Lister, and Terry Cummings, who combined for 25. Game 2 was more of the same, but closer, as Boston won 122–111 with all five starters scoring 20 or more points. The Celtics then mercifully finished off the Bucks in Milwaukee. In Game 3 Bird led the Celtics with a triple double, and then outscored the Bucks team, 17–16, in the fourth quarter of Game 4, closing the series with a three-pointer from the left corner (on the way to the locker room) as time expired. As the Celtics headed into their locker room, Walton collapsed in a chair, a big grin on his face, and said to no one in particular, "Larry Bird! Oh, my God!" Nelson was impressed with Bird and everyone else. "I'm not sure that Boston isn't on a different planet than us mere mortal teams," he said. And the Big Three? They had been one-two-three in scoring, with Bird averaging 25.3, McHale 21.5, and Parish 17.8. They also had been one-two-three in rebounding, as Boston dominated the boards.

The anticipated matchup with the Lakers never materialized, however, as the Houston Rockets stunned the defending champs in five games, setting up the second Boston-Houston final of the decade.

There were some interesting subplots to the matchup. Bill Fitch, who had left Boston after the sweep by the Bucks in 1983, was now with Houston. And, after successive number one draft picks, the Rockets boasted a front line tall enough and strong enough to match up with the Celtics' trio. The Rockets had 7-4 Ralph Sampson and 6-10 Akeem (now Hakeem) Olajuwon; though Sampson was taller, he was the power forward. They were dubbed the Twin Towers.

The power forward had been a league staple for years and he usually was a 6-8 to 6-10 bruiser. But for a lot of teams, so was the center. The Knicks' Willis Reed was no taller than 6-9. Dave Cowens was 6-8. Westley Unseld played center for the Bullets and he was no taller than 6-7. Even Russell was only 6-9, an unacceptable height for an NBA center today.

Using two big men became quite fashionable in the mid-1980s, but it was neither new nor revolutionary. The Golden State Warriors had, at times, used George Johnson and Clifford Ray together in the 1970s. And in the 1960s, the Warriors, then based across the bay in San Francisco, put together a humongous frontcourt featuring Wilt Chamberlain, Nate Thurmond, and Wayne Hightower. It was good enough to get them to the NBA finals in 1964, but the Celtics easily dismantled them, winning in five games.

In the 1980s, two teams tried, with limited degrees of success, to use Twin Towers.

The Rockets had the most visible and talented unit in Sampson and Olajuwon. Sampson came to Houston in 1983, as the Rockets finished with the worst record and won the coin flip, giving them the number one pick. But Sampson did little to help Houston and the Rockets again were big losers, finishing last in the West in 1984 and winning the coin flip again.

Even though Michael Jordan was available, and even though Houston had a center in Sampson, the Rockets didn't hesitate a moment and drafted Olajuwon. Houston has never, ever taken any heat for that decision, mainly because Olajuwon turned into an All-Pro. The Portland Trail Blazers, who took Sam Bowie with the next pick, however, have been badgered incessantly ever since.

The first year Sampson and Olajuwon were together, the Rockets went from twenty-nine victories to forty-eight. The next year, they stunned the defending champion Lakers and reached the finals.

The Lakers briefly flirted with the idea of restructuring their team after the Houston elimination. They talked intently with Dallas about a deal that would land them Roy Tarpley, a seven-footer, to play alongside Kareem Abdul-Jabbar. The price was James Worthy, and the deal never materialized. The Lakers instead made a midseason trade the following year in which they landed 6-10 Mychal Thompson without losing a key member of the team. With Thompson, L.A. won two straight titles, and he played a key role, both as a substitute for Abdul-Jabbar and as an occasional accomplice.

The Knicks also took a stab at the concept, but they were less successful. Their two components were both centers, pure and simple, which made the task that much more difficult. Starting in 1986–87, Bill Cartwright, the Knicks' number one pick in 1979, who had missed most of two seasons with foot injuries, was teamed with Patrick Ewing, who had been named Rookie of the Year the year before. There was much optimism in New York and coach Hubie Brown thought the two seven-footers could play together, combining Ewing's athleticism and Cartwright's defense in the post. On paper, it looked promising, but when Ewing's effectiveness was limited by injuries in his first two years, the Twin Towers experiment in New York failed—or, at least, couldn't be sustained.

There was a delay to accommodate television before the Boston-Houston series opened and the Celtics were frisky, feisty, and ready when Game 1 began. The Big Three dominated up front, with Parish scoring 23 and Bird and McHale adding 21 apiece. A third-quarter spurt turned a close game into a rout and the Rockets, with Sampson delivering a Still Life Special (1 for 13), could not recover. Boston won 112–100, but the game wasn't that close. "We were trying to bother the big guys," Parish said. They succeeded with Sampson. Olajuwon was undeterred, however, and had 33 points and 12 rebounds in thirty-eight minutes. In Game 2, mindful of the dreaded two-three-two playoff format, the Celtics turned to Bird to ensure they'd head to Texas with a 2–0 lead. Bird scored 31 points, using Rodney McCray as a prop in a steamy Boston Garden as the Celtics romped, 117–95. Fitch noted that General Custer had made no speeches, "so I'm not going to, either. We were humiliated.'' Boston led by 10 at the half and then ran the lead to 25 after three. And Sampson got a five-stitch gash under his left eye, courtesy of an errant Parish elbow.

It was time for the Celtics to go for the jugular in the Summit and they were prepared to do so. And had they merely taken care of the ball over the final three minutes, they would have won and gone up 3–0. But their offense slipped into a coma, and the Rockets erased an 8-point lead to win, 106–104. Sampson finally surfaced with a 24-point, 22-rebound gem after being thoroughly outplayed by McHale in the first two games. And the Celtics simply could not stop the relentless Olajuwon or Mitch Wiggins down the stretch. ''We haven't given one away like this since Christmas,'' sniffed Parish, who had a regrettable day (3 of 15). Only McHale had any touch: he was 12 of 19 and had 28 points. The rest of the Celtics shot 40 percent, with Bird (10 of 26) being the chief bricklayer.

Boston regrouped in Game 4, due to some memorable collaborations between those basketball brothers and purists, Bird and Walton. The game was close for the entire forty-eight minutes and was tied at 101–101 when Walton, who usually spent the ends of games watching Parish from the bench, grabbed a rebound and fed Bird, who drained a three-pointer. After a McCray follow-up, Walton, who was 5 of 5 from the field, rose to grab a Dennis Johnson miss and converted a reverse lay-up. ''Games like this are why I came to Boston,'' Walton said. McHale then made two key defensive plays to preserve the 106–103 decision, giving the Celtics a 3–1 lead. All that remained now was for the Rockets to choose the site of their execution.

Game 5 will be forever remembered as the game in which Sampson got ejected for punching Jerry Sichting, a 6-1 guard. But the Rockets used Sampson's expulsion as a firestarter, and won convincingly, 111–96. Houston had a 56–37 rebounding edge, including 23 offensive boards. No Celtic had more than 8 rebounds and only McHale, who had 33 points, could mount any serious offense. Afterward, Bird and Sichting ridiculed Sampson, and Bird said he was looking forward to Game 6. ''Ralph had better wear his hard hat,'' he said. He wasn't kidding.

The Celtics were steamed. They had been embarrassed in Game

5 and they wanted swift retribution. Bird was hot. He had arrived for Game 6 against the Rockets seeking not merely a victory, but an absolute, unconditional conquest. "Everything's gonna be all right," he said before returning home.

Despite their uplifting victory in Game 5, the Rockets faced the sobering prospect of having to win twice in Boston in a matter of days, something the entire league could not do over six months. The Celtics were so incensed over their fortunes in Houston that coach K. C. Jones called off practice the day before the game. Bird still couldn't wait; he slept only two hours the night before the game.

"I never quite had a feeling like that before in my life," Bird said. "I was so pumped up for that game that I think I hit my max. I never was fired up for a game like I was for that one. I didn't play all that well"—he had only 29 points, 11 rebounds, 12 assists, and 3 steals in forty-six minutes—"but I know one thing: I hit my max. And I'll never forget walking off the court that day with my heart pounding so hard I thought I was going to have a heart attack. I never reached that milestone again. There just isn't a greater feeling than winning a championship on your own floor and walking off the court at the end."

Bird put his own inimitable signature on the game early in the fourth quarter when he took a behind-the-back pass from Walton, dribbled away from the basket past several startled Rockets as if he was taking a driving test, ended up in front of the Houston bench, and then knocked down a three-pointer in front of a seated Robert Reid as the shot clock expired. The basket gave Boston an 87–61 lead and sent the Garden into utter pandemonium. Boston went on to win, 114–97.

"I was everywhere that day," Bird said. "But we simply had to have that championship. It was our best team. By far. If we hadn't had to worry about the playoffs, we could have done whatever we wanted to do all year. That was as good as it gets."

Jones allowed the veterans to leave the floor before the game ended, a concession to the state of delirium and the chaos bound to follow.

The locker room was already prepared for the celebration. Locker stalls had been covered with sheets of plastic; a makeshift platform was in place to officially anoint the new champions and give them the appropriate congratulations and hardware. Outside on the parquet floor, the scrubs mopped up and the crowd waited, counting down the final ticks in raucous unison.

Once the game ended and the locker room filled with people, champagne, tributes, and tears, Ainge went from player to player exchanging high fives and shouting, "Forty-five grand, babe, forty-five grand." That was their playoff payoff, the winners' share for steamrolling through the postseason at a 15–3 clip. The amount meant more to some than others. To Bird, it was walking-around money. To the twelfth man, David Thirdkill, a player who would be released the following season, the stash was significant, representing almost half his annual salary. McHale held aloft a T-shirt, ready made, noting that the Celtics were the world champions. Such T-shirts are now a staple at events of this kind, but this was the first time one had been made. The Celtics were a safe bet that day.

Someone asked Bird amidst all the jubilation how many years he had remaining on his contract and he held up four fingers.

"Guess that means we will be seeing you this time for the next four years, right?" he was asked.

"Guess so," he said. No one could think of a reason to dispute him.

And, at the time, there was nothing to indicate that the good times would not continue unabated. Bird was in his prime and only twenty-nine. McHale was twenty-eight. Parish, the senior citizen, was thirty-two. They were close. They were tight. They were confident it could go on forever, which, of course, was not the case at all.

"That was honestly just about as much fun as you can have playing basketball," McHale said. "And that summer, I was euphoric thinking we'd all be back together and would do it again the next year."

Then the Celtics drafted Len Bias with the number two pick in the 1986 draft and forty-eight hours later were mourning his passing. The death started a chain of events that haunts the franchise to this day.

CHAPTER 6

The Last Call
and Kevin at His Best

The Big Three had now been together, as starters, for a solid season and had an NBA championship to show for it. All three players were in their prime, and the club also had the number two pick in the draft, courtesy of the 1984 trade that had sent Gerald Henderson to Seattle. But two days after the Celtics drafted Len Bias, the Maryland forward, who was expected to lead the club into the 1990s, died of a cocaine overdose. Then, bad things started to happen to a very good basketball team.

A new rival, Detroit, emerged as a serious threat to the incumbent Celtics, showcasing a brand of basketball that stressed defense and physical play. Even more disturbing was the unending litany of injuries that dogged the Celtics all season. Walton broke a finger in a pickup game and then, riding the exercise bike to stay in shape, broke a bone in his right foot. He was limited to ten games and some token appearances in the playoffs. Scott Wedman played in just six games because of heel problems and had a season-ending surgery during the year. Danny Ainge missed eleven games, Bird missed eight, Jerry Sichting was waylaid by an intestinal parasite, and even the durable Parish had to sit out two games because of his chronically sore elbow.

There still, however, was no one in the division or conference to

mount a serious regular-season challenge to the team. Their dominance in Boston Garden continued unabated; they lost there only
once all year, to the Lakers. They also lost in Hartford, although
purists have never considered games there to be true Celtics home
games. The Celtics took over first place for good on December 13
and won the division by fourteen games, posting a 59–23 record.
The one glaring blemish was an inability over the second half of the
season to win on the road. The Celtics always prided themselves on
being a good road team. However, they started to slip and dropped
eleven of their last sixteen on the road, finishing with their first
sub-.500 road record (20–21) since Bird arrived.

But the Big Three in general, and McHale in particular, again
were dominant night in and night out as no frontcourt had ever been.
Early in the season, they went into Chicago Stadium and scored 96
points in a 110–98 victory. In a twenty-two-game stretch from late
January to mid-March, all three players registered double doubles
(points and rebounds) in the same game on nine different occasions.
The Celtics were 8–1 in those games, the only defeat coming in
overtime to the Hawks in Atlanta. Six of the nine games were on the
road.

Parish was never more consistent, and he probably had his best
season since joining the team six years earlier. He scored in double
figures in each of the first seventy-six games. In his previous years
as a Celtic, he had never scored in double figures more than thirty-
three times in succession. "Everyone talks about Kevin and Larry,"
the Lakers' Mychal Thompson said that season, "but ever since I've
been in this league, I've noticed Robert. They need him. You take
him out of their lineup and there would be a huge hole." He was a
participant in the All-Star game for the seventh straight year and, in
one memorable outing, ransacked the Kings for 28 points and 25
rebounds. He also had a triple double against Philadelphia, the only
one of his NBA career. Bird had one the same night. Bird averaged
28.1 points, but wore himself out playing 40.6 minutes a game. He
also got himself thrown out of a game by referee Billy Oakes with
Wayne Gretzky in the Garden audience. "If I had known that," he
said, "I never would have gotten thrown out."

But while 1986–87 was an excellent year for those two, McHale

was, at times, on a level all by himself. He scored 20 or more points
in the first twenty-eight games of the season and in sixty-nine of the
seventy-seven that he played. He was, quite simply, the most effi-
cient and simplest method of producing a basket in the NBA that
year. He became the first (and still only) player in the history of the
league to shoot 60 percent from the field and 80 percent from the
line. He averaged 26.1 points and 9.9 rebounds, again improving
his scoring average from the previous season, as he had each year
since coming into the league. And he also achieved a notable daily
double, making the All-NBA first team and the All-NBA Defensive
first team. Among his contemporaries, only Michael Jordan, David
Robinson, and Hakeem Olajuwon can make such a claim.

"There were a lot of times that year where it was hard to tell who
was better, Kevin or Larry," Danny Ainge said. "Kevin was just
coming into superstar status and he really, at that time, didn't have
a weakness in his game."

McHale worked at his game constantly, although he always led
people to believe his series of twists, squirms, scoops, down-unders,
reach-arounds, and other moves were as much on impulse as by any
grand design. He may have improvised a lot; that is the nature of the
game when someone is trying to take something away from you.
But the evidence that he also knew what he was doing most of the
time is the simple fact that it worked. He could beat you inside
thanks to his amazing footwork or with the jump hook that he first
learned in Hibbing. He had the soft fadeaway jumper that was
virtually unblockable and usually on target, and the face-up fifteen-
footer, which he used to soften up the inside. It was a remarkable
arsenal, and it got stronger and more diversified each year. It was
almost as if Saudi Arabia discovered diamond mines under its oil
wells and gold deposits under the diamond mines.

McHale was such an automatic basket that it overshadowed the
importance of his defense. But it was his skill as a defensive player
that enabled the Big Three to dominate at both ends of the floor.

There was little doubt in most people's minds that Bird was the
glue that held the Big Three together, and the Celtics as well. He ran
the offense and was the one person who could make the entry pass

to McHale at precisely the right time, place, and speed. He was the one who worked the pick-and-roll with Parish and made it deadly. He was the one who would get the defensive rebound and start the fast break when the Celtics felt inclined to run. Without Bird, statistics told us, the Celtics were, at best, a .500 team.

"As the Big Three, we all had games which complemented each other and we were held together by Larry's overall game," McHale said. "Robert and I in our own right are very good basketball players. If I hadn't played with Larry, I would have scored a lot more points, won a lot less games, and had a lot less fun. Larry could do everything. He could pass, he could rebound, he could shoot and dribble. And Chief [Parish] was just a tremendous, steady force. We all complemented each other well, but the glue was Birdy."

Bird could rebound, shoot, pass, and dribble as well as or better than anyone. His leadership abilities were beyond reproach. He was the captain and conscience of the Celtics. He may have been the glue. But McHale was the foundation for the Big Three as a basketball trio. He made it possible for them all to coexist and to subsist as the sport's nonpareil frontcourt.

McHale will never, ever receive the credit he deserves because he spent virtually his entire career in Bird's pterodactyllike shadow. But without McHale, the Celtics' front line would have become a defensive liability that could have easily been exploited. Instead, McHale went out night after night and guarded the opposing small forward.

McHale didn't see his ability to make the defensive switch as a big deal. He is alone in that assessment. Rival coaches marveled at it, possibly because it was so unusual. Here was a 6-11 guy out on the floor guarding a 6-6 cheetah—and stopping him. The arms made it hard to shoot over McHale. The wingspan made it hard to go by him.

"I could go out and guard people on the perimeter. Larry couldn't," McHale said. "That was just my ability. I didn't have to work at it. It was something that I could do. Playing those guys was second nature to me and I never thought there was anything odd or special about it. I'd always played against guys who were six-five or six-six. It was easy to do. It was something I'd done all my life and I didn't see any big deal about it."

But it *was* a big deal because no other power forward could do it. Bird wasn't a bad defensive player. He was not a world-class one-on-one player, and he played the passing lanes as well as anyone, anticipating entry passes and getting in the way. But not only would McHale take on the Dominique Wilkinses of the world, he would do it alone, giving Bird even more leeway to be a defensive pest, disrupting things and double-teaming.

"Offensively, it really doesn't make a bit of difference what they play," said former Knicks and Hawks coach Hubie Brown. "Where the negative part comes in is where one of the two forwards is asked to defend players who are quicker athletically—and not just foot quickness and dribbling quickness, but also quicker jumpers. That's what makes it so unique for Boston: Kevin played the small forward. That whole thing could never have come down if Kevin McHale didn't accept the learning experience and didn't grow as a defensive player. And what about the stamina? The toughest position to defend was the small forward. And then people not only expected you to defend the high scorers, they also expected you to score. So it was an exhausting position to play. There was no rest time. That's why McHale made it work. And I always found it interesting that people took it for granted."

Defensive assignments during the Big Three's heyday were like a predictable joke. Bird, the titular small forward in the offensive scheme, never guarded the other small forward unless it was someone either bigger or slower than he was.

When the Atlanta Hawks came to town, Bird would guard cipher centers Jon Koncak and Tree Rollins while McHale tangled, often *mano a mano*, with Dominique Wilkins. When the Washington Bullets came to town, Charles Jones, the team's low-scoring center, was Bird's guy. He guarded Bill Laimbeer when the Celtics played the Pistons and let McHale worry about Adrian Dantley or Mark Aguirre.

Charles Barkley longed for Bird to guard him, and with good

reason. Before Barkley arrived, Bird usually guarded Marc Iavaroni or Caldwell Jones.

"Charles loved having Larry on him. But he had no idea how to deal with Kevin," said Jerry Sichting. "It used to drive him crazy."

Bird was a wonderful team or "help" player on defense. He cheated like a devious older brother playing Monopoly and he got away with it when the league was lax in enforcing illegal defense violations. He would funnel his man into the middle, confident that either McHale or Parish would systematically swallow up the unfortunate lad should he consider taking a shot. And the system worked.

McHale never thought much of it, but that is totally in keeping with his unique form of self-deprecation whenever he and Bird are compared. Or when someone suggests that he may have been slighted, however unjustly, because of all the attention focused on Bird. That was the way it was and the way it would be, now and forever. He knew that as well as anyone. As he put it the night he retired, "People say I played second fiddle to Larry Bird. That's still a pretty good fiddle." At times, however, the attention given to Bird was ludicrous.

When Bird had back surgery in 1991, the Celtics announced it a day ahead of time, held a press conference after the operation, brought out the doctors, released biographical information on the surgeons, and had a printed transcript of the press conference available. When McHale had surgery, the team released a one-paragraph statement after the fact. When Bird and his wife adopted a daughter, *The Boston Globe* put the story on the front page. Not the sports page. The real front page. McHale's four children all entered the world without fanfare. (He and his wife had a fifth after retiring.)

That McHale and the other Celtics may have suffered slights given Bird's enormous appeal and popularity isn't surprising, but the Celtics didn't even know that McHale had scored his 15,000th point until it was pointed out to them a few games later. Before that, they had stopped a game to give Orlando Woolridge the game ball when he scored his 10,000th point.

When Bird wanted a new contract, he'd make it known in no

uncertain terms that he expected it to be finalized by a certain date, or else. McHale would simply try to get it done quietly, but sometimes wondered if being a public tough guy might get it done sooner.

Privately, there were times when McHale would fume. But he was intelligent enough to understand the laws of Boston Celtics physics. For every Bird action, there most definitely was not going to be an equal or opposite reaction on his behalf. McHale thought of Bird as the better player, period. And if he made sacrifices along the way, well, so did others. And the end result was three world championships.

"Kevin never rocked the boat," Ainge said. "It was just one of those situations where Larry was the star. It just wouldn't happen."

Added Parish, "There were two sets of rules on the team, no question about it: there was one set for Larry and one for the rest of us."

And they all understood it. The big picture was what mattered. Even though McHale and Parish were critical parts of the picture, they tolerated the double standard and subjugated their egos. They were not undone by petty jealousies or envy.

"Robert and Kevin accepted Larry and subordinated their egos to Larry," Alan Cohen said. "And you can see it in everything in life, that that isn't always easy, to take a step back and be number two, especially when you have the talent to be number one, as they did. But they did it. And that is what is so extraordinary."

As uneasy as Bird and McHale were in their personal relationship, and as much as McHale's carefree approach sometimes conflicted with Bird's basketball *über alles* approach, there is no doubt that Bird's three championship rings would be on someone else's fingers had only one of the Big Three been in Boston. Parish noted, "They had success when Larry was a rookie, but I think the *real* success came when Kevin and I came. That's when the championships started to come."

Bird at least understands that.

"If it weren't for Kevin, I know where my career would have went. We would not have won a championship," he said. "He is definitely the best low-post player I've ever seen. Everyone cries that he can't get the ball out to the open man when he's double- or triple-teamed. But you gotta understand something: we wouldn't have thrown the ball to Kevin if we didn't want him to shoot it. Kevin is one of the hardest workers that we ever have had around here. It's just the little things that bothered me. I always put him in the same category as my little brother. I always try to push him. Kevin is sort of the same way.

"I've always had a great deal of respect for Kevin as a person and a player. The things that irritate me about a player, Kevin usually does. One thing: he always shows up to catch the bus thirty seconds before it leaves. Or goofing around a little bit too much. But that's very minor compared to what he's done on the court. If it wasn't for Kevin McHale, I don't think I would have won a championship. Without Robert Parish, I know we wouldn't have. If one of those guys had gone somewhere else, we would have been suffering. I know what Kevin brought to our team."

And, in 1986–87, McHale brought the full menu to the table, soup to nuts. His game had evolved to the point where he was being mentioned as a potential Most Valuable Player. Bird had won the last three MVP awards, and deservedly so. But now people were finally recognizing how good Kevin McHale could be—and it was a frightening prospect to anyone who didn't play for the Celtics. "It was as good as I can play," McHale said.

The notion of naming McHale MVP that year was not farfetched in and of itself. It was, however, never going to happen because of the mere fact of Bird's presence. When Portland made its annual visit to Boston that season, and coach Jack Ramsay was asked about McHale's MVP chances, he simply shook his head and said, "There's only one MVP on this team and it isn't Kevin McHale."

Everyone shared Ramsay's view—everyone, it seems, but Bird. The player who constantly expected more of McHale still does not understand why McHale didn't chase the MVP.

"I was disappointed in him because he didn't want to go for the MVP award when I thought he had just as good a shot as anybody," Bird said. "He just took it nonchalantly. Down the road, he's going to wish he went after it. He's got kids, and the kids are going to say, 'Daddy, why weren't you the MVP? Why weren't you the star?' And that's what bothered me. I wanted these guys to have fun as we went along because we had great teams. I wanted them to get some recognition and do the best they could while they had a chance to do it. You can't get them days back—they're gone. That's why you do it while you have the opportunity. I think it would have helped our team if Kevin had got it or maybe came in second. I think it would have helped us down the road. If Kevin had won MVP, I think it would have helped all of us for a few more years.''

Bird had wanted the MVP and he had won it three straight times (although the actual hardware never meant much to him—he kept his first MVP trophy in the back of his mother's pickup truck). Why didn't McHale chase it with the same tenacity? ''He said it was no big deal to him,'' Bird said almost contemptuously. Well, it wasn't.

''I could have cared less,'' McHale said. ''I could never have won the MVP, no way. And rightfully so. And I don't have any problem with that. I'm not a long-term guy. I'm a short-term guy. I'm not worried about what will happen down the road. I'm worried about who we play tomorrow night.''

Parish could conceivably have been considered an MVP candidate, especially in the early 1980s. But he, too, thought his and McHale's chances of winning the award were ridiculous with Bird in the picture.

''No matter what type of year Kevin had, he wouldn't have won the MVP, not over Larry,'' Parish said. ''Larry always felt that Kevin had the potential to be an MVP, which he did, and any other place he would have been. But because of the way he played, no way he was going to be the MVP with Larry around here. No way. In Larry's mind, Kevin could have won it one year. But no way. Not while Larry was on this team. Anyplace else, Kevin would probably have won it two or three times, at least twice.''

But Parish also understood what drove Bird to make such a statement: it was Bird's way of trying to get more out of what he saw as an unfinished work. To paraphrase George Bernard Shaw, Bird looked at McHale and saw things that could be and asked, ''Why not?'' McHale looked at McHale and saw things that were and said, ''It's enough.''

''I think Larry respected Kevin as a person,'' Parish said. ''I think that Larry always felt that Kevin could be a lot better than he was. And I think that respect diminished somewhat over the years because Kevin, as we all know, had a tendency to coast. He had a very strong first quarter and fourth quarter and we rode him. But he'd always coast in the second and third. Larry always felt, 'I'm out here busting my hump, Chief [Parish] is out busting his hump, Kevin should be busting his hump also.'

"You look at Kevin's stats, he still had twenty-five points. But he could have had thirty points if he had pushed it for the whole time he played. It's like he [Bird] said, Kevin always had that mental cushion; he'd go out there with the mind-set in the first period, get ten or twelve points, and coast."

McHale has heard it all before and, frankly, thinks it's all rubbish.

"People thought I was coasting, but I wasn't," he said. "I've always had the ability to focus when I want to focus and to get narrow real quickly. And also to get broad two seconds later. It may have been during a time-out and I was talking, but when it was time to do something, I was completely focused on it. That's me. That'll be me for the rest of my life. I think you bring your personality to the court. You can't check it in the locker room and go out. That's part of me. Some people can't do that. They have to have a game face. I have a game face, but it's not there all the time. It's on the court when the play is going on. When the play stops, I find some humor in a lot of stuff. People get that perception [that he doesn't care], but it is a misperception. I know how hard I work at it and I know what I have to do to play. One thing I've always been proud of is that I've always prepared myself to play. If I'm not shooting well, I won't think anything of spending an hour or two in the gym and shoot. People never see that, but my teammates do. And they know I'll be the best basketball player I can be."

The whole McHale-as-MVP question became moot and irrelevant after March 11, when Larry Nance of the Suns stepped on McHale's right foot, causing a hairline fracture. Had McHale stopped playing then and rested—it was only a stress fracture at that point—he might have never faced surgery. But he also might not have played again that season. He didn't know he had a fracture; he suspected it, but the medical response said otherwise.

"People kept telling me, 'It's in your head.' I said, 'No, it's not. It hurts all the time. It hurts at night, during the day, all the time.' At that time, our medical staff would say, 'Ice it and forget about it.' But that was not going to work. I had played on it so long. I shouldn't have. In the Detroit series [the Eastern Conference finals], it fractured all the way through. I went to turn on it and it felt like someone stuck a poker in my foot. It was white hot. I should have probably stopped then. I would have been in a cast for four weeks and been fine for the next season."

But he didn't stop there. In the first round of the playoffs, some six weeks after the Nance incident, he was still uncertain why he was in constant pain. Then the Chicago Bulls' team physician, Dr. John Hefferon, took a look at the X rays while the Celtics were finishing off Michael Jordan & Co. in the first round and found the fracture. Hefferon had spent the last year looking at X rays of another important broken foot—Jordan's—and he knew what to look for.

Once word of the break leaked out, a decision had to be made: to play or not to play? One of the true inanities of the Celtics organization is its policy toward injured players. The organization leaves the final decision to the player because, allegedly, he knows his body better than anyone else. Consequently, no one stepped in to tell McHale, "Uh, Kevin, you've got a broken foot and you're going to the hospital." Instead, McHale selected the basketball court over the OR.

He went through the 1987 playoffs limping and wincing. After missing one game against the Bulls and another against the Bucks, he remained in the lineup throughout both the Pistons and Lakers series, while his foot worsened by the day. It was absurd, but McHale kept listening to his inner voice—the one Bird always doubted he had—saying, "Go for it," as he pushed himself forward. His playoff numbers were, and still are, astounding. He averaged 21.1 points and 9.2 rebounds and shot 58 percent from the field, all in 39.3 minutes a game. "I never knew how good I was until I had to play on one foot," he joked. "I'd still get twenty points and eight or nine rebounds. I said to myself, 'Damn, if there was a league for one-footed players, I'd be All-Pro.'

"I had never been hurt up to that point. I think back now, and you don't want to sound greedy, because I have had a great career, but boy, I wonder what would have happened if I hadn't gotten hurt. That was the first time I realized what happens when you get hurt in this league and you have a major injury. It really takes a lot out of you. The league takes a lot out of you when you're healthy. It all wears on you.''

The Big Three's dominance was never more apparent than in Game 7 against the Bucks. The Celtics had won three of the first four games and then, inexplicably, lost Game 5 at home, their first home defeat in thirty-three games. Parish sprained his ankle and missed Game 6, which the Bucks also won.

Game 7 was close all the way. The Bucks got a huge break when Sidney Moncrief's shot at the end of the third quarter—clearly taken after the buzzer—was allowed to stand. Milwaukee led by 8 with 5:22 remaining after a basket by Ricky Pierce and things looked bleak for Boston. To make matters worse, or so it appeared, Ainge injured his knee and did not return. But Sichting came in and provided a big spark. And the Big Three stepped up with their final frontcourt trifecta of the year as Bird (31 points and 10 rebounds), McHale (26 and 15), and Parish (23 and 19) were relentless. Ten of McHale's rebounds were offensive; 11 of Parish's were. Second chances begat third chances, which resulted in baskets. And Boston rallied down the stretch to win, 119–113.

That victory set the stage for one of the three most memorable, nerve-racking, emotionally draining playoff series of the Big Three's days. The first was the conference final against the 76ers in 1981, when the Celtics rallied from a 3–1 deficit. The second was the 1984 finals against the Lakers. In 1987, there was a new adversary, the Detroit Pistons. And there was no one on the Sixers or Lakers who could anger the Celtics more than Bill Laimbeer. That alone made the Boston-Detroit series noteworthy.

Inevitably, the Celtics' dominance in the East had to end sometime. The conference had had champions in bunches in the 1980s. Philadelphia was the early kingpin, save only for its uncharacteristic collapse in 1981. The Celtics won four straight titles from 1984 to 1987. And the Pistons were next, breaking through for three straight conference titles to close the decade.

Detroit was in many ways an implausible pretender, given its dearth of basketball tradition or success. The team had been in the NBA since 1948, only two years after the league formed, starting as the Fort Wayne Zollner Pistons (after the owner, Fred Zollner) before moving to Detroit in 1957. Once it became the Detroit Pistons, the franchise became the very embodiment of futility, posting exactly three winning seasons in twenty-six years. Chris Ford was drafted by the Pistons in the second round of the 1972 draft and played for six full seasons. He got an idea of how things would be when coach Earl Lloyd was fired seven games into his rookie year. Ford played for five coaches in his six years in Detroit.

"There was always constant turnover," he said. "There was no direction to the franchise. When M. L. [Carr] came in [1976], everyone said it was going to be different, but it wasn't. Still, though, we made the playoffs four of the six years I was there." In two of those four years, however, the Pistons had a losing record. But in 1973–74 the Pistons won fifty-two games, had the fourth-best record in the NBA, and lost in the conference semifinals to Chicago, losing Game 7, 96–94.

Until Chuck Daly came aboard as coach in 1983, the Detroit Pistons had never even had consecutive winning seasons. It was, as they say, not your ideal situation. But Daly had been through hoop hell in Cleveland two years earlier, lasting forty-one games during Ted Stepien's reign of terror as owner and going 9–32. By comparison, Detroit, even with its historical suffering and on-the-court inadequacies, was like the old IBM.

The Celtics and Pistons had no basketball rivalry whatsoever until their fateful clashes in the 1980s. This was due to Detroit's year-in and year-out hopelessness and also to the fact that, until 1967, the Pistons were in the NBA's Western Division. They settled into the East when the NBA admitted San Diego and Seattle, but until the 1980s they had only one playoff meeting with Boston, an uneventful six-gamer in 1968, which the Celtics won. But the Pistons helped the Celtics on occasion throughout the years, sending them Ford (for an unwanted and unused Earl Tatum) and then giving up the two number one draft picks for Bob McAdoo to complete the M. L. Carr compensation deal.

The 1987 Pistons were vastly different from the team the Celtics had beaten only two years earlier. Daly had presided over a dramatic personnel and philosophical make-over. Gone were Kelly Tripucka, John Long, Kent Benson, Earl Cureton, Terry Tyler, and Dan Roundfield. All that remained from that squad were Laimbeer, Isiah Thomas, and Vinnie Johnson. Daly had acquired Adrian Dantley for Tripucka and drafted Joe Dumars in 1985. Then, in 1986, two rookies arrived to complete the transformation: John Salley and Dennis Rodman. The Pistons beat you with muscle, defense, and opportunism. They had just eliminated the division champion Atlanta Hawks in five games and were confident and ready to dislodge the Celtics. Thomas had even gone on a local cable show in New York and predicted a Detroit sweep.

The series produced some incredible tension and outright animosity. But the first game was neither tense nor acrimonious—it was awful, the *Ishtar* of the series. The Celtics were without Danny Ainge, who was still bothered by a knee injury, but the Pistons could not capitalize. (Ainge, as it turned out, also had a dislocated finger. That, too, had happened in the Milwaukee series when he caught the finger in Jack Sikma's wristband.) Parish was immense in the opener, scoring 31 points. Detroit started strong and had 12 points off fast breaks in the first quarter, but then fizzled. Rodman was hit with four quick fouls in ten minutes trying to guard Bird, and the Celtics won, 104–91. Afterward, Daly said his team appeared hyper and overanxious and Thomas, who was 6 for 24 and looked dreadful, even suggested that the Celtics' injuries were more imagined than real. "Tell him I've got some X rays he can look at," McHale said, shaking his head.

Thomas then tried to take over Game 2. He scored 25 points in the first half and the Pistons led 65–56 in the third quarter. Four minutes later the Celtics had a 68–67 lead after a 12–2 run, and Boston led 82–81 after three. In the fourth quarter, the Celtics tried every way imaginable to give the game away. They went six minutes without a basket. They fouled the Pistons at the wrong time, but Detroit missed seventeen free throws. The Celtics even had to resort to using Greg Kite down the stretch, but he converted a huge dunk in the closing minutes and Boston somehow won, 110–101. Boston took a 2–0 lead out to Detroit, knowing that no team had ever beaten the Celtics after trailing 2–0.

Ainge was still out for Game 3, but his absence was insignificant. The Pistons took the lead for good, 12–10 on a spinner by Adrian Dantley, who had all 25 of his points in the first half, 16 via the fast break. The hoop was part of a 22–6 Detroit run and pushed Detroit out to a 20-point lead at the break. Parish sat out the second half after aggravating his sore left ankle and, with 10:08 to play, Bird used one of his familiar up-fakes under the Detroit basket to get Rodman airborne. But as Bird waited for Rodman to descend, Laimbeer pulled Bird to the floor in a most awkward way. Bird was furious, falling on Laimbeer and then punching the Pistons center. When they were separated, Bird flung the ball at Laimbeer's head and connected. "Just like all of Larry's passes. Right on the money," Jerry Sichting noted. "I was just throwing it to the referee and Bill's face got in the way," Bird said. "But this is the first time I can remember being in a fight when I wasn't in the wrong. Wholly." The fight did nothing to alter what was already an obvious outcome; the Pistons won 122–104.

Game 4 was the next day. When the teams lined up for the center tap, Bird refused to shake Laimbeer's hand. Boos rained down from the football stands in the hideous Silverdome. Laimbeer then exacted his revenge on the floor. Detroit led from wire to wire before the largest playoff crowd in Pistons history (27,387) and used a 15–2 run in the third quarter to turn a reasonably close game into a runaway. Detroit led by 16 after three and got the lead out to as many as 32 in the fourth before settling for a 145–119 rout. The 145 points represented the most allowed by the Celtics in a playoff game, a stinging insult. Even worse, Laimbeer had 20 points on 10-of-13 shooting from the field. Parish had to leave the game with 8:45 left in the third quarter when his ankle acted up again. Dantley had 32 points and Vinnie Johnson added 25 as the Pistons shot 64 percent. The five Boston starters attempted only 5 free throws.

If this wasn't a lost weekend, what was? Reserve Sam Vincent led the Celtics in scoring in both games. The Celtics led for only 3:44 of the ninety-six minutes, all in the first quarter of Game 3.

Bird said the only thing he got out of the weekend was a good punch on Laimbeer.

As the Pistons prepared to come to Boston for Game 5 with the series knotted at 2–2, Laimbeer became an obvious lightning rod for the Celtics and their fans. He already had gotten into it with Bird. He was loathed in Boston (and virtually everywhere else, too, except Detroit). "I hope the crowd doesn't do anything drastic," said Bird. "I don't like him, but I don't want somebody to hurt him, either. Our crowd didn't like him before this whole thing started." It was also announced that Bird had been fined $2,000 and Laimbeer $5,000 for their fight in Game 3.

The scene shifted back to Boston for what would be one of the most unforgettable playoff games in the franchise's history. Two members of the Big Three would be showcased in this game, but for vastly different reasons. Laimbeer was a central figure in each subplot.

Before they got to know Laimbeer, the Celtics thought he was just someone to be mocked and derided. They mimicked his deliberate and pensive free-throw shooting style and his crybaby antics. And he wasn't the only Piston who was belittled. Vinnie Johnson was derogatively known as the Link (as in "missing link"). Terry Tyler, the Celtics felt, might one day be a real NBA player if he ever learned to dribble. But once the teams started playing for high stakes, the Celtics' attitude toward Laimbeer changed. They quickly discovered that he was not simply someone to mock. He was someone to watch out for, because he might hurt you.

In Game 5, Parish finally snapped. Tired of Laimbeer's incessant elbows and the general trend of the series, he unloaded four punches on an unsuspecting Laimbeer. To this day, the only thing he regrets about the incident is that he couldn't make a complete fist because he had tendinitis.

"He had elbowed me in the back once. Then, he elbowed me in the rear another time. The only thing I said to him was 'Watch your elbows.' Because we all throw them. I've thrown my share of them. And he told me to go fuck myself. So I just let him have it," Parish said. "There's no excuse for losing your composure. And that was very unlike me because I always pride myself on being in control.

I can't ever remember any other time being in an altercation like that. Of that magnitude.''

Incredibly, Parish was neither penalized or ejected. Referee Jess Kersey seemingly had a perfect view of the barrage but did nothing. Despite the obvious noncall, the Pistons kept their composure in the game and led by 4 with three minutes left. Boston rallied to lead again and things seesawed until Thomas hit a tough turnaround jumper from the foul line over Sichting with seventeen seconds left. Boston trailed 107–106. Bird, who had 36 in the game, got the call and drove the lane for a runner. Rodman came flying out of nowhere and blocked the shot and Sichting could not keep the ball in play. There were five seconds left and the Pistons had the ball, the game, and the series. Or so it seemed. Diagonally across the floor, Daly screamed for a time-out. His call went unheeded. Thomas had the ball and was preparing to inbound it, thinking the Celtics would quickly foul.

"I should have called time out," he said. "I should not have thrown the pass. You can see I should not have thrown the pass. Or I should have thrown it harder. Or Bill [Laimbeer] should have come for it. All I can say is they stole the ball and won the game.''

The "they" is Bird, who was lurking unsuspected at the foul line as Thomas made the fateful pass to Laimbeer. He then bolted to the end line, where Laimbeer was waiting for the pass, snatched the ball, and, remarkably, stayed inbounds while off balance. Bird briefly thought about shooting; there were four seconds left. But Dennis Johnson made a beeline for the basket, and Bird saw him and made a perfect pass. Johnson was forced to his left hand by Dumars, but still managed to make the basket. The Celtics won the game, and all anyone could talk about was Bird's steal.

"We got lucky," Bird admitted. "I was going to foul Laimbeer real quick, but then I saw the pass was lobbed and I had a chance to steal it. It seemed to hang up there forever.'' And the Celtics, instead of facing elimination, now had the Pistons on the brink.

The next day, Pistons general manager Jack McCloskey ripped the referees and also took some shots at Red Auerbach for influencing the officials by going on television as an expert analyst and moaning about the Pistons' strong-arm tactics. Auerbach denied such underhanded behavior, though, of course, he did just that throughout the series, on television and to anyone else who asked. Daly even got into it, calling Parish's attack on Laimbeer a "sucker punch" and wondering why Laimbeer was the target instead of the more ornery Rick Mahorn. The insinuation, of course, was that Mahorn would hit back.

When Parish arrived in Detroit for Game 6, the league had done what Kersey had failed to do. It fined Parish a then record $7,500. It suspended him for Game 6, meaning he had to turn around and fly back to Boston. Laimbeer got nothing. Said Jan Volk, the Celtics' general manager, "It's a shame the consummate provocateur is still roaming the hardwood." The way the series was progressing, or regressing, it would have been foolish and even dangerous to bring Parish into the Silverdome that night. Bird was told about the fine at the Celtics' hotel and responded quizzically, 'What? All that for that Boy Scout deed?'' (Whenever Laimbeer made the All-Star team, Bird rued the day, because that meant he'd have to be his teammate and try, unsuccessfully of course, to be quasicordial. It never worked. Bird was elated one year when he found out that Laimbeer did not make the All-Star team. "Then I won't have to get on the bus and listen to him say, 'Good morning, Larry,' and I won't have to say, 'Fuck you, Bill,' back to him.'')

Parish received a ton of mail after the Laimbeer incident, all of it positive. "I never realized how popular I was," he said. He respected Laimbeer's dedication to the game and competitive drive, but that was where it stopped. "One reason he is not liked around the league is because he is not a clean player. We all fought, kicked, held, and threw elbows, but no one out there was trying to cause the other guy bodily harm. He's the only player I've ever seen that is actually trying to hurt you. What he does is not basketball. I understand he's trying to compensate for his shortcomings, athletically, but his behavior has no place in basketball. I think that's one reason nobody likes him. You have to respect him as a player. But as a person? Very little respect. He's the only person I've ever met that has a negative reputation and actually gets off on it. That tells you something about the person right there."

Without Parish, the Celtics were again outplayed in the Silverdome and lost Game 6, 113–105. It was time for another climactic Game 7. And it would measure up against some of the great ones.

Once again, the Pistons seemed cursed by the Boston Garden fates. Dantley and Vinnie Johnson dove for a loose ball and banged heads. Johnson went to the bench, Dantley to Massachusetts General Hospital with a concussion. Those who watched Dantley wondered why he picked that specific time and place to dive for a loose ball for the first time in his career. Still, the Pistons stayed close. Dumars was on an incredible roll—he finished with 35 points—and the game was tied with four minutes to play. The next sixty-five seconds defined the game and the series. Once again, the Big Three rose to the occasion.

The telling stretch started when Danny Ainge missed a jumper. Bird got the rebound, one of his 9, but missed. McHale got the next rebound, got the ball to Bird, but Larry missed again. McHale got another rebound, kept it above his head, but missed a short follow from the lane, still on his tiptoes. Then Parish stepped up and got McHale's miss, but his putback was blocked by Rodman. The ball went to Bird, who took the ball out and eventually, sixty-five seconds after the sequence started, got the ball back to Ainge. He swished a three-pointer. The hoop gave Boston the lead for good. The Celtics held on to win, 117–114, and an exhausted Bird admitted afterward, "I wish we didn't have to play another series."

The Pistons, meanwhile, were a ticking time bomb. Daly had warned his team to think before it spoke to reporters. Some did. Thomas and Rodman did not. They ignited a firestorm by suggesting that Bird would be considered just another good player if he were black instead of white.

Bird never saw the tempest for what it eventually became, but everyone else did. And, a week later, during the showcase NBA finals, commissioner David Stern brought Thomas out to Los Angeles to stand by Bird for a *mea culpa* news conference. Bird pretty much deflated whatever controversy may have lingered by insisting that the perceived slight did not bother him and, seeing as how he was the target, if he was not offended, why should anyone else be? Thomas tiptoed through the tumult and left Los Angeles and the crisis, if there ever was one, finally resolved. But the Pistons in general and Laimbeer in particular had made themselves the Celtics' hated rival not only for what they said, but for the way they played.

"I definitely looked forward to playing them," Parish said. "I think I enjoyed kicking their butts more than, say, Philadelphia or Los Angeles because of their attitude. They were a team of bullies. The thing about Detroit, the thing I didn't like about them, you know they're bullies but they know you can't do anything about it because of the heavy fines that would be leveled against you. So that made them even bigger bullies because they'd do something they shouldn't do and then stand back and say, 'What are you gonna do about it?' You know, like egg you on and dare you to retaliate."

The Celtics-Lakers final looked to be a mismatch. Los Angeles had picked up Mychal Thompson and won sixty-five games in the regular season, taking its division by sixteen games. It had lost one playoff game in three series. Magic Johnson was on pace to win his first Most Valuable Player award and the Lakers were healthy and bent on another title.

The 1987 NBA finals would be the third Celtics-Lakers meeting of the Bird/Magic era and the worst of the three. The first, in 1984, was clearly the best, although the rematch a year later provided the Lakers with sweet revenge. This time, however, the teams were not on an even playing field. The Lakers clearly were the superior team, and the Celtics' injuries only exacerbated their plight. Had this been the 1986 team, the series would have been truly great. But now, instead of Bill Walton, K. C. Jones had to rely on Greg Kite. Instead of Scott Wedman, he had Darren Daye. And, for the first time since Bird arrived in Boston, the Celtics entered a playoff series without the homecourt advantage.

The Lakers gave an indication of how things were going to be when they opened Game 1 with 7 straight points as Kareem sank a baby hook, James Worthy converted an offensive rebound, and Magic went coast to coast for a three-point play. Bird had 32 points, including eleven straight shots in the second and third quarter, but Boston could not stop the Lakers' running game and L.A. prevailed, 126–113. Game 2 was even more lopsided, as the Lakers outscored the Celtics by 15 in the second quarter and led by an eye-opening 75–56 at halftime. Five Lakers scored between 21 and 24 points and

Johnson, who had 22, also added 20 assists. Michael Cooper killed the Celtics with six three-pointers and the Celtics looked hopelessly outclassed. Bird seemed to sum up Boston's destitute condition. Asked how to stop the Lakers, he shrugged and said simply, "I have no idea."

Boston returned home and promptly fell behind 29–22 at the end of the first quarter of Game 3. Parish was in foul trouble and Boston was in real trouble. But the game turned soon after Kite entered and started bumping people, rebounding (he had 9 in only twenty-two minutes), and blocking shots. He had no points, but that seemed immaterial. Somehow, he rejuvenated a lifeless team. McHale went forty-three minutes on his broken foot and had 21 points and 10 rebounds. Bird went forty-four minutes and had 30 points and 12 rebounds. The Celtics converted on fifteen of sixteen possessions and Kite even blocked Magic. Boston won 109–103.

The Celtics came out smoking in Game 4, leading by 16 in the third quarter and by 8 with 3:30 to play. The Lakers kept chipping away, though, and took a 104–103 lead in the final minute of the game. Bird responded by nailing a three-pointer with twelve seconds left, giving Boston a 106–104 lead. Then Abdul-Jabbar was fouled and had a chance to tie the game. He made the first free throw and missed the second, but McHale wasn't able to control the rebound and the Lakers had one more chance.

With seven seconds left, Worthy was the Lakers' first option, but he was covered, so Magic drove the lane and launched a short hook. As the shot sailed toward the basket, it summed up the series symbolically as it floated over the outstretched arms of Parish, McHale, and Bird and hit nothing but net. The Lakers sweated out a last-second miss by Bird at the buzzer, and the game belonged to Los Angeles.

When he was asked about his dramatic and surprising last-minute hook shot, Magic said, "I learned it from Kareem and practiced it all the time. What can I say? In the last two minutes, you saw some of the best basketball ever." Afterward, referee Earl Strom had to weather some Auerbachian bombast, prompted by the Lakers' 32–16 advantage in free throws. Strom dismissed the outburst. And

Bird was left to speak wistfully of what might have been. "I've been up three–one a lot and I know what it feels like," he said.

The Celtics regrouped to take Game 5, as all five starters scored at least 21 points and the Lakers looked wrung out from having to spend a week in Boston. In their minds, they had won the series on Magic's hook. All that remained was the formality of wrapping it up in the Forum.

While the Lakers looked forward to the trip home, the flight to Los Angeles for the Celtics seemed to have a perfunctory and futile air to it from the beginning. Things seemed even worse when the Celtics boarded the bus after losing the series in Game 6, 106–93, and drove down Century Boulevard for the flight home. McHale was limping home, awaiting surgery for the first time in his life. Parish had tendinitis in his right elbow and did not have the full extension of his right arm. His ankles, too, were shot. Time and again he hit the floor, stayed there, rose to one knee, paused some more, then, ever so gingerly, rose to both feet and walked delicately back into the play.

In one short year, everything had gone from the sublime to the surreal. Many thought that something needed to be done, a house-cleaning or, at worse, cleaning of a few rooms. General manager Jan Volk was not thinking along those lines. In his mind, this was the best starting five in basketball. It had been a case of injuries and unexpected delays. How could they have anticipated Walton's quirky year? Or Wedman's? And who would ever have imagined McHale's problems? No, Volk thought, everything is OK. "I think we have the nucleus," he said, "that can last several more years."

And he was correct. Five years later, the only players left from the team that had ceded its title to the Lakers were Larry Bird, Kevin McHale, and Robert Parish. Every other player was somewhere else.

But what was starting to unfold was the gradual, inevitable deterioration of the Big Three. McHale was the first to unravel. He had made the decision to play hurt and he would never again be the player he was. He no longer could go out on the floor and guard the small forwards with the effectiveness he used to have. He lost his thrust, although he would remain nearly unstoppable in the post unless he was double-teamed. Injuries always happened to the other guy, he once thought. He now knew better. He would never mock Walton again, as he frequently did in 1986, when Big Bill couldn't play. Then, McHale had watched Walton cross the floor and remarked that he would probably starve if his mailbox was not attached to his house.

McHale's foot operation was a biggie. It also was the beginning of what became almost an annual ritual: summer surgery. He had major foot surgery in the summer of 1987, an operation on his left thumb in 1990, and one on his ankle in 1991. "Kevin ended every season with some kind of medical problem," said team physician Dr. Arnold Scheller. "The season never officially came to an end until we operated on Kevin."

And it wasn't much longer before Bird, too, became a regular patient. And when the Big Three started to make as much medical news as basketball news, the Celtics became a team in limbo, unwilling to rend asunder what they had so carefully brought together, and unable to stop the ineluctable slide into mediocrity. There was time, however, for one final stand.

CHAPTER 7

The Downfall

The extensive surgery on Kevin McHale's right foot in the summer of 1987 was a procedure from which he would need months to recuperate. The navicular bone had split like a piece of firewood under the repeated strain of NBA playoff bumps and grinds. A short screw was implanted to keep the bone together. The screw remains and probably will never be removed. There also was a bone graft.

While McHale was getting accustomed to crutches and a cast, Larry Bird was home in Indiana, working like a zealot to come back and win another championship. It seemed possible. The Lakers had needed six games to beat the Celtics, and that was as good a Lakers team as Magic Johnson directed in the 1980s. The injury problems from the year before would be over. And maybe K. C. Jones, who had been accused of relying too much on his starters, had learned his lesson about the value of substitutions.

Before Bird headed home, Dan Dyrek presented him with a four-inch-thick notebook filled with flexibility exercises, strengthening exercises, cardiovascular exercises, and nutritional guidelines. Bird followed the recommendations like a dutiful schoolboy. "He came back lean and mean," Dyrek said of Bird. Indeed he did.

One of the great what-ifs of Larry Bird's career is what he would have accomplished if he had finished the 1987–88 season the way he began it. He was, without question, in the best shape of his life. He was still only thirty. It is neither presumptuous nor farfetched to suggest that he might have eclipsed any and all that he had achieved until then had his body not rebelled.

There were early signs that Bird's rigorous summer regimen had paid handsome dividends. In an exhibition game at Brigham Young's Marriott Center, Bird displayed his new spring and bounce by following a Jerry Sichting miss with a two-handed dunk, something Dominique Wilkins does with regularity but Bird rarely even tried. The stunned Boston bench erupted, and Bird tried to hide a smirk.

This was something new and, for Celtics opponents, something quite frightening. In addition to all the other facets of his game, Bird now had added a quick first step to his repertoire. What would be next? Left-handed threes? In the second game of the season, Bird scored 47 points against the Bullets, which included a three-point field goal to tie the game and another hoop in overtime to win it. Two games later, he became the first Celtic ever to post a 40/20 game with 44 points and 22 rebounds against Indiana.

But six days later, with the Celtics playing in Cleveland, Bird attempted a behind-the-back dribble and strained both of his Achilles tendons on the same play. He already had bone spurs in the area and they snapped at the base of the tendon. Although the bone spurs were nothing new, the double Achilles strain pushed his injuries from the "I can live with it" stage to the "We're going to have to do something about this" stage. He would miss only four games, but the spurs would be a growing concern.

The Celtics' new trainer, Ed Lacerte, quickly discovered Bird's aversion to discussing injuries. Bird told Lacerte to say nothing and Lacerte said nothing. Bird was a difficult patient because he would ignore the cause of his discomfort—even lie about it—until he absolutely, unswervingly trusted the person in charge. He barely knew Lacerte at that point. Team physician Arnold Scheller was in the same position. Both had come on board in 1987 after the disastrous handling of McHale's foot the previous spring.

"We started as an adversarial relationship, until I realized that he was challenging you and then gauges you on how you respond," Scheller said. "But he got me mad. We're fine now, though."

While Bird started the season on fire, McHale was on the injured list, a situation that was neither unanticipated nor alarming. He missed the first fourteen games of the season and then was activated at the end of November. The Celtics were 10–4 in his absence and comfortably ahead of the pack; no one else in the division was even at .500. And when he returned against Atlanta on December 1, he promptly lit up the Hawks for 22 points in twenty-two minutes, converting 7 of 13 field goals and 8 of 9 free throws. ''I don't know how much he's practiced,'' Hawks coach Mike Fratello said before the game, ''but if you're asking me if you're worried he's going to score every time he touches the ball, the answer is, of course you are.'' McHale was back in the starting lineup the next night against the Nets and was even more destructive, scoring 23 points on 9-of-11 shooting and grabbing 8 rebounds while going 5 for 5 from the line. He had 20 and 23 points in his next two games, signifying, if nothing else, that he had not lost his shooting eye over the summer.

McHale went on to lead the league in field-goal percentage that season, matching his 60.4 percent from the year before. His 22.6-point average marked the first drop-off since he'd entered the league; unfortunately for him, it was a trend that would continue in the following seasons. He again made the All-NBA Defensive first team, though he admitted now that his reputation may have had something to do with it.

Bird missed the four games with the Achilles injury and two more inconsequential late-season games with a bum ankle. He won his third straight three-point shooting title, besting Dale Ellis in the finals. (Ellis would win the following year, in Bird's absence, prompting Bird to say, ''One day everyone will notice that one year and wonder where I was.'') He never liked the three-pointer, but he used it again and again, at one point going fifteen straight games with at least one. Against the Mavericks, he nailed one in the closing seconds to give the Celtics a 1-point win. Unbelievably, he was left uncovered as the Celtics made their final assault on the Dallas basket.

In February, he again had gone on the road and delivered a beauty in arguably his favorite haunt, Memorial Coliseum in Portland, scoring 40 in a Boston win. Five days later, the teams met again in

Boston and Bird scored 16 points in the fourth quarter—and 44 in the game—and the Celtics won 113–112. Those were just two of the eleven times he scored 40 or more in a game that season and he concluded his second straight 50/90 season, shooting 52.7 percent from the field and 91.6 percent from the line, both personal bests. His scoring average of 29.9 was also a career high.

And he also revealed his legendary toughness later in the season. In early March, he collided with Cleveland's Dell Curry and suffered an eye injury. How serious it was could not immediately be determined because Bird was, well, Bird, and Scheller still was the new guy.

"When I first saw him, he had double vision," Scheller said. "He was seeing two rims and he was still making the shots. But he wouldn't tell me. Then, he went into the shower and blew his nose and his eye dropped out of the socket. I said to myself, 'Now he's got a problem.' It wasn't a major fracture, but it had to heal. And then he didn't want to wear the goggles. Robert and D.J. [Dennis Johnson] told him to wise up. There just was a lot of emotional change spent trying to get it right while dealing with people who didn't."

Bird wore the goggles for the next four games, reluctantly, just long enough to get his goggled face on the cover of *Sports Illustrated*. At the foul line, he would push the goggles up on his forehead while he shot free throws. Nothing changed there; he made 53 straight at one point.

Parish saw his minutes decline dramatically with the addition of Mark Acres and, later, Artis Gilmore. Only in his first year in Boston did he average fewer minutes. Still, he shot a career-best 59 percent from the field, although his scoring average was his lowest as a Celtic, 14.3. But those numbers did not reflect Parish's defensive presence. They did, however, reflect the cakewalk the team had during the season.

The Celtics' only challenge in the regular season seemed to be that of Mother Nature herself. Bird missed the six games. McHale was out eighteen, most due to his late return from rehab. Parish missed five games. Bill Walton, who had hoped to be back after missing virtually all of 1986–87, underwent summer surgery and never returned. Still, the Celtics won fifty-seven games and, incredibly, were the only team in the Atlantic Division to play .500 ball. They won the division by nineteen games. New York and Washington tied for second with 38–44 records.

The Knicks, in their first year under the hyper Rick Pitino, beat out Indiana for the last playoff spot, and that meant facing the Celtics in the first round. The two teams had not met in the postseason since the memorable series in 1984, mainly because injuries had destroyed New York in subsequent years.

And the two teams had changed personas in that span. In 1984, the Celtics ran the ball while the Knicks preferred the slow tempo. In 1988, the Knicks pressed everywhere and relied as much on gimmicks as anything else. The Celtics liked to slam the ball down an opponent's throat.

Boston won the first two games easily, 112–92 and 128–102. The only concern in those first two games was the status of McHale, who suffered a corneal abrasion in Game 1 when his eyeball was scraped by Bill Cartwright's fingertip. Blurred vision or not, McHale went out in the second half and finished with 19 points, 7 rebounds, and 3 blocks. He was taken to the hospital after the game and was cleared to play for the rest of the series.

Before the series resumed in New York, it was announced that K. C. Jones would leave the bench at the end of the season and that longtime assistant Jimmy Rodgers would take over for the 1988–89 season. Jones had been criticized for playing the starters too many minutes and ignoring the bench, particularly Reggie Lewis and Brad Lohaus. No one explained whether Jones had jumped before he was pushed or whether he had made the decision without any pressure.

In Game 3, Bird had 20 points and 12 assists, but was unable to contain the slippery Johnny Newman and went into a shooting drought as the Knicks turned an 8-point deficit into a 10-point lead. Patrick Ewing then went 10 for 10 from the line in the fourth quarter and the Knicks carved out a 109–100 victory in Madison Square Garden. Two nights later, the Celtics reverted to form and closed out the Knicks, 102–94, setting the stage for their second meeting with the Hawks in three years.

The Atlanta Hawks still basically looked like the NBA champions in warm-ups but became something quite different in games. They had a "Body by Fisher, Mind by Fisher-Price" reputation, which they did little to dispel. They always seemed to be on edge, afraid to make mistakes. But when their undeniable athleticism emerged, they could be a joy to watch with their running and dunking exhibitions.

In the opener, Bird set the tone with a 24-point first quarter, making his first nine shots, starting with a runner in the lane. The quarter represented a Celtics' playoff record and was enough to keep the Celtics on top all the way, resulting in a 110–101 victory. It was sloppy, however, as the teams combined for 44 turnovers. Parish also came up big, with 22 points and 14 rebounds. Boston won Game 2, 108–97, but neither triumph was convincing, and the sense was that had either game been played anywhere but Boston Garden, the Hawks easily could have won both.

In Game 3, the Celtics shot atrociously: they made only 8 field goals in the entire second half (or 1 less than Bird had made by himself in the first nine minutes of Game 1) and went one eleven-minute stretch without a basket. In that span, Boston had 24 possessions without a basket, shot 0 for 11, and had 3 turnovers. They stayed close due to free throws before collapsing, as the Hawks won 110–92. The Celtics had another horrifying stretch in Game 4, losing a 10-point led in the second quarter. They turned the ball over 22 times, which led to 30 Atlanta points. Doc Rivers set an Atlanta playoff record with 22 assists and the Hawks prevailed, 118–109, tying the series at 2–2.

Game 5 victories for the Celtics had become a tradition at Boston Garden, especially in series that were tied 2–2. The Big Three had played five such games and won them all. Would the trend continue? Kevin Willis emerged as a monster with 27 points and 14 rebounds, offsetting a 24-point, 13-rebound gem from Parish. Rivers hit a huge basket at the end and the Hawks won, 112–104. Atlanta now led the series 3–2 and could close out the Celtics at home. And, with Jones retiring, this very well could be his last game. But Boston eked out a 102–100 victory; Parish preserved the win at the end when he disrupted a shot by Cliff Levingston. Atlanta's party, if there was to be one, was going to have to wait.

Bird, who had quieted down considerably since his Game 1 *tour de force*, told the Hawks and their fans to forget it. "They had a chance to beat us and they didn't. I think Sunday is going to be a big win for the Boston Celtics." And it was. It will be remembered as one of the classic Game 7's, which, had it been against a traditional foe like the Sixers or Lakers, would have qualified as the Game of the Century.

The Celtics were now getting accustomed to Game 7's. The year before, they had played two in a row, becoming just the sixth team in NBA history to go the distance in consecutive series and the third to win both deciding games (against Milwaukee and Detroit). Now, in their first seven-game series the following year, they were again pushed to the maximum. McHale had 33 points that day, including 21 in the first half, along with 13 rebounds and 4 blocked shots, but no one remembers any of that. This was the Larry & Dominique Show, and it was as good a performance of "Anything You Can Do, I Can Do Better" as you're likely to see.

Both teams were exceptional all game, shooting a combined 59 percent and committing only 15 turnovers. In the fourth quarter, the teams combined to shoot 72 percent, with the Celtics connecting on 12 of 15. One of those misses belonged to Bird. So did nine of the baskets.

"Larry just took over the game," McHale said. "It had been awhile since I saw that look in his eye, the one that says, 'Give me the ball and get out of the way.' But he had it."

Bird had 20 points in the fourth quarter and 34 in the game. Wilkins had 16 of his 47 in the fourth. The shoot-out began with what Bird called "a lucky shot," a turnaround in the lane. He also was fouled by Antoine Carr and made the shot. The Celtics led 93–90 with 8:56 to play. Seventeen seconds later, Wilkins camped on the sideline and drained a three-pointer, tying the score.

With 5:57 remaining and Boston leading 99–97, Wilkins tied the game on a twenty-foot sideline fallaway. Fifteen seconds later, Bird answered with a ten-foot, left-handed leaner. Wilkins was back seventeen seconds later with a jumper from the top of the key, tying the game at 101. On and on it went. Bird hit a seventeen-foot turnaround (103–101, Boston). Wilkins banked in a ten-footer

(103–103). Bird snapped the game's final tie (105–105) with a fourteen-foot turnaround from the lane. That started a 7–0 run, which he memorably capped with a nerveless three-pointer directly in front of the Atlanta bench, making the score 112–105 with 1:43 to play. But Wilkins kept the Hawks going, making a turnaround and then adding two free throws to pull the Hawks to within 112–109 with forty-seven seconds left. Bird wasn't through. He somehow invented a left-handed running scoop while splitting the Hawks defense like a fullback, giving Boston a 114–109 lead. Wilkins came back and scored off his own miss in just six seconds. Boston led 114–111 with twenty seconds to play.

Neither player made another basket after Wilkins's putback, but the Celtics kept things in control from the free-throw line and finished with a remarkable 118–116 victory. Wilkins had even deliberately missed a free throw with one second left, hoping for a rebound basket, which would have sent the game into overtime.

Red Auerbach, who watched the game on television while awaiting an honorary degree at American International College in Springfield, Massachusetts (the ceremony was delayed until the game ended), later called it "the greatest quarter I've ever seen in forty-two years of basketball" and lauded Wilkins as a latter-day Jerry West, going down valiantly and then saying all the right things afterward. McHale said the only thing in his personal scrapbook that could top Game 7 was his first eagle on the golf course, though he claimed, unconvincingly, not to know what he had done that day. "The guy I was playing with told me it was two better than what I was supposed to shoot. I said, 'I like the sound of that.' " Afterward, Bird was told that Wayne Gretzky & Co. would be playing in the Garden later that night in the Stanley Cup finals. "This is my building," he snapped. Who could doubt him?

The dramatic win extended K. C. Jones's coaching career another two weeks, but the Pistons were waiting for him and the rest of the Celtics. They had a full week's rest after eliminating the Bulls. The Celtics, meanwhile, had to do something about their bench. The five starters had averaged between 37.3 and 44 minutes against the Hawks. The most utilized sub was Jim Paxson. He averaged 7.4 minutes. Jones had two frisky, promising rookies on the team in

Lewis and Lohaus, but he was disinclined to use either of them for any prolonged or consistent stretch. Had he integrated them into the mix early—as Chuck Daly had done with Dennis Rodman and John Salley the year before—he might well have had two valuable assets by playoff time. Instead, he just had two more benchwarmers.

The nine-deep Pistons, meanwhile, were essentially the same team from the year before, with one notable exception: 7-1 James Edwards, an NBA veteran who had come over from Phoenix in midyear wearing a "Yard Sale" sign around his neck (the price was someone named Ron Moore and a second-round pick) and who would soon be regarded as indispensable. With Ricky Mahorn's back acting up, Edwards was needed for defensive help against McHale and Parish. And his back-to-the-basket game gave the Pistons something they lacked: a legitimate low-post scorer, although Adrian Dantley could also post up, an incredible feat given the fact that he was only 6-4.

The Celtics again had the homecourt advantage and the Pistons, who had gone six years and twenty-one games in Boston Garden without a win, were determined to end the jinx. The two teams had split the regular-season series, 3–3, with an NBA record crowd of 61,983 witnessing one Detroit victory in the Silverdome. That game may be remembered for something more than basketball. Coach Chuck Daly, a fashion plate, was horrified to discover he had neither a coat nor a tie for the game. That's akin to Yehudi Menuhin showing up at a concert without his violin. So he dispatched assistant Dick Versace to find him threads and Versace succeeded, driving like Gene Hackman in *The French Connection* on the way back to the Silverdome through the gridlock.

The Pistons wasted no time ending the jinx, winning Game 1 104–96 behind Isiah Thomas's 35 points. There was no gloating or glee in the Detroit locker room. They had learned their lesson from the year before. Daly repeatedly referred to the Celtics as a snake that would not die, no matter how many times you chopped off its head. Crude, but true. Or so he tried to believe.

Then came the Phantom Three in Game 2. The game stretched into two overtimes and the Pistons figured they had things under control when Isiah Thomas nailed a huge trey with seconds left, giving them a 109–106 lead. Boston then botched the inbounds play, as Bird fumbled the pass. McHale scooped up the ball, promptly let it fly, and made the shot. The referees signaled a game-tying three-pointer. The Pistons screamed that McHale's foot was on the line. Replays were inconclusive. The Celtics went on to win in the second overtime and tied the series.

"Even a blind pig can find an acorn once in a while," said McHale, then a thoroughly unlikely three-point threat, as he had not even attempted one all season and was 1 for 16 in his career, the only conversion coming in November 1983 in a game at Utah. "The key to my success in basketball is to never think."

The Pistons were hot, but kept their cool. Years later, Daly said in jest, "I should have good things to say about him [McHale]? After the way he tortured us over the years? With the three that wasn't a three?" But it counted. Parish had come up huge with 26 points and 13 rebounds while Bird clearly was struggling with his shot, going 6 for 20 in Game 2. He had gone 8 for 20 in the opener, which, as it turned out, would be by far his best game of the series.

The series was evolving into another out-and-out battle of the trenches. Mahorn played McHale incredibly tough and the two were assessed double technicals in the first and third games. Dennis Rodman was all over Bird. It worked because the referees let the Pistons get away with it. By comparison, the Western Conference semifinal between Dallas and Los Angeles looked like a scene from *Swan Lake*. McHale watched one L.A.-Dallas game and saw Mark Aguirre get called for a bump foul while defending James Worthy in the post. He got so disgusted he turned the channel and watched golf. "It's more exciting," he said.

"It was a changing of the guard in the NBA," McHale went on. "The guards started to dominate and the big guys beat the hell out of everybody and played defense. That was their job. In some ways that hurt the league, because it allowed guys who probably were less talented to get away with so much murder. I respected Laimbeer and Mahorn because they did play hard, but there was so much holding and pushing and grabbing and clutching going on out there. The post was a disaster. It was like hand-to-hand combat. There was no grace or fluidity in the post-up game. You got it, you missed it, and they either called a foul or they didn't. But you got fouled every single time.''

The Pistons returned to the Silverdome, where with 26,481 screaming for Boston blood they took a 2–1 lead with a 98–94 victory. Parish got into foul trouble and did nothing. McHale had 32 to lead all scorers. But the big question was Bird. He was rebounding well but his shooting was awful. He was 6 for 17 in Game 3 and rumors started circulating that he might be sick. He dismissed them, but did admit to having something wrong with his shot. "Maybe I've been watching Jim Rice too much," he said, a reference to the struggles of the then declining Red Sox star. "I'm doing something wrong.''

No one knew it then, but Bird's feet were killing him. The bone spurs that were lodged in his Achilles tendons were painful and piercing. Yes, the Pistons were holding him, grabbing him, bumping him, and taking away what mobility he had. But he couldn't free himself up because every step was a laborious one.

Boston managed to tie the series with a 79–78 victory in Game 4, an ugly spectacle in which the Celtics shot 40 percent and won, attempting just 65 shots. Laimbeer led the Pistons with 29, but passed up an open shot down the stretch that would have won the game. "I don't care if I had missed my last hundred shots. I would have taken that one," Bird said, jabbing his hated nemesis. When the Pistons returned to Boston, a sign hanging from the balcony noted that "When the pressure mounts, Laimbeer passes.''

At the end of Game 4, Danny Ainge emphatically spiked the ball at midcourt, a gesture that let the Pistons and their fans know that Boston had regained the edge and upper hand. At the end of Game 5, Laimbeer did the same thing in Boston Garden after a 102–96 overtime victory. Bird was 9 of 25, including 4 of 15 after halftime. The Celtics bench contributed only 2 points. Detroit trailed by 14 at the half, then went on a 19–2 run to take the lead. The Celtics managed 6 field goals in the final seventeen minutes and were 12 of 48 in the second half and overtime. The Pistons now had a chance to end things at home.

And, of course, they did, taking Game 6, 95–90. Parish collided with Vinnie Johnson, injured his knee, and left early in the game, never to return. Bird closed out his wretched series with a 4-of-17 effort; he made only 40 of 111 shots in the series. "It's the worst series I've ever had shooting the basketball," he said. No one disagreed. McHale was the only consistent scoring threat, averaging 26.3 points and shooting 56.3 percent. Take away his percentage and the rest of the Celtics shot 37.2 percent. They had never, ever seen defensive pressure like this before. Daly had totally remade the Pistons in just five seasons.

As the clock ticked down, McHale sought out Thomas, who had played a terrific series. In full view of the 38,912, he whispered words of encouragement into Thomas's ear. "Don't be satisfied with this. Go for it all. You guys are good enough to do it," he said.

It was a classy gesture and Thomas recognized it for what it was. It was the symbolic passing of the torch. For the Pistons were on their way to the first of three straight NBA finals, and the Celtics would never again win a seven-game series with the Big Three intact.

"We learned so much from them," Thomas said. "If we hadn't played them year after year the way we did, I'm not sure we would have won our championships. They were so mentally tough. So many games we thought we had them beat, but they'd do something incredible or spectacular to steal it from us. After a while, we started to realize they weren't stealing it. They felt they *owned* those games. When we started playing that same way, we started winning championships."

"I have a lot of respect for those Detroit teams," McHale said. "They played hard. Chuck Daly did a great job. And the way they looked at it for a lot of years was 'If we can't beat Boston, then we can't do anything.' They played their whole year to see what we were doing and, finally they beat us."

Bird was given orders to rest during the off-season, the hope being that the irritation and aggravation inside his heels would stop. But Bird did not rest in the summer; to him, *rest* is a four-letter word. "He was machoing it out there in Indiana," Scheller said, "and we had no clue. Then he comes in one day the following season and says, 'I can't deal with it anymore. Let's take the spurs out and get it over with.' But at the time he had no idea the extent of the injury.''

The only option was surgery, and Bird figured he might as well have both feet done as long as he was going under the knife. There was some opposition to the surgery. The owners of the Celtics saw the season going down in flames with Bird out and wanted every assurance the operation was necessary. Dyrek feared the operation would be the beginning of the end, sapping the strength from Bird's legs, never to be regained. Bird trusted Dyrek implicitly, but he had to have the spurs removed—he was in constant pain. He decided to have the surgery in November.

Scheller forecast a three-month rehab program. Everyone assumed Bird would be ready by March at the earliest and certainly by playoff time in mid-April.

Bird had been in a cranky mood since he reported to camp and the feet were one, or two, large reasons. Another was his contract. He still had two years and an option remaining on the deal he had signed in 1983. But late in the 1987–88 season, after a lopsided win over New Jersey, he brought up the new, record deals being given to Michael Jordan and Magic Johnson. He figured he should share in the wealth, too.

Before the Achilles problem led to surgery, Bird publicly rebuked general manager Jan Volk for not producing a new deal. Again, this was classic Bird. Did he deserve the money? Sure. Did he need to pop off? No. He was going to be paid $1.8 million in 1988–89 and $1.8 million in 1989–90. In 1990–91, the option year called for a $1.5 million payout. But by 1988, there was a lot more money available for players' salaries. Four new expansion teams were playing. Television revenues had skyrocketed. Jordan's new deal put him in the $3-million-per-year-and-up category. Johnson was getting similar money.

Alan Cohen took over the negotiations. Although regarded as tough, cheap, and sometimes ruthless, he has always paid the Big Three handsomely. And he did not disagree with Bird. Cohen has sat across the table from some of the most powerful and influential people in the business and entertainment industry, ranging from the late Steven Ross to entertainment mogul David Geffen, and only one person has ever actually intimidated him. That person is Larry Bird.

"He was the only one who could intimidate me because there was no downgrading his worth or value," Cohen said. "Forget what he's worth to the Celtics. Think about the league. There's no number you can put on that. It's like a priceless work of art. I may have been tough with him, but at the same time I also recognized that Larry Bird and Magic Johnson have done more for this league than anyone else."

The numbers being considered were huge; the Celtics had not even considered paying a player as much before. The kind of money Bird wanted was the equivalent of their entire payroll when Cohen bought the team in 1983. Of course, then the team cost $19 million; it was probably worth six times that amount now, and the main reason was Larry Bird. Cohen knew that. The team made hefty profits every year, and Bird was the main reason. Cohen knew that, too.

The two met for four hours at Cohen's apartment at Longfellow Place, a high-rise complex down the street from Boston Garden. By then, the league had already decided that Bird had to play his option year and that his contract could not be thrown out and superseded by a more lucrative one. In other words, Larry Bird took a pay cut in 1990–91, from $1.8 to $1.5 million.

The talk then turned to one big balloon year and how to structure it. The three years he had remaining would pay him $5.1 million; Bird wanted $12 million over four years. Cohen wanted to make sure Bird fulfilled the terms of the contract (Bird originally planned to retire in 1991), and the extension would cover Bird through the 1991–92 season. Bird would then play the 1991–92 season for the astonishing figure of $7.07 million—$2.2 million in salary and a delayed $4.87 million signing bonus.

"In totality, he got what he wanted," Cohen said. "To me, Larry has never been a hick from French Lick. He likes people to think that he is sometimes. But he turned to me during our negotiations and said, 'Mr. Cohen, I know you have to do what you think is right for the good of the team and to protect the franchise. I realize that.

But at the same time, I don't think I'm being unfair. I know I'm worth every penny and would not take a penny more than I'm worth.' ''

Cohen believed him then. And four years later, when Bird retired and insisted on fixing the document so he would not receive his 1992–93 salary, Cohen again saw that Bird was true to his word. And when the surgery sidelined Bird, he offered to send back the contract because the timing made it look as though he had put the team under the gun knowing he would not be able to play. The Celtics told him to forget about it.

Prior to 1988, Bird had missed twenty-seven regular-season games. The Celtics were 16–11 in those games. They were 0–2 in the two playoff games he had missed. But facing an entire year without Bird was something new—a wonderful way for first-year coach Jimmy Rodgers to break into the big leagues.

The remaining members of the Big Three had different responses to Bird's absence. McHale struggled all year, despite scoring 22.5 points a game and making the All-Star team. He talked candidly about having to restrain himself on the floor because he was afraid to get into foul trouble. He openly pined for help, going so far as to ask why the Celtics had not taken a stab at Walter Berry. He finally got the help he wanted in February, a day after the Celtics completed a nightmarish 1–5 road trip. Two sturdy players arrived from Sacramento: Joe Kleine and Ed Pinckney. The price was steep, especially for McHale, who lost his best friend: Danny Ainge was sent packing, along with Brad Lohaus, whose game had virtually disappeared under Rodgers.

Two months earlier at the team's Christmas party, when McHale himself had been rumored to be on the block, Auerbach took him aside and told him that he would not be traded. Ainge was with McHale and said Auerbach told him the same thing—in effect, ''You guys are lifters. Don't worry about it.'' Then, as the trading deadline approached and McHale went public for help, the deal with the Kings was consummated.

If Ainge was unhappy with the trade, he had no one to blame but himself. He had all but orchestrated the deal, although he probably would have preferred a better team. He was unhappy with his contract (he had signed a six-year deal that quickly became ridiculously outdated) and also with his role—Rodgers had decided to start rookie Brian Shaw and Dennis Johnson at the guard positions and bring Ainge off the bench. Not only did Ainge not like that, he also didn't like being on the bench in the closing minutes of a close game after being one of the key contributors for the last five years.

"I was not real happy with the situation," Ainge said. "I felt like I was in the prime of my career, and I'd be on the bench and we'd be losing. I didn't understand that. I never said anything publicly. I did talk to Jimmy and Jan about a trade. I didn't discourage a trade, but I didn't demand one, either. But I was the only guy they could trade. I didn't understand at the time that I was being used. I think Jimmy and Jan and [team owner] Alan Cohen wanted to trade me. I think they felt they were solid in the backcourt."

McHale lost a buddy. "Trading Danny really pissed me off," he said. "He was so much fun to have around and he played hard every night. But we weren't going anywhere." And McHale and Bird not only lost a friend, but also a message courier.

"Everybody always thought Larry and Kevin were best friends because they played together so long," Ainge said. "But they weren't. They're just totally different personalities. They never hung out. They never talked to each other. They would tell me to go tell the other one this or that. Then the other would say the same thing. I was the go-between."

Parish, meanwhile, characteristically stayed away from controversy and merely reverted to his early Boston form, submitting his most complete season as a Celtic. He registered career highs in rebounds (only Akeem Olajuwon had more that season), assists, free throws made, and free throws attempted. His 18.6 scoring average was his highest in six years. He was named Player of the Week after one monster stretch in December that was punctuated by a 34-point, 15-rebound masterpiece against the Knicks. He had 20 or more points on thirty-six occasions (as opposed to fifteen the year before) and fifty-six games in which he had double figures in points and rebounds (as opposed to twenty-eight the year before). The reason was simple: he was now a critical part of the offense. He was now getting 13 shots a game. The year before, he got 10. And he missed only two games, both due to elbow trouble at the end of the season.

Parish, the oldest of the Big Three, was, remarkably, also the fittest, despite his later admission that he smoked marijuana. He was one of the first Celtics to specialize in nutrition. He gave up red meat in 1976, with one memorable slip: a hamburger with his son. He was sick for three days afterward and so incapacitated he had to summon a baby-sitter because he couldn't get out of bed. He also discovered that alcohol and fatigue were related and gave up wine almost cold turkey. He had never associated the two, but quickly discovered he was rejuvenated when he stopped drinking. "Something had to give," he said. "I felt I was drinking too much over the course of a season." He has been a zealous martial arts practitioner for more than a decade.

The exploding NBA salary scale had more than convinced Parish to stay fit. Even then, at thirty-six, he still was one of the top six or seven NBA centers, though his off nights were more frequent and, at times, malodorous. He was making $2 million a season. For that price, he felt it was his duty to stay in shape. He installed a gym at his home and maintained his martial arts, diet, and drinking habits (ginseng tea, daily). He still finds the money ludicrous, especially for the work.

"It is unbelievable. And, not to mention, it's only for two hours a day. And sometimes we don't even go for two hours," he said. "We work hard when we are there, but for how long? An hour? An hour and a half? I don't care how many games you play, that's a lot of money. You only got to do it two or two and a half hours a day and then you can spend the rest of the day doing whatever you want to do? I can't complain about that. Even if I don't feel like it—and there are nights when you do stink out the joint—I just tell myself, 'You should be embarrassed for complaining about what you're doing.' "

He can afford to be so glib because his long career has been remarkable for its durability. He has never had a serious injury. He has never had to undergo surgery. He has never missed more than eight games in a year, and he has played in 97 percent of his teams' games.

He is blessed with a healer's body. When his ankles go, as they do periodically, there is little swelling. When Ed Lacerte came on board in 1987, he found that Parish's right elbow had only 80 percent extension and had been that way for a number of years. Regular treatment by Lacerte soon restored the elbow to its normal mobility. And Parish, like Bird and McHale, also is blessed with a high pain threshold. He can block out pain, play through it, and simply ignore it, oftentimes eschewing medicines that might make it easier for him.

"The key to Robert is that he keeps himself ultraconditioned," Dan Dyrek said. "He's knowledgeable about nutrition. It has been important to him to keep himself fit and healthy. His thing has always been, let nature heal. He was always resistant to anything else. Medication? Nah. X rays? Nah. Therapy? Nah. And his foot structure is such that he's always walking on eggshells."

Parish started martial arts (tae kwon do) when he reached the age of thirty after he discovered that his reflexes and hand-eye coordination had started to slow down. He was missing rebounds. He was dropping passes. "The quicker person was getting those balls that I should be getting," he said. "The martial arts taught me about reflexes, timing, and being focused. And you really have to concentrate because martial arts is not something that comes naturally to most people."

The Bird-less Celtics were 24–28 when they made the Ainge trade. They then won nine of their next eleven games to get back over .500, but they needed a final win over Charlotte to clinch a playoff spot. By now, McHale was sharing the scoring load not only with Parish, but also with second-year forward Reggie Lewis, who got plenty of playing time and averaged 18.5 points a game. Still, the team had little luck on the road, which is exactly where it found itself as the playoffs began. Even more disconcerting was the locale: the brand-new Palace of Auburn Hills, home of the soon-to-be-world-champion Pistons.

There was never any doubt about the outcome of the series. The Pistons had made a midseason deal, bringing in Mark Aguirre for Adrian Dantley. Bird had hoped to be ready—the team had put him on the playoff roster, displacing Ron Grandison—but he was still unavailable. The Pistons won the first game, 101–91, and then, in Game 2, blunted a Celtics rally led by Brian Shaw and won by 7, 102–95. Game 3 was more of the same, an even more convincing Detroit win in Boston, 100–85. The Celtics shot 44 percent and averaged only 90.3 points against the stingy Pistons. McHale shot just 48 percent, a huge dip for him. Parish, too, slumped to 45 percent. The series was similar to the one the two teams had played the year before, but this time the Pistons' dominance was unquestioned.

After a season ends, the players head back to their practice site to clean out their lockers. Reporters wait on stakeout to see who shows up and who is inclined to talk. In 1989, Bird showed up and talked plenty. Given his minimal contributions that year, his explosive comments seemed both unwarranted and ill advised. He talked about players not working hard enough (McHale, again, was the unnamed target) and of the need to set better picks, like Detroit. (He always pronounced it "*Dee*-troit.") It looked like a cheap shot, coming when it did and from a player who had played only six games all season. But there was no response or retaliation from the unnamed players; they had scattered and the season was over.

Before the 1989–90 season began, the Celtics found themselves in the unlikely position to improve their unfortunate situation. They had an unusually high draft pick (thirteenth), but wasted it on Michael Smith, a 6-10 forward from Brigham Young. Right player, wrong decade. He could not play NBA defense. His alleged forte, offense, surfaced in spurts, though he was jerked around as a rookie. His work habits were questioned. "He's another Larry, I hope," Auerbach said, announcing the pick. Smith lasted two years and was waived. Even worse, the Celtics passed up some very good players, including Tim Hardaway, Shawn Kemp, Vlade Divac, and B. J. Armstrong.

The Smith selection typified the season to come. What looked good wasn't necessarily so. How many times does a team win fifty-two games and underachieve? That was the situation with the Celtics in 1989–90. Jimmy Rodgers was honored as the NBA's Coach of the Month in April. He was fired two weeks later.

The Celtics were in turmoil much of the season. The main sources of contention were Rodgers's laudable but impractical plan to diversify the offense and Bird's efforts to remain the team's offensive leader, despite having missed the previous year due to the dual Achilles surgery. Rodgers's plan didn't work. The team opened against Milwaukee, and Bird scored 32 points in his first game in almost a year as the Celtics routed the Bucks, 127–114. Yet afterward, he wondered aloud if he could adjust to this new spread-the-wealth philosophy. Bird had played only thirty-three minutes that night and Rodgers seemed determined to scale back his playing time.

McHale didn't say anything after Bird's comments, but couldn't help wondering if his remarks heralded something sinister down the road. A week later, everything hit the surface. An unidentified Celtic had said that Bird was killing the team by trying to do the things he used to do but could not do anymore. It was a classic case of an older superstar unable or unwilling to adjust. The unnamed Celtic was never identified, but speculation abounded that the remarks had McHale's fingerprints all over them. Bird, however, singled out Jim Paxson, who professed his innocence throughout the year.

"That was the toughest period because it became public," said Chris Ford, then an assistant coach. "No one gets along all of the time. Larry was unhappy because his game wasn't at the level he wanted it to be. He still wanted to take the big shot, do everything like he did before. He should have taken more time. It was an adjustment for him and I think he learned from it."

It was a painful learning process. During one game at Detroit, Bird repeatedly refused to shoot, instead throwing the ball into the post, even when Joe Kleine was the center. It was a very public temper tantrum by someone who, while paying lip service to Rodgers's attempts to get more versatile, still preferred the old way, which, essentially, was described by K. C. Jones as "give Larry the ball and get the hell out of the way."

"That was the one time I got mad at Larry," McHale said. "He tried to do everything and it was hurting the team, as opposed to just letting it happen. And that's a hard thing. At the time, he was trying to do too much. But in his heyday he did the same thing and he could usually pull it off. But that was the only time I can remember saying to myself, 'C'mon, Birdy, play the game.' Because when he played the game, he was the best. But I thought we needed something. I don't know what it was. Jimmy wanted something, too. He saw what was happening. Our management at that time wasn't all that together. Jimmy was put into an almost no-win situation. His first year, Birdy goes down [with the Achilles]. And he tries to get Brian Shaw some time, which results in Danny being traded. Then Brian goes to Italy [for the 1989–90 season]. There were so many things out of Jimmy's control. And out of our control, too. Maybe that's why it was so frustrating. Before, we were always good enough to keep everything under control, and now, maybe we weren't that good.''

Parish, too, thought Bird overdid it.

"It was a difficult year for everyone," he said. "They were trying to work Larry back in and Larry felt he could pick up where he left off, carry the load. And after a while it got disrupted, until Larry finally realized, 'I can't do it.' Once he started to realize that and when he was willing to accept a lesser role, that's when things started to calm down. But he had that attitude like, 'I'm going to show everybody that I can still do it, that I'm still the man, that I can still hit the big shots and that I can carry the team.' It was a rude awakening for him. He had thought he was invincible and that injury just messed up his whole psyche. There was a long readjustment period for him. And, for a while, he was like in a shell. He just could not believe he got hurt. I guess he started believing all his clips.''

Bird took the criticism surprisingly well. When *Sports Illustrated* ran a cover story on the Celtics' simmering feud, Bird was pictured with the question "What's Wrong, Larry?" When he saw it, Bird said, "That ain't so bad." He absolved McHale, not by name, but by description, saying no one who had fought the long and hard battles with him would ever stoop to such underhanded tactics. Or maybe it was his own way of jabbing McHale, for it soon became one of the worst-kept secrets in town that McHale was, as he described, upset with Bird's jumping back into the fray and trying to take over.

"It really didn't matter to me who it was," Bird said. "I always use that stuff to motivate my game. It's just sad to have played so many years and it comes down to that. But that's part of it. Whether they were upset with their game or whether I was the cause, I don't know. I was just upset it came out when it did. I was struggling at the time. I didn't have my feel back. We were struggling as a team and I was forcing a lot of things. But they had to expect that. I was out for a whole year. We had a new coach, different roles, and I was going through an adjustment period, too. I just thought the timing was bad.''

Bird, despite Rodgers's efforts, ended up playing big minutes (39.2) and led the team in scoring (24.2) and dramatic finishes. He beat the Bulls, in Chicago, with a short jumper with 3.6 seconds left. He beat Philadelphia in Hartford with a jump shot with .5 seconds left. He made two free throws to beat the Clippers in Los Angeles, inviting the crowd to jeer him, which, of course, it did. He scored 20 points in the fourth quarter on two occasions, the most memorable in a game against Orlando, which Bird won with a jumper with 27.1 seconds left. He averaged 31.5 points a game in his last fifteen games and he threatened Calvin Murphy's free-throw record, making 71 straight before missing in the first game after the All-Star break.

But Dyrek had been right. Bird's legs weren't there. His rebounds were down. He still could be Larry Bird, but not every night.

Parish, meanwhile, settled back into his "only as a last resort" role. His numbers dropped, as he knew they would. What he couldn't have anticipated was the internal melodrama that seemed to escalate by the days. There was an easily discernible schism on the team: McHale and Jim Paxson occupied one group and Bird and Dennis Johnson the other. Parish leaned toward the Bird/D.J. camp.

After the Celtics started a key western swing in February with wins in Houston and San Antonio—with John Bagley running the team instead of D.J.—Rodgers inexplicably returned to Johnson on the third game in Portland and the team got smoked. From that point on, the team drifted aimlessly throughout the season. Rodgers lost the players' respect by seemingly yielding to D.J. (who had complained about his playing time in the two Texas stops), and the conflict never got resolved. Rodgers was close to losing his job in

March (Cohen had wanted to fire him after the first, Birdless, year, but was talked out of it).

Then came the kicker. Boston, unable to overtake Philadelphia, lost the division. The Celtics ended up meeting the Knicks in the first round. New York, another underachieving team—it had lost twenty-one of its last thirty-four—had not won a game in Boston Garden since 1984.

The Knicks looked as if they were in trouble. The Celtics, in contrast, had finished strong as Rodgers had hoped and wanted, and took the first game, 116–105, as Bird had 24 points and 18 rebounds. Game 2 was a rout, a record setter, as the Celtics scored 157 points, led by McHale's 31, and Boston won by 29. The Knicks were humiliated and embarrassed. They headed home and vowed to get Patrick Ewing involved. Ewing was so manhandled by Parish in Boston that the Knicks' radio analyst, Walt Frazier, called him a quitter. Ewing took his revenge once the Celtics arrived at Madison Square Garden.

In Game 3, a supercharged Ewing erupted for 33 points and 19 rebounds. The Knicks held on in the end for a 103–99 victory, getting a big bucket from an unlikely source—Kenny Walker. The Celtics had had a chance to tie the game at the last moment, but Bird missed an open three-pointer that floated away like a Hoyt Wilhelm knuckler. "It looked like one of those shots you take outside and gets caught in the wind," said Bird. "It was terrible." In Game 4, it was the Celtics who looked terrible. In a game that seemed like the exact opposite of Game 2, Ewing exploded for 44 points and 13 rebounds as the Knicks won by 27.

The series came down to the deciding fifth game. Even though they had been beaten in Boston in twenty-six straight games, the Knicks liked their chances. Once again Boston had no answer for Ewing (31 points) or Charles Oakley (26 points, 17 rebounds) and lost 121–114. The seminal moment came when Bird drove the baseline and went for a reverse dunk—and missed. Bird, who had scored 31, was in shock after the game. "I'll wake up tomorrow and still be in shock," he said.

Well before the Boston flameout against New York, Cohen was upset about the franchise's direction. The team was in chaos; it was going every which way but the way he wanted. He met with Auerbach in his New York office and the two decided that something had to be done. Auerbach, now seventy-three, was the only real basketball mind in the front office, and he spent most of his time in Washington, D.C., where his wife and daughters lived. (Auerbach always kept his official residence in Washington, even when he was coaching. He had an apartment in Boston.) The only other person with NBA experience who had been in the front office was K. C. Jones, who was named vice-president for basketball operations after quitting in 1988. The job was that of a glorified scout, however, and Jones left in 1989 to take an assistant's job in Seattle with old friend Bernie Bickerstaff.

"I think had K.C. stayed, his job power would have increased," Cohen said. "But he wanted to coach again and that surprised me. He is, by nature, a reticent person and it would have taken an aggressive stance on his part to create the job. He is not aggressive in that regard."

Jan Volk, despite having been the general manager since 1983, was a lawyer who still was regarded as more bookish than basketball-wise. "Jan is great in terms of a lot of the rules," Cohen said, "but Jan is not such a basketball maven that he could tell a coach what to do or tell a scout about a player or disagree with a scout. We needed somebody like that."

Auerbach and Cohen agreed they needed someone who would be at practice every day (which Auerbach would not and could not do), who would run the daily basketball operation (which Auerbach did not want to do), and who, basically, would shepherd the Celtics into the nineties. What should they do?

Auerbach said, "Here, let me make a call," and picked up the phone on Cohen's desk. He made a call to Providence, Rhode Island, but the other party was not there. Auerbach left a message.

Cohen asked whom Auerbach was calling.

"Dave Gavitt," Auerbach said. "He's the best guy I can think of."

Cohen needed no explanation. Nine years earlier, when he was one of the New Jersey Nets' two principal partners (the other was Joe Taub), he had wanted Gavitt to take the team's head coaching job. Cohen thought he had an excellent shot at landing Gavitt (the Big East, which Gavitt had launched, was just starting to grow at that point, and Cohen felt Gavitt might want a change), but Taub insisted they hire a coach with professional experience. The Nets hired peripatetic Larry Brown, whose pro experience at that point was limited to three years with the ABA Denver Nuggets. He was gone after two seasons in New Jersey.

"I was a little surprised when Red said he was calling Dave," Cohen said. "I told Red, 'He'll never take it.' "

Gavitt was arguably the most powerful man in basketball, especially in college basketball: he oversaw the Big East, was president of USA Basketball, and was universally respected. Cohen spoke with Gavitt. Fellow owner Don Gaston, who did not know Gavitt, met him and the two bonded. "We need someone like you to save us from ourselves," Gaston told Gavitt. But there never was a formal, sit-down, "What do you want to be doing in five years?" type of meeting.

"Dave isn't the kind of guy you actually interview," Cohen said.

Cohen already had made the decision to fire Rodgers at the conclusion of the playoffs. Gavitt was privy to the decision, but did not participate in making it. He also did not stand in the way of it, either. The firing was announced early in May of 1990. Gavitt by then already knew he was coming on board; the Celtics officially hired him at the end of the month to avoid the appearance of any linkage with the Rodgers move.

The Big Three, meanwhile, contemplated the 1990s with equal parts urgency, skepticism, and concern. Bird and McHale both talked of how bad they felt to end a season that had seemed at times to be promising.

"We should never, ever have lost to New York," McHale said. "But those five games were probably a microcosm of the whole year. The frustration. The shit feeling. When that season was over, I said to myself, 'I don't ever want to do that again.' "

CHAPTER 8

Reconstruction, False Hopes, and Reality Therapy

A couple of months after he joined the Celtics, Dave Gavitt was standing in line at a fruit stand near his home in Rhode Island. As he waited, he suddenly felt something whack him in the back. It wasn't just a careless shopper brushing a bag against him; someone wanted to make a forceful point.

He turned around and saw an elderly lady holding the bag of apples she'd used to get his attention. She looked the Celtics' senior executive vice-president squarely in the eyes and sternly said, "Don't you ever trade Kevin McHale! Ever!"

Gee, figured Gavitt, if sentiment for the Big Three was this strong down here, he could only imagine what it must be like in Boston. The clamor to do something with Robert Parish, Larry Bird, and/or Kevin McHale was unending. And it also was inevitable. The Celtics' season had ended in ruins and Gavitt had been hired to clean up the mess. He wouldn't be in the position he was in had there been no need to rebuild the teetering team. There was an urgent need, and he had agreed to oversee the project.

It wasn't as if the Big Three had collapsed against the Knicks in the first-round loss, although the loss was as bitter as it was unlikely. McHale had averaged 22 points in the five games and shot 61 percent from the field. Parish had averaged 15.8 points and 10 rebounds, but was no match for Patrick Ewing, who had averaged 31.6 points, including 36 in the three New York wins. And Larry Bird had averaged 24.4 points a game, but had shot poorly (44.4 percent) and missed the key dunk in Game 5.

Finally, people thought, the Big Three had run their course. The league was getting smaller and faster. The Twin Towers had quickly become an outdated concept. Yes, the Celtics had been good enough to win fifty-two games that year, but they had done so on an uneven keel and they were knocked out of the playoffs in the first round for the second straight season. And they didn't have a coach.

Like the New England real estate market, the Big Three peaked in the mid-1980s and then went through a steep decline as the decade came to a close. By the end of the decade, their value was far greater to the Celtics than to any other team. There simply was no way the Celtics could have gotten fair market value for any of the Big Three, even if they had considered trading them.

And by then, the Celtics were paying for their decision of a few years earlier to keep the Big Three intact as a nucleus. As the 1990s arrived, that decision came back to haunt them as they tried to find adequate replacements and maneuver around the salary cap. But the Celtics would make that same decision again and again, because these three were special players. Lifers. The Celtics might not be the Celtics without the Big Three. But unless they got something for them, would they still be the Celtics in the future?

The problem for Gavitt was that the three were basically untradable because of exalted status (Bird), mystifying salary cap restrictions (McHale), and age and salary (Parish). As Gavitt noted, "If you trade Bird, you end up facedown in Boston Harbor." And, he figured, McHale probably wouldn't play for another team unless the deal gave him a realistic shot at another championship ring and more time for golf. Of the three, Parish always felt he would be the one to go, perhaps because he had been the only one of them ever to have been traded. Red Auerbach had always maintained that the three would not be broken up and stayed true to his word.

"Those players didn't want to go anywhere," he said. "As long as I had something to say about it, I wasn't going to trade any of the three. They were going to be like Russell and Heinsohn and Havlicek and everyone else. They'll finish here. Of course, you always listen. I mean, if the Lakers had offered us Jabbar for Parish, I would have taken it. So you gotta listen.''

But it was McHale whose name always surfaced in trade rumors because he was an elite player without Bird's cachet. He could be traded without a fan uprising. Bird could not. And, after Bird, McHale drew the most interest. There were strong rumors of an impending deal with Dallas in 1988, but the names mentioned (Sam Perkins and Detlef Schrempf) and the contracts involved made the deal unworkable. Although McHale made $1.3 million, he was not worth that much to the Celtics in a man-for-man trade. Because of a restriction in the rules, McHale, at the time, could be traded only for someone who didn't earn more than $450,000.

He could, however, be traded for draft picks, provided a team could fit his $1.3 million salary into its payroll. The day Rodgers was fired, McHale figured his days might be numbered, too. The Dallas Mavericks owned three number one picks that year and were presumed to be close to an NBA title; McHale seemed like a logical choice to put them over the top. "If I were the Celtics, I'd check that one out,'' McHale said.

But the Mavericks went in another direction (Fat Lever and Rodney McCray were acquired for the three picks) and there was little interest in any of the Big Three around the league. The Orlando Magic had the fourth pick in the draft that year. Pat Williams, their general manager, said he would in no way surrender the pick for McHale.

Parish? He was thirty-seven. Was there a market for a thirty-seven-year-old center making $3 million a year? The Celtics decided to find out. Auerbach wondered if K. C. Jones, now the head coach at Seattle, might be interested in taking on Parish. It made sense. The Celtics figured they might try to get some youth and muscle while there was still someone available to trade.

Years before, Don Nelson had seen Bob Lanier and Brian Winters retire nobly in Milwaukee, but the Bucks got nothing in return. When Marques Johnson and Junior Bridgeman were nearing the ends of their careers, Nelson pulled the trigger, trading the popular duo (and Harvey Catchings) to the Clippers in a blockbuster deal for

Terry Cummings, Ricky Pierce, and Craig Hodges. The theory was that you simply can't have players, however great, retire on you year after year without replenishing the team. And the Bucks, while never able to get past Boston and Philadelphia, still remained strong and successful.

Seattle made sense. The Sonics needed a center. (They had masqueraded Michael Cage and Olden Polynice as centers, gone 41–41, and finished out of the playoffs.) And Jones was now their head coach, having spent a year as an assistant. Jones and Parish were extremely tight; Parish still harbors some antipathy for Don Nelson because of some comments he made that were critical of Jones in 1984, when the Celtics and Bucks played in the Eastern Conference finals.

"I didn't like his attitude, the arrogance he showed, saying that the Bucks were better coached and that they were smarter than the Celtics," Parish said. "He didn't give us any respect, or K.C. I think K.C.'s record speaks for itself. And what did Nelson ever do? He hasn't even come close. He may have got the most out of what he had, but I don't remember seeing him in any championship series. How can he sit back and criticize K.C.? That's why I don't care for the man."

Asked about the prospect of playing for Jones in Seattle, Parish replied, "lovely."

To this day, the Celtics maintain that while there was talk with Seattle over Parish, it was all generated by Seattle and it never got to a serious stage. Parish thinks otherwise, and his source, Jones, is fairly reliable. He figured he was headed to the Great Northwest.

"I thought it was pretty much written in stone that I was going there," Parish said. "And I'm sure the only reason I didn't go to Seattle was because the Celtics were asking for the whole team in return. That's the reason I didn't go. K.C. said the Celtics simply were asking too much."

Boston's shopping list included Xavier McDaniel, Cage, Nate McMillan, and Derrick McKey. The Celtics were willing to throw in Ed Pinckney, who at that time had zero value. The Sonics said thanks, but no thanks.

"Could you blame them?" Parish said. "They were going to get two or maybe three years out of me at the most. I wouldn't have made the trade either. If I had been thirty, maybe I would have kicked it around. But I feel they did the right thing for that team. I wouldn't have taken me, either.''

There also was a gaping hole at center in Golden State, but Nelson, now coaching the Warriors, said he never even bothered to call. As an ex-Celtic, and one who had played long enough (eleven years) and well enough to have his number 19 retired, maybe he knew what the answer would be before he picked up the phone.

''There were times when you might have thought one of them might be available, but I never called them. I always had too much respect for the Celtics,'' he said. ''I only made one deal with them and it's either my best or worst. It was [Quinn] Buckner for [a retired Dave] Cowens. My team then [1982] was ready to win a championship and I thought Dave would be the guy to get it done. I think we could have won with that team, but Dave got hurt and it never happened. But I never bothered to inquire about the Big Three. I always assumed the Celtics philosophy was intact at that point. They don't trade their great players away. And even if they traded one of them tomorrow, his number will still go up in the rafters.''

The Celtics aren't the only team that treats its stars that way. They just seem to have had more stars than anyone else and to have been doing it longer than anyone else. But Jo Jo White was traded. So was Ed McCauley. They have had their numbers retired. And even after Dave Cowens and Bob Cousy had retired, the Celtics still held their rights. Both players attempted ill-advised and unrewarding comebacks: Cousy had a seven-game stint as Cincinnati's player-coach seven years after he retired from the Celtics; Cowens played in only forty games for the Bucks in 1982–83.

So the Celtics made a decision: the Big Three, while slowing down and nowhere comparable to the force they had been in the mid-1980s, still were worth having around. Despite the ruinous season, McHale had played in all eighty-two games for the first time in six years. Bird, coming off his Achilles surgery, had missed seven games, Parish only three.

Having basically succeeded Auerbach as the keeper of the Celtics' eternal flame, Gavitt also sensed an obligation not to dismantle something that had taken years to build. He was not planning on destroying the city to save it. He agreed with Auerbach that the Big Three were special and were worth preserving, protecting, and defending, Seattle notwithstanding.

After he took the job and got a crash course in Celtics Mystique 101, Gavitt told the owners two things. First, he told them it was not going to be easy reconstructing a team built on principles of the 1980s to compete and win in the 1990s. He was proven right on that score. Then he gave them his view of Bird, McHale, and Parish. It paralleled that of Auerbach and was consistent with the team's long-standing tradition.

"I told them I thought it was very important that it has to end well for all three of them," Gavitt said. "For it not to end well would be a violation of trust with the Celtics' fans that would take a long, long time to forget."

He mentioned the Bobby Orr situation with Boston. Orr may have been the most popular athlete ever to play in Boston, even more so than Bird, but when his knees were shot and he wanted to keep playing in Boston, the higher-ups basically told Orr to forget it. Orr ended up signing with Chicago, but he played for only a small stretch before retiring. The public relations damage had been done, however. Orr had been a deity. The Bruins were horrible when he arrived and, within a few years, had themselves a Stanley Cup (though only after the Bruins pulled the hockey equivalent of the McHale/Parish trade by getting Phil Esposito and two others from Chicago). Bird had revived the Celtics in a similar fashion.

"That thing with Orr, it took a long, long time to heal," Gavitt said. "And I think that Bird, McHale, and Parish were such a cornerstone of this franchise for so long that for it not to end positively for them, for it to end in some form other than great, and them feeling good about the Celtics and the Celtics feeling good about them, and the fans feeling good about both, I think would be a disaster. Like it or not, there is a tradition and a trust that exists with the fans, and we are going to do things the right way. And for it not to happen in a positive way for any of the Big Three would not be a good thing. I told them that.''

Gavitt had to retool the team, beginning with a new head coach. When the Celtics lowered the boom on Rodgers, they also fired assistant Lanny van Eman, a Rodgers confidant and longtime friend. But they held on to Chris Ford, suggesting they had something in mind for him.

Ford is the living embodiment of the company man. His idea of giving a reporter a scoop is to pull him aside and tell him the sun is going to set in the west tomorrow and you can go ahead and go with it. When Gavitt went on a very public fishing trip to try to hook Mike Krzyzewski, Ford patiently waited to see what would happen, twisting in the wind while saying nothing that could be construed as damaging or disloyal. He was even prepared to be Krzyzewski's top assistant. Parish and McHale both came out strongly for Ford, who they knew understood the dynamics of what made the Celtics and the Big Three tick better than anyone else, especially someone from that minor league known as the NCAA.

Gavitt figured it might be wise to sound out each of the Big Three before he actually hired a new coach. So after word filtered up from Duke that Coach K was staying put, Gavitt phoned Bird to ask his thoughts about Ford. The NBA finals were under way, a marquee matchup between Michael Jordan and the Bulls and Magic Johnson and the Lakers. Bird answered the phone and Gavitt asked him what he thought of the game. Bird said he liked Georgia's chances. He was watching the College World Series. But he got around to endorsing Ford, as did Parish and McHale. And Ford got the job, as he should have all along. The Celtics were understandably wary about hiring another assistant, given the Rodgers disaster. But Ford was a former player, bled Celtic green (even if it was tainted from his time in Detroit), and was ready for the chance. Ford also had the benefit of having Gavitt to lean on. Rodgers had no such luxury.

With no trades in the offing, Gavitt and Ford had to find some way to rebuild the team. After spending hours and hours poring over tapes, they decided that the Big Three weren't the problem. The

problem, they both agreed, was that there was no speed, athleticism, or quickness around them. Dennis Johnson was the point
guard and he preferred walking the ball up the floor, letting the play
develop, and, more often than not, finding Bird underneath. The
reserves—Jim Paxson, Joe Kleine, and Michael Smith—were also
slow afoot.

Gavitt looked at Ford and said, "We gotta get quick around these
guys." Ford heartily concurred.

"We all felt the Big Three had the ability to continue to play and
play well provided they remained healthy," Ford said. "That was
the biggest gamble of all. It always was 'Is this going to be their last
year?' But they kept on coming back. Skillwise, and that's what you
judge, is that if they are healthy, can they get the job done? And the
answer kept coming back yes. They were still near, or very near, the
top of their games."

Gavitt and Ford then swallowed Celtic pride and convinced Brian
Shaw to forget his ill-advised plan to return to Italy. Shaw, who the
team thought had great promise, had unexpectedly bolted the Celtics
and the NBA after the 1988–89 season, signing a two-year deal with
Il Messaggero of Rome. The Celtics persuaded him to return after
his first year and Shaw signed with Boston for the 1990–91 season.
But after doing so, he changed his mind, figuring another year
overseas would enhance his market value because he would return
to the NBA as an unrestricted free agent, able to choose his team.
At the time, Shaw said he preferred to honor the second year of his
Italian contract, which he'd never bothered to cancel. The matter
went to court and got extremely ugly. Shaw vowed to play anywhere but Boston and Il Messaggero sued the Celtics. But a federal
judge in Boston not only ruled in favor of the Celtics in the Shaw
matter, but also fined Shaw $5,000 a day for every day he did not
extricate himself from the Italian contract. Shaw returned to the
Celtics, the lawsuits were dropped, and soon the matter was forgotten by fans (although never by management).

Shaw was one piece of the new puzzle. Gavitt then plucked a
slender slice of mercury named Dee Brown out of the draft. Paxson
was released, paving the way for the quicker Kevin Gamble. And
suddenly the Celtics had some athletes.

Their new style, too, would reflect that fact, would again revive
the Big Three, and would make the Celtics front office look like
geniuses. Ford wanted to run, and would not pay lip service to the
concept. He would do it, and he made that point emphatically (and
profanely) to a skeptical Bird early in the 1990–91 season. It helped
that Ford had greyhounds where Rodgers had had manatees.

Ford also moved Bird to power forward and kept him there, using
Bird's prowess as a defensive rebounder to trigger the running game.
McHale returned to the bench, willingly and cheerfully, and was
used more as a backup center as the team constantly succeeded
using a small lineup. The Big Three were involved, but rarely
together. Ford had to find time for the young whizzes, Shaw, Reggie Lewis, Brown, and Gamble. The Celtics were playing the NBA
style of the 1990s and it worked for thirty-four games. They were
29–5 and the talk of the league.

There was cautious optimism in Boston. Miraculously, Ford and
Gavitt had turned around a team with Shaw, a new point guard (who
was never a true point guard, but played the role as best he could),
and Brown being the only newcomers of any consequence. Bird's
back, while known to be bothersome, was not impeding him. Then,
calamity struck. Bird missed twenty-two of the next fifty-one games
with the bad back.

Bird's bad back was congenital. As Dr. Alexander Wright of
New England Baptist Hospital put it, "For Larry, the die was cast
a little bit by heredity. He always was susceptible." The constant
wear and tear from years of basketball had also exacted a toll. One
of the underlying problems was a basic instability. Certain joints
had too much motion, and a shift in the joints would cause a disc to
swell and put pressure on a nerve. Once the pain arrived, it never
left. It varied only by degrees. The condition was officially called
spinal stenosis. Basically, Bird's nerve root was constantly getting
scraped by a protruding bone. The disc problem was in the same
area.

Bird had had back problems throughout his career (most notably
in the fall of 1985), but this was worse than ever. He had injured his
back in a collision with Michael Jordan at, of all things, the Kenny

Rogers Celebrity Tournament in Atlanta in September 1990. The back, shaky to begin with, would never be the same again.

By midseason, he could no longer stand the pain. It was unbearable, and he was held together by steroids, therapy, antiinflammatories, and his steel will. "What I went through I wouldn't wish on anyone," he said. "I always felt I was born with a gift that I could take a lot of pain. That I could play with a lot of pain. I loved to play the game and that's why I kept playing. I felt I would let the fans down if I didn't show up. Fans come in from Connecticut and Florida and they want to see the Celtics and they want to see Larry Bird play. I felt obligated to do that, but some nights it was just too unbearable. I know there are people out there in worse shape, but they didn't have to run up and down the basketball court."

Bird missed fourteen games, but was ready for his favorite annual rite, the western swing. Then, at the end of the third quarter in the trip opener at Seattle, McHale came down on Sedale Threatt's foot and turned his left ankle. McHale's ankles were already fragile. Now one of them was shot, never to be the same. Only a few nights earlier, McHale and his wife had gone out to dinner during the All-Star break and he was upbeat about the second half of the season.

"I was telling her how excited I was and how I felt really, really good." He had even bought some new clothes for the upcoming western trip. "Then, the next game, I tore up my ankle and it was basically the end of my career."

Like Bird, McHale had high arches. He tended to run on his toes, which is not the most stable position. He had had an Achilles strain in 1986, a battered foot in 1987, and periodic ankle woes over the years. This, however, was something worse. His ligaments by then were so frayed that they couldn't hold on to or support anything. And this latest sprain was a beauty. Lacerte called it a two-plus out of a maximum severity of three. But with McHale's ankles, a two-plus amounted to about a six on the same scale.

"I limped into the locker room"—and at the Seattle Center Coliseum, that is a long way to limp—"and within thirty seconds there's this thing the size of a golf ball on my foot," McHale said.

"I told Eddie [Lacerte] to tape it and I'd run it off. He said, 'Uh, I don't think so.' It was tough. I wanted to play. That's just me. It's something that was instilled by my father. He'd go to work every day, never take a day off. I was making a ton of money. If seventy percent of me is better than what we have, I'll go out there. It's tough not to play for me. Sure, you do some dumb things. And you play when you shouldn't. It's probably not very smart. But if it's the worst thing they can say about you, well, then I'd say you've had a good career."

McHale missed the next eight games and, true to form, returned earlier than he should have. He played in nine more games, managing a 31-point performance against the Heat, then missed six more games because the ankle still bothered him. Still, he finished with a more-than-respectable 18.4 scoring average and was third in the balloting for the Sixth Man Award.

But between January 3 and the end of the 1991–92 season, April 19, McHale and Bird were available for the same game only fifteen times in fifty-three games. And that made things doubly difficult for Ford. It was like opening a potential letter bomb every day, be it practice or a game. "It was an adventure every time out," Ford said. "First, they had to get through the game. That's assuming, of course, that they were able to play at all. Then, the next step is the following morning. How are their bodies going to react? Are they OK? I had no idea where it was going to go."

"There were times when I'd ask them why they were playing," Ford said. "I'd tell them to take the night off. They didn't want to hear it. There really was no holding them back. You listen to what the doctors say, you put in your own two cents' worth, but the ultimate call is up to the player. You ask them, 'Do you wanna play?' The response was always the same: 'Yeah.' As a coach, you can't stop them. They were playing a game that they loved, and they felt they owed it to the fans and to their teammates. And they also knew that as every day went by they got older and there would be less of a chance to go for that title. They all wanted to win. To be champions. They were willing to play hurt. They wanted to give the fans an honest day's work, the owners an honest day's work, and they felt that playing hurt was part of the game. I don't think we'll ever know how much.''

Gavitt, too, was awestruck by what he saw. "For someone who had been in the sport for thirty years, what struck me the most was the price that they would pay. We'll never know how badly they were hurting.''

Bird ended up playing in just sixty games and averaging only 19.4 points, career lows if you throw out the 1988–89 six-game season. The team was 10–12 in the twenty-two games he missed (it was 8–6 without McHale). It was not a season bereft of achievements or highlights, however. On March 31, a week before he would again be sidelined with more back pain, Bird played fifty-two minutes in a double-overtime 135–132 victory over Chicago. He had 34 points, 15 rebounds, 8 assists, and 3 blocks. In the second overtime, he had 9 points. He even managed three triple doubles during the season. But now, despite the heroics, the Celtics and Bird were showing their warts. The team had a losing month, its first since Bird arrived. And Bird managed a meager 5 points in a loss to Milwaukee, his worst performance in a game untainted by injury or ejection since his oh-fer against Golden State in his second season.

Parish simply continued on, missing only one game and getting selected to the All-Star game for the ninth time in eleven years. Now the league's official elder statesman, he established career highs in field-goal percentage and free-throw percentage. Parish enjoyed a spectacular western swing in February, making up for the loss of McHale. In five games, he averaged 19 points and 12.4 rebounds while shooting 67.2 percent from the field. The highlight was a 29-point facial on Vlade Divac in the Forum, including 21 in the first quarter.

The giddy start had given way to stark reality by the time spring arrived. But it also had enabled the Celtics to get such a comfortable lead that a 27–22 finish, including a 4–6 April, did not drop them out of the top spot. However, they did lose their last four games and, with both Bird and McHale ailing, the prospect of facing a young, frisky Indiana Pacers team in the first round of the playoffs was not at all appealing.

Indiana was light-years removed from the Celtics in both tradition and success. The playoffs for the Pacers were a big deal. For the Celtics, they were a given. The Pacers had never won a playoff series since joining the NBA in the merger in 1976. They had some scary players in Chuck Person, Reggie Miller, and Detlef Schrempf, but generally lived up to their reputation as a team with a lot of players who are good enough to get you beat.

The first game was thoroughly entertaining, forecasting a lively series. Bird and Person were friendly foes; Person liked to talk and Bird liked to talk back, pointing to the championship banners and wondering if Person would ever get one, let alone three. Bird had missed four days of practice—for him, that was criminal—but was in the starting lineup. He then went out and missed his first six shots and ten of his first thirteen. But he hit a big hoop down the stretch and then stripped Person on a critical possession, and the Celtics won, 127–120. Bird had one of those trick-or-treat triple doubles with 21 points, 10 rebounds, and 12 assists, but he was 6 of 20 from the field. He shrugged off the shooting, saying it was hard for him to get his rhythm without practicing. And he had gone forty-one minutes and lived to tell about it.

Then, incredibly, Bird was ordered to New England Baptist Hospital to spend the night in traction. Now things were truly getting preposterous. If the guy had to go into traction, what was he doing on the basketball court? But this was Bird and his confined world: basketball. He was never more at ease or more content than when he was playing basketball.

And there was another factor at work as well. The mere thought of losing to the Pacers was something Bird would not, or could not, contemplate. He was thinking then that if surgery—which had been decided on—did not work out, he did not want to retire having lost his last basketball game to, ugh, the Pacers. (As it was, he lost to the Cavaliers, which may be more palatable to him, but to most everyone else, the distinction is lost.) He figured this might be his swan song, and he wanted to go out playing, not watching.

"A lot of games I played where I couldn't feel my feet. I knew it was stupid, but I had to do it," he said. "I knew I didn't have many years left and I had to try and push through it. It's tough.

You're laying on the floor for eight days at a time. And not even moving. Eating all your meals on the floor like a dog. You look back, sure it's stupid. But at the time I'm glad I did it, because I wanted to play basketball.''

Person destroyed the Celtics in Game 2 with 39 points, including 7 three-pointers, and Indiana squared the series. The teams split in Indiana, as McHale secured a victory in Game 3 with a big block on Schrempf. Person then woke up again in Game 4, scoring 12 straight points (at Bird's expense) and leading Indy to a come-from-behind 116–113 win. For the second straight year, the Celtics faced a Game 5 at home, winner take all. The Pacers were confident and cocky. The Celtics were restrained and ailing. The game was proceeding at a frantic pace when, late in the first half, Bird dove to recover a loose ball. His head hit the floor in whiplash fashion and he lay there, still, for a few scary seconds. He then slowly rose and headed to the locker room. Ice was applied to the zygomatic arch under his right eye. He did not come out with the team for the third quarter, though the Pacers figured this was a ploy.

Midway through the third period, Bird made his triumphant return, and it was almost MacArthuresque. The crowd went crazy. Over the next twelve minutes, he simply took over the game, scoring 14 points, dishing out 3 assists, and giving the Celtics a 14-point lead with seven minutes left. He then got a breather, although he wanted to remain in the game, and eventually he had to return when the Pacers staged a late, desperate rally. But four Brian Shaw free throws sealed the win for Boston, 124–121, and Bird, who had 32 points and 9 rebounds, again showcased his inexhaustible supply of grit and bravado.

He would have little of either left for the Pistons, who were the next opponent, and, in fact, he missed the first game with back spasms. Detroit won that one, then lost the second, which was played the following afternoon because the Celtics were determined to avoid playing back-to-back games. ''I know I couldn't go back to back,'' said McHale, whose ankle injury was, of course, overshadowed by the daily coverage of Bird's back situation. Bird did play the final five games, but was a nonfactor, averaging just 13.4 points and shooting 38.2 percent. The Celtics won Game 3 in Auburn Hills then lost Game 4, even though Isiah Thomas was ailing. Detroit then won Game 5 in Boston, helped by an ankle injury that kayoed Parish, and came home to end the series.

Parish could not play in Game 6. He was still limping and the ankle had not responded as quickly as he had hoped. It was only the second time Parish missed a playoff game due to an injury. (The other was Game 6 against the Bucks in 1987, which snapped his string of 116 straight playoff games.) McHale, however, played and was immense, battered ankle and all. He had 34 points, but a key late-game tap-in was ruled offensive goaltending by Jack Madden, a hideously bad call. The Celtics rallied from a 17-point hole to force overtime, but succumbed, 117–113, ending their season.

By then, Bird's surgery was a foregone conclusion. The only question was when. At the team picnic at the end of the 1990–91 season, Dr. Alexander Wright, who would be in on the operation, saw Gavitt and gave him the grim news. There was no dispute on this procedure; Bird needed it if he was going to do anything athletic over the rest of his life, from golf to horseshoes.

"When I saw Larry the first time," Wright said, "quite honestly, I don't see how he continued to play. He had complete foot drop. By that I mean he was unable to lift up his toes. He could walk on his toes, but his toe or leg would flip-flop under stress. He had had physical therapy and [cortisone] injections but there was nothing to alleviate the disc problem. It was a routine procedure except for the person involved. It's not very often that you operate on a seven-million-dollar back."

The surgery freed up the nerve root, shaved the bone, and removed the disc. Bird left the hospital the next day, was soon walking ten miles a day, and, incredibly, was ready for training camp in the fall. McHale waited until July 17 to have his operation, and although the team thought he would be ready for training camp, that was not the case. "The operation gave the foot a boost, not a cure," Dan Dyrek said. McHale did not play one minute in the exhibition season, spending his time on exercise machines to keep his conditioning. The ankle did not visibly improve.

"The surgery didn't work," McHale said. "It probably made it worse."

Bird wondered why McHale waited so long to have the operation, especially since he was not ready to start the season. Scheller defended the delay. "Kevin needed time to smell the coffee," he said.

Prior to the start of the season, both Bird and McHale signed two-year contract extensions. McHale, finally getting a long overdue big hit commensurate with his stature, would receive $7 million. Bird's deal was for $8 million and contained guarantees. It also did not kick in until the 1992–93 season.

Bird was ready for the season opener and, in fact, led the team in scoring in eleven of the first twenty games. He had 31 points and 14 rebounds in an overtime loss to Washington. In the eleventh game of the season, he had 26 points and 19 rebounds against the Pacers. Then Shaw undercut him at practice and the back flared up again. He missed the December 14 game against the Knicks, though he returned for the next game. But after the team's December western swing, he was unable to continue, and he missed the next two months. As Wright had feared, the disc problem was back. The sciatica was back. The back was back.

"When you put pressure on a nerve," Wright said, "it causes numbness. What causes the pain is inflammation. So you have to get rid of the inflammation. You do that with drugs, traction, bracing, anything that takes the pressure off. We know how to treat it. But we don't know how to stop it from reoccurring, and that's where the problem lies.

"And," Wright added, "Larry's problem isn't all that unique. It's just that he plays basketball for a living. And, like the rest of us, he only has two legs."

The Celtics tried to keep Bird going. The medical staff felt enormous pressure. "It's like the *Memphis Belle*," Scheller said. "All we're trying to do is keep everything and everyone together for one last ride." Gavitt felt pressure, too. "Not from me that he had to play," he said, "but from me saying, 'Are you sure it's all right that he is playing?' I don't think anyone, anywhere, could have persevered like Larry did."

The Celtics even went to the trouble of leasing a plane, something that most teams do now but that was rare in 1990. The cost was considerably more than that of commercial travel, but the benefits were many, ranging from catered food to avoiding airport crowds. But a more immediate reason for the Celtics' decision to use their own plane was Bird's back. He could lie down on flights in a special bed in the back of the plane. The worst thing he could do was sit, especially for prolonged stretches. That deprived the disc of the small amount of nutrition it gets (a disc has no blood supply). The longer he sat, the worse it got. That was why he would often lie down on the sidelines when he wasn't playing. "I don't think we would have seen Larry as long as we did without the plane," Dyrek said.

The Celtics made sure Bird was on such an aircraft when he flew coast to coast to join the team in Los Angeles to participate in the ceremony retiring Magic Johnson's jersey. Even though he was not going to play, Bird made the trip, practiced with the team in Playa del Rey the day before, and then accompanied the team to the Forum for the ceremony, which was scheduled for halftime. Bird was going to speak and he also was going to have to look smart—the game also was on national television—and that meant wearing a coat and tie. There was one slight problem. He did not know how to tie a necktie.

As he began to get dressed, he asked around the locker room if there was anyone who could help him with this problem. Before he got an answer, he unzipped his carryall and found his ties inside, already tied, ready to slide over his head. His wife had done the dirty work for him before the trip.

"Will you look at that," Bird said. "Ain't she wonderful?"

Walking out onto the floor, he told assistant coach Don Casey to sit next to him on the bench and talk to him a lot. Why? "Because the whole world will see you then."

Two weeks later, he returned to the lineup. Two weeks after that, he summoned up a Last Hurrah with a fifty-four-minute virtuoso performance against his favorite tormentee, Portland. He had 49 points, including a controversial three-pointer to tie the game. (Either it was a two-pointer or he traveled.) He also had 14 rebounds and 12 assists. It was, indisputably, the last time he was really Larry. Three weeks later, he again was disabled, and he missed the last eight games of the regular season and the first six of the play-offs.

While Bird was on again, off again, so too was McHale. He played in the first ten games, missed the next nine, missed a month with a torn calf muscle, and, in all, played in only fifty-six games. He was, however, reasonably healthy when the playoffs arrived, which had been his goal from the outset. And although he was a key contributor down the stretch, when the Celtics won fifteen of their last sixteen games to clinch the division title, he had started to come to grips with his own basketball mortality. His minutes were down. His thrust was gone. He was no longer able to defend or rebound as he once did. It was a transition Bird could not have made. But McHale made it dutifully and without complaint.

"It is tough being an impact player in this league and then re-signing yourself to being a part-time player," McHale said. "I've always tried to be pragmatic and be a realist. I would have liked to have gotten back to playing effectively, whatever that is. It's hard to explain to people. It take so much out of your legs and energy. You just don't have that boom, boom, boom that you've always had."

Lacerte and McHale became daily companions, to the point where McHale cracked that he was spending more time with the trainer than with his wife and children. It was monotonous and boring. He started to reminisce about the old days, enjoying the road with Robey and Bird. And about being able to stretch for a couple of minutes before going out and playing without ever once worrying about getting hurt. With the injuries came a greater appreciation of the game—and of others' misfortune. He recalled a chat he had had with Walton.

"Bill said I had to go to this big rock somewhere in Haiti," McHale said. "And he said he had a map and that this rock would get the curse off. It's down some dirt road and you come to a shack and there's this guy who will remove the curse. I laughed at Bill when he first told me. After I hurt my foot, I told him, 'You better make me a copy of that map.' "

Parish, meanwhile, continued to be the NBA's version of the Timex watch and accumulated milestone after milestone along the way. He scored his 20,000th point in January against the Sixers. He grabbed his 12,000th rebound against Charlotte in the season opener. He blocked his 2,000th shot against Minnesota in January. He played in his 1,200th game against Seattle in February. And he missed only three games. One of them, a January 11 game at New York, marked just the second time that the Big Three all were unavailable for the same game. (The other occasion had been a game against Portland in the 1988–89 season.) Against Miami in the division clincher, he had 22 points and 19 rebounds.

The Celtics had figured to be playing Detroit in the playoffs, but the late surge again paired them up with Indiana. Bird was still out, although the Celtics' late-season success had started to raise questions about his value to the team among some fans. The media soon picked up on the obvious question: were the Celtics better off without Bird? What was undeniable was that the medical staff was on orders to keep Bird out as long as the team was winning. There was no use risking the good karma or Bird's bad back. To that extent, the Celtics felt that bringing Bird back might not be the best thing. And the Bird they were talking about was not the Bird of 1986, but a ticking time bomb who hadn't played in some time and was unable to practice.

Were the Celtics better off without Larry? "What do I look like, an imbecile?" Ford cracked when asked the question. The players wouldn't touch the issue publicly. When Bird was healthy, the question was ridiculous. When he was not, the question was problematic. The undeniable fact was that the Celtics had found a cohesive unit without him and then swept the Pacers, increasing their non-Bird winning streak to eleven straight games.

The Cleveland Cavaliers were next. And Bird was still out. Cleveland won Game 1 in a rout as Brad Daugherty overpowered Parish. The Chief took a lot of abuse, then came back in Game 2 and scored 27 points, leading Boston to victory. He also refused to talk for the remainder of the series, something he frequently did during the playoffs. When the teams returned to Boston, Bird was cleared to play for Game 3. But he would be used in a reserve capacity until Game 6, by which time the Celtics were trailing and facing elimination. Ford then made the obvious switch and started Bird, a move that sent the Boston Garden into a frenzy.

It was to be his last game on the floor and, perhaps sensing that, Bird got everyone involved early. He scored 16 points, but, more important, he had 14 assists, getting the ball to Parish and McHale down low or to Lewis on the wing. The Celtics won easily, 122–91, and as the game ended that night, Dinah Mattingly Bird snapped, "Where are those people now who don't want him to play?"

Boston then returned to Cleveland for yet another Game 7. Once upon a time, the Celtics were automatic winners in these situations. Opposing teams crumbled. Legends stepped up. The Celtics Mystique kicked in and Boston prevailed. "Hey, it'd be great if we could have Bill Russell and John Havlicek playing for us," McHale said, "but the last time I checked, they were retired."

On the way to the Richfield Coliseum, a sign said simply, "Larry's Last Game" and pointed to the building. It was not the way he would have scripted his finale. On Boston's first possession, Parish dribbled the ball off his foot and out of bounds. It set the tone for an ugly afternoon, as Cleveland won a laugher, 122–104. Bird had 12 points and 5 rebounds, roughly his averages for the four games he did play. McHale averaged 16.3 points a game. Parish had his 27-point outburst in Game 2, but managed only 49 points in the other six games.

After the game, Bird said he would enlighten everyone on his future plans in September. He didn't even wait that long. Three months later it was official.

May 5, 1993

Larry Bird's first year as an ex-player didn't exactly go as planned. He did watch some tape of top college players, raving about Purdue's Glenn Robinson. But his back continued to bother him even without the day-to-day strains of basketball. He found it amazing that he was even able to finish off his career as a member of the first United States Olympic basketball team to include NBA players. And he almost didn't make it to Barcelona.

Shortly before the Olympics, Bird's back was so sore that he called Dan Dyrek and suggested the unthinkable: he was prepared to ask the selection committee to remove him and send someone else.

"I can't do it," he told his longtime therapist. "It just hurts too bad. If I go, I really need someone who can take care of my back. [Long pause.] Do you think you could go?"

Dyrek had not been planning on any such trip. He was teaching graduate classes at summer school and he knew that the basketball team was in capable medical hands. The trainer would be Ed Lacerte, the Celtics' trainer. What more did Bird need?

Bird made another appeal. And Dyrek went. There were three bad back episodes in Europe, the first on the flight over. Bird could still lie down—the Olympic team had a larger version of the Celtics' plane—but the travel was not good for his back.

And while the Olympics were hardly a grueling enterprise, there still were games and interview sessions, and Bird had to be a part of them. These were not taxing activities, but neither were they benign. And it was no surprise to Dyrek that Bird's back again became a problem, or that the decision to call it quits came so quickly after the Olympics. In addition, the mental strain at that point was overbearing as well, to the point where Dyrek offered to shoot Bird in the foot, a form of Clint Eastwood acupuncture.

Bird played in all eight games in Barcelona as the Dream Team easily won the gold medal. He averaged 8.4 points and 3.8 rebounds a game and was the team's leading scorer with 19 points in a 111–68 victory over Germany. He did not score, however, in the gold medal victory game against Croatia.

By fall, Bird was not alone in his discomfort. McHale reported to training camp and reinjured his troublesome ankle before the exhibition season even began. This was exactly what he did not want. And he thought seriously then and there of retirement, but decided against it.

One night that October, he sat in bed with his wife and the two chatted about what seemed now to be inevitable. Why go through another year like the previous one? What was the purpose? Kevin and Lynn McHale pretty much decided that night to call it a career. But they did not anticipate the reaction from two people: sons Joey and Mikey. They were due to be ball boys this season, and that meant their dad had to be on the team and not angling for walleyes in Minnesota or working on his golf game. McHale relented, seeing the disappointment on his kids' faces. He had always put his personal life well ahead of basketball, and this was another example.

From a pure basketball standpoint, however, the decision appeared to be the wrong one. McHale had nothing out of the box and endured the most frustrating season of his career. During the middle of the season, with the team struggling and McHale seeing sporadic and limited time, he again decided to shuck it. Never was his frustration more public or visible than the time he actually left the bench in disgust and headed for the locker room as the Celtics were in the final throes of getting routed by the Pacers in Indianapolis. He made the pitch to Gavitt, who, while sympathetic, requested that McHale postpone the decision because the timing would make it look as though he was taking the last lifeboat on the *Titanic*. Again, McHale shrugged and agreed to stay on, though at times he wondered why.

He was being phased out of the regular rotation, mainly due to his declining skills and deteriorating body. He averaged only 10.7 points a game. His shooting percentage dropped to a dismal 45.9 percent. In one brief appearance during a rout of the Warriors, he did not even attempt a shot.

"I tried to regenerate it," he said. "And I got it generated a couple times. But for the first time in my career, the injuries took a toll on me mentally. I've always been able to stay really mentally strong and fight through the injuries. This year the injuries got to me, and I just got tired of being hurt, and I lost that fire. You can be physically hurt if you're mentally strong. I mentally lost it and I didn't have the fire anymore."

Complicating McHale's situation was the apparent implosion of the team. He had little in common with the modern MTV athletes who now graced the NBA. He saw little of his unimpeachable work ethic in any of the newcomers. He was, by his own admission, a dinosaur in the league. How could he empathize with Sherman Douglas removing his sneakers during a game and briefly leaving the team in a snit over playing time? Or understand that talented but raw rookie Marcus Webb, who would skip doctors' appointments and prefer a nightclub to the basketball court? He couldn't and wouldn't try.

Everything, however, was forgotten in a monumental nostalgia blitz on the night of February 4. Bird, who had been an occasional visitor to home games and even made a road trip in December, had his number retired and raised to the Boston Garden rafters in an elaborate yet tasteful two-and-a-half-hour extravaganza that raised more than $1 million for charity. For one night anyway, the team, the hazy future, and the injuries all faded as Bird's career was relived through videos and personal tributes. At his retirement news conference, Bird had said he wanted his number retired in the old Boston Garden. That was not a problem. A new Boston Garden would not be ready until 1995 at the earliest. And the Celtics made sure Bird went out in style, dropping about $500,000 to honor Bird.

There was no game that night. The building was reserved to honor Larry Bird and his family, although daughter Corrie was not present, despite having written twice to her father to ask if she could be there. Season-ticket holders were given a chance to purchase seats and a lottery was held for the remaining 486 tickets. It drew almost 12,000 requests. There were 243 lottery winners (each winner got two seats).

The members of the 1981 championship team returned, minus Wayne Kreklow and Terry Duerod. The 1984 team, minus Carlos Clark, was there. The 1986 team, save for David Thirdkill, was there, too. The coaches, save for the excised Jimmy Rodgers (who was invited, did not attend, then was omitted when Auerbach mentioned Bird's coaches), were there. Danny Ainge sent his regards via tape; he had a game the following night in his new home, Phoenix. Greg Kite also couldn't extricate himself, being similarly occupied with the Orlando Magic on a West Coast trip. That night, Auerbach admitted for the first time that his only regret was that he never got to coach Bird. He never got to coach Dave Cowens, either. Or McHale. Or Parish.

The tributes, predictably, were endless. No one talked about Bird's fight with Erving, or his altercation in a Boston bar during the 1985 playoffs in which he may or may not have hurt his hand. (He shoots righty, but punches lefty.) Ainge talked about the time that Bird tied K. C. Jones's shoes together while Jones, unaware, was giving a pregame talk in New Jersey. Ainge never mentioned the time Bird got on the team bus, started an impromptu game of Simon Says, and told everyone to raise his right arm, which made legendary broadcaster Johnny Most the loser (as Bird intended all along) because Most had suffered a stroke and couldn't raise his right arm.

Magic Johnson was the guest of honor, as Bird had been eleven months earlier when the Lakers retired number 32 and hung it on Retirement Row in the Forum next to the uniform numbers of Jerry West, Elgin Baylor, Wilt Chamberlain, and Kareem Abdul-Jabbar. Magic went over his early years with Bird and said that the two did not get along at first but eventually came to be friends after shooting a Converse commercial in Indiana in the mid-1980s. Now they were all but picking out curtains together.

"When I was playing," said Johnson, "I always told people that Larry Bird was the best all-around player that ever played the game. But more than that, he was the one player I feared and respected more than anyone else. Because if there was any time left on the clock, that man would find a way to win the damn game.''

Bird would have more company in the Boston Garden rafters than Magic had in the Forum. His number 33 would join Dennis Johnson's number 3 on the third flag with retired numbers. His would be the eighteenth name or number to be retired and he would be the sixteenth player. (Auerbach and former owner Walter Brown are also represented, Brown by number 1 and Auerbach by number 2.)

The night, however, was physically taxing on Bird, who, despite his retirement, was still in constant pain. He rarely stood in one position for more than a few seconds. Mentally, he was also uneasy. This retirement gig wasn't so great, although he had found a new Shangri-la in Florida in the Gulf Coast community of Naples. He soon sold his home in Brookline, Massachusetts, even though he had recently refurbished it and had planned to hang on to it because, as he put it at his retirement news conference, ''there are just too many great memories of that house.'' He sold it to Bob Woolf's daughter.

One month after his retirement bash, Bird underwent another back operation, this one a spinal fusion. Again, it was portrayed as a major news happening. The news that Bird was reentering the hospital led the evening sportscasts and was reported on the front pages of both Boston sports sections. The surgery itself also produced a front-page story. Unlike the previous operation, this one required a week's stay in the hospital with no activity for at least six months. And this operation, doctors said, would be more painful than the first, not that Bird wasn't used to pain by then.

Dan Dyrek had argued for a fusion operation the first time around, even though such a procedure would have made it highly unlikely that Bird would be able to play again. ''But if anyone could, it would have been Larry,'' said Dyrek.

Bird spent much of the winter in Florida and by springtime was back in Boston. He soon became the subject of rumors regarding the head coaching job of the Indiana Pacers. His back made him unable to consider anything, however. He's always said that he would not like to coach. But his restlessness was apparent. The new challenge he spoke about at his retirement party still was not there in his life. He was in limbo, both professionally and personally. But he did participate in the Celtics' 1993 draft in June and he ran a miniclinic in July for some of the players.

McHale and Parish had some fun with Bird's retirement party. Asked how he expected to be honored, McHale cracked, "Probably during a twenty-second time-out." His number was to be retired in January 1994.

Parish has always felt he was number three on the Big Three priority list—it was hard to dispute that—and he probably is anticipating seeing his number retired in Hartford. There was some speculation about his future in Boston—he thought he was history—but he re-signed for another season in late June.

Parish quietly accumulated more milestones during the 1992–93 season, again showing his remarkable durability by missing only three games at the age of thirty-nine. He already had played more games in a Celtics uniform (1,032) than either McHale (971) or Bird (897). Only the sainted John Havlicek has played more games (1,270) as a Celtic.

But Parish's season was most memorable for one bizarre off-the-court incident just after the All-Star break. In February, three days after Bird's bash, a Federal Express package from Hayward, California, arrived in Natick, Massachusetts, addressed to Parish at his comfortable, secluded Weston, Massachusetts, home. Drug-sniffing dogs had smelled something in the Federal Express package and the Weston police were summoned. It was marijuana. The Weston police also found more marijuana—two ounces—when they searched Parish's home. Parish confronted the embarrassing situation head-on, saying he felt humiliated for his friends and family. He was given six months' probation with the stipulation that the charge be dropped if he stayed out of trouble. It was the customary sentence for a first offense in Massachusetts. Parish's girlfriend, Heather Graves, also was charged and given the same sentence. The whole thing came and went in two weeks.

Parish never denied using marijuana and, in fact, admitted that he enjoyed it for relaxation purposes while listening to jazz, his favorite music. As for President Clinton's remark that he had tried marijuana but didn't inhale, Parish said, "Obviously I did. What's the sense of using it if you don't? But I am not a chronic user. Otherwise it would show up on the court."

Parish was greeted by sympathizers when he showed up at court, including advocates of even more lenient marijuana laws or outright legalization of the drug. One sign typified Parish's long road to respectability: it spelled his name "PARRISH." This was a common mistake. Every year during the Celtics' West Coast trip, writers collected box scores to see how many NBA teams also misspelled the name. Several invariably did. Parish was always amused at the error; he was, after all, a perennial All-Star on a marquee team. But his response always was the same: "As long as they spell it the right way on the check."

Parish's marijuana problem quickly faded from public view. It was 1993 and no one cared. The president had even admitted he tried the stuff. The NBA's policy on drugs doesn't even bother with marijuana, focusing instead on the more dangerous cocaine and heroin. "If it wasn't me," Parish said, "it never would have been an issue. It was only because of who I am and my relationship with the Boston Celtics. But the sensationalism soon passed and everyone found someone else to look at."

Interestingly, despite their workingman, blue-collar roots, Parish and McHale had both settled in Weston, the wealthiest suburb of Boston. And one of the snootiest, too. Weston is the only Massachusetts community that regularly and resolutely refuses to build state-approved "affordable housing." This refusal costs the town thousands in state aid. Weston figures it doesn't need the money, and it knows it doesn't want the perceived undesirables that affordable housing might bring in to contaminate its sylvan setting. Bird had chosen Brookline, one of the more liberal-thinking suburbs, but only because he found a house close to his agent, Bob Woolf, and to the Celtics' practice site at Hellenic College.

The off-season also would renew a painful side of Parish's private life: his futile attempt to see his son Justin. Parish has been divorced from his former wife, Nancy, since 1988 and Justin has lived with his mother. Parish has not seen Justin since the divorce because, he said, his wife won't abide by their custody agreement. And Parish said he does not want to go to court because he feels it will traumatize the child. In the summer of 1993, he didn't even bother making a request. "What's the point? It'll just hurt Justin and make his mother angry," he said.

The former Nancy Parish refused to discuss the custody agreement, and her attorneys said the situation is vastly more complicated than Parish described it. Parish said he thinks that time eventually will resolve the custody issue.

"One day Justin is going to be old enough to decide for himself, just like my daughters," Parish said. "One day, he won't be under the influence of his mother. Then he's going to be able to see for himself what the situation is."

Parish has a similar situation with another son, his namesake, Robert III. The child, born in 1981, lives in the Bay Area with his mother. Parish and the mother have a strained relationship and he has not seen the boy in years. Parish may never be a candidate for Father of the Year—he has four children by three different women, none of whom he was married to at the time the children were born. His one marriage, to Nancy, rapidly deteriorated and eventually ended in divorce. But he said the marriage made him more tolerant and empathetic.

"First of all, being married to Nancy definitely made me a better person," he said. "It made me more understanding, even though we screwed things up at the end. It was a learning experience. Before I got married and had Justin, I didn't have a lot of patience. I wasn't very understanding. Being married taught me to communicate and work things out. In the past, when I felt things weren't going right, I just walked away from it. So I definitely learned and grew and became a better person. But I'm glad it's over."

And, since 1988, it can be argued that Robert Parish has not regressed on the floor. He may even have gotten better. He attributes much of his late-career success to his marital split.

"It was like a relief. I wasn't angry all the time. My last year with her I was angry. I was mad. I was always in a bad mood, and it showed, too. Right out in public it showed. You can feel that. I guess you call it air, energy, whatever. Negative energy. I was in a bad mood for a year and a half. For the first six months, the marriage was great. After that, it went right down the toilet and I became a very angry person. But it could be worse. I could still be with her. Think about that.''

While Parish remained a steady constant throughout the 1992–93 season, McHale occasionally surfaced to submit a performance that validated his presence on the team. In a game against Minnesota, the franchise he would join after retirement in a media/coaching capacity, he had 22 points, 6 rebounds, and 4 blocked shots. He gave rookie Shaquille O'Neal a crash course in fourth-quarter heroics by scoring 7 points in sixty-five seconds, helping the Celtics take an overtime decision in Orlando. But those were blips on a screen dominated by otherwise unremarkable stints.

In early April, the Celtics went into a five-game tailspin and McHale finally cracked. He played only twelve minutes against the Pistons and then only eight minutes in a nationally televised loss to the Knicks. He did not even play in the first half of that game and ended up with 4 points, all on free throws.

McHale called the cameo appearances ''an embarrassment.'' He said he had no idea what coach Chris Ford was doing. ''Even in my All-Pro years, I couldn't have accomplished anything in five minutes. It's hard enough when the team is winning. But when you're losing, it's doubly tough,'' he said.

What Gavitt had hoped—that all of the Big Three would go out with grace and dignity—seemed to be coming undone. The next day, he met with McHale and told him to cool it. Both men knew the end was near. Assistant coach Don Casey came up to McHale and added, ''Don't go out kicking and screaming. You'll regret it five years from now.'' And then McHale did something unusual: he apologized.

Although he knew his game was declining, he felt he still could help the team. But he understood Ford's position, and he hoped he had not put a strain on the coach or their relationship, which had been tight. He was frustrated. He was confused. But those sentiments should be aired in private, he said.

It was a catch-22 situation. He wasn't able to do the things he used to do. But because he couldn't, he wasn't given the time to try to see if he could.

"I have never, ever put myself ahead of the team and I'm not going to do it now," he said.

Then, three weeks later, after missing three games with a new ailment, back spasms, he treated the fans to one final moment of glory in his final regular-season home game: a marvelous 17-point, 11-rebound performance over thirty-two minutes. He received a standing ovation when he left and the message board said, "Thanks, Kevin." He had not announced his retirement, but it was an open secret. And then his son Joey, in his cherished role as a ball boy, asked what the commotion was all about. McHale said, simply, "No big deal," and kissed the boy on the head.

McHale then put an exclamation point on his career with a 1987ish performance in Game 2 of the team's playoff series with Charlotte, a valiant effort in a game the Celtics lost. In what turned out to be McHale's last appearance in Boston Garden, he scored 30 points and grabbed 10 rebounds, resurrecting Sir Kevin the Fourth in the process.

After that, the team went to Charlotte needing one win to send the series back to Boston. It got routed in Game 3 and was headed in the same direction in Game 4 when Boston staged a late, utterly implausible comeback and almost won the game. McHale was, again, front and center during the drama, scoring 19 points. He finished, incredibly, as the team's leading scorer in the playoffs, quite a feat for a player whose status was iffy from the beginning.

And history will record, somewhat ironically, that McHale's final act as a player for the Boston Celtics was a pass. He was never known for his passing ability and was, in fact, jokingly known as the Black Hole because when the ball was passed in to him it never came back. But in his last act as a Celtic, he made one final pass, which was as good as any that Bird had made at any time in his career. With only four tenths of a second left, McHale was the inbounds passer at halfcourt. The play was an alley-oop to Dee Brown, who would be forty-five feet away. The pass had to be perfect for the play to work. One foot off and the Celtics' season was over. McHale held the ball over his head with his long arms, looking as if he was ready to make an inbounds pass in a soccer game. The pass was perfect, but Brown got fouled and there was no call. And Kendall Gill of the Charlotte Hornets diverted the ball on its downward path, which the rules say is goaltending. There was no call. The Celtics lost.

McHale, seeing injustice, ran and pleaded his case with the officials, to no avail. He then walked slowly off the Charlotte Coliseum floor with Casey, never again to play for the Celtics.

A few minutes later, he was back on the floor of the Charlotte Coliseum, announcing his retirement on the radio and then elaborating on the game, the decision, and his remarkable career while seated at midcourt. It was a bizarre scene. The Coliseum, a building that represents the music video aesthetic the NBA seems intent on embracing and that is repugnant to McHale, was in a state of suspended joy. The Hornets had eliminated the Celtics for the first playoff series win in the team's young history. Diminutive point guard Muggsy Bogues was looking for his kids. And a future Hall of Famer was calling it quits, grateful only that those few late-season, turn-back-the-clock performances had surfaced to make palatable an otherwise frustrating and unrewarding season.

"The last few games made up for the whole year," he said. "And you know how tough this year has been on me. After a long, hard, arduous year, it made it kinda nice. If I could find that kind of energy every game, I'd play another year. But I can't do it.

"Those last games, I found that energy again. I found something deep inside me that made me love this game again. And I said, 'I'm not going to worry about getting hurt. I'm not going to go out there and play passively. I'm going to go out there and play aggressively. And try to make things happen.' That was the thing that I was most disappointed with this season. I became a passive player because I was so afraid my feet were going to go on me again. They hurt. And the pain and everything got to me."

Typifying his career, McHale's vintage effort should have been bigger news than it was. He was entitled to a moment in the sun after being in Bird's shadow for so long, was he not? He had earned the right to have the owners and executives by his side, lauding his work ethic, his commitment, his approach to the game. But he again, through no fault of his own, was second-page news when the situation demanded otherwise.

This time, McHale's play was dwarfed not by Bird, but by Reggie Lewis, who had collapsed in Game 1 and did not play for the rest of the series. And while McHale was giving his retirement briefing, the assumption was that Lewis had a serious heart problem and might never play basketball again. That diagnosis later was changed, but Lewis's heart problem remained. (Tragically, Lewis collapsed and died of massive cardiac arrest while shooting baskets a few months later.)

McHale understood the temporary imbalance. He had quashed the notion of a farewell press conference and he had deliberately held back on any official announcement until the end of the season, fearing nostalgia and sentiment would dominate. He didn't say, "Wait until September." He didn't say, "I'm going to talk it over with my family." When his career was over, McHale said it was over and time to move on.

"He played the game for all the right reasons," said Chuck Daly, the former Pistons coach. "He had great clarity of thought and he knew what was important and what was not. He must have been a joy to have around."

McHale has three championship rings from his years with the Celtics, but he doesn't wear any of them. Why? They signify past glory and he is interested in tomorrow, not yesterday. He will have to endure one more round of yesterdays when the Celtics officially retire his uniform number in January 1994. The number will be raised and the memories revived during an extended halftime ceremony. He will have played his entire career for one team. He will be going to the Hall of Fame. He will know that no one ever again will wear number 32 for the Boston Celtics.

"It is almost overwhelming, really," he said. "Any of the three is. The Hall of Fame. Playing your entire career in one place. But what means the most to me is putting my number up there in the rafters. Because over the years I've gotten to meet a lot of those guys and there is something about them that has 'winner' written all over them. And to be up there with them, that will mean more to me than anything else."

Parish, too, will see his number, 00, retired, although in keeping with his self-deprecating side, he has said he doesn't care if some-one else comes along and wears the uniform. "It would be a great compliment to me and I'd be honored, but to me it is not an issue. If someone else wants to wear it, that's fine with me. If they didn't retire the number, I won't be campaigning to get it raised." He won't have to, though. It's a *fait accompli*.

Parish first wore 00 in junior high because no other number was available. He kept it through high school, college, and the pros.

He will leave as one of the best centers to have ever played the game. He will have more championship rings than Wilt Chamber-lain and will have played in more games than anyone but Kareem Abdul-Jabbar.

"In my mind, he was one of the four greatest centers to ever play," said Dave Wohl, a former NBA head coach and assistant. "He was more versatile than Moses [Malone]. He was as good a rebounder as you'd want. He ran the floor as well as anyone. He could set a good pick. He was a good passer. He never seemed to make a mistake. Defensively, he was all that you could ask. And there was a tenacity in him, day in and day out. I always thought he was one of the best who ever played the game."

And then, finally, all of the Big Three will be able to take their proper place in basketball history. There will be stories about how they destroyed the Chicago Bulls, outscoring their front line by combining for 96 points in one game and 81 in the next. Or the ten times they submitted double doubles in points and rebounds in the same game, the final time being February 12, 1988, a 105–104 victory in Dallas secured by a Bird three-pointer. Or the time Bird walked onto the Chicago Stadium floor, asked coach Doug Collins what the building scoring record was, and then almost broke it. Or the time McHale and Bruce Springsteen yukked it up after a game in Atlanta and McHale noted that the Boss was just another guy. Or the time Bird deliberately held the ball late in a game against Mil-waukee, refusing to give it to McHale, and then made a game-winning three-pointer. Or the countless times they made a difference in other ways, through leadership or experience or in the manner in which they carried themselves.

"They just epitomized the word *professionalism*," Daly said. "And that is something that we're missing today. Already we're starting to miss it."

NBC and TNT, the two national networks that televise the NBA, will miss them too. In 1993–94, the Celtics are scheduled for only four TNT appearances, down from ten the year before. It represents the largest dropoff in the five years since TNT began covering the NBA. And NBC, which broadcasted five Celtics games in 1992–93, has scheduled only one Celtics game in 1993–94.

The greatest frontcourt ever? Without a doubt. Under the right circumstances, each one could have carried a team. The quirks, twists of fate, and gambles that produced pro basketball's most fabled front line are many and bizarre. That the three came together was unique in and of itself. That they improved, persevered, and excelled is even more remarkable.

"Theirs was an extraordinary combination of people and personalities," Jan Volk said. "Each one is so different in their personality, their approach to the game, and their style of play. But they all shared some important values. Their work ethic. Their recognition of team goals over individual goals. That's what is unusual about them. It's a combination that, regrettably, we in Boston won't see again. Or anyone else. But it's terrific that we had a chance to see it for as long as we did. And, like a lot of things, we probably never appreciated it fully while we had it. The way it was, it can no longer be."